BIRDS
of the
PACIFIC NORTHWEST
Washington, Oregon, Idaho
and British Columbia

BIRDS
of the
PACIFIC NORTHWEST
Washington, Oregon, Idaho
and British Columbia

by
Earl J. Larrison

Assisted by
Michael D. Johnson
Stanlee Miller

Illustrated By
Zella M. Schultz
Amy C. Fisher
Gregory A. Pole

A NORTHWEST NATURALIST BOOK
The University Press of Idaho
A Division of
The Idaho Research Foundation, Inc.
1981

ISBN 0-89301-078-2
Library of Congress Catalog Card Number 80-54649
Copyright © 1981 by Earl J. Larrison
Manufactured in the United States of America
Printed by the
News-Review Publishing Co, Inc., Moscow, Idaho
Published by the University Press of Idaho
A Division of the Idaho Research Foundation, Inc.
Box 3368, University Station, Moscow, Idaho 83843

Dedicated
to the memory of
EARL LARRISON, SR.
(1885-1976)

CONTENTS

PREFACE

BIRDS OF THE PACIFIC NORTHWEST is an extensive revision and expansion of the book WASHINGTON BIRDS by Earl J. Larrison and Klaus G. Sonnenberg which was published by the Seattle Audubon Society in 1968 and now out of print. Many of the illustrations are new, the descriptions have been checked and modified where necessary, and the range summaries entirely rewritten on the basis of information gathered since the preparation of the earlier book.

The present volume embodies the results of studies on the birds of the Pacific Northwest made by the author for some 50 years, during which time he has been almost continuously a resident of the region and has carried on field work in all parts of it. Intensive work on this book was begun some twelve years ago.

The great mass of field data on bird distribution as well as marked changes in the ranges of many species brought about by increased exploratory movements on the part of the birds, plus many more birders, have together necessitated a complete reappraisal of the avifauna of the region and the geographic and seasonal occurrences of many forms. The author, therefore, has tried to include in the present book as up-to-date an understanding of our native Northwest birdlife as is possible. Therein lies a major contribution of this work. We must realize that such distributional changes are most interesting to record but also that many individual birds slip through the Northwest undetected, so that any book as this is only an approximation of actual conditions. It is hoped that readers will be inspired to increase their field studies in order that eventually we may come to possess a clearer and more detailed knowledge of the BIRDS OF THE PACIFIC NORTHWEST.

*   *   *

Many persons have aided in the preparation of this book and the author tenders a blanket thanks to them all. Certain individuals, however, must be singled out for special acknowledgement. Michael D. Johnson spent many months in sifting the literature and various field reports for distributional data. Stanlee Miller checked descriptions against specimens. Preliminary drafts of the range summaries were checked and criticized by Philip W. Mattocks, Jr., Charles Trost, Dennis Paulson, Richard Johnson, Thais Bock, John W. Weber, Hazel A. Wolf, Grace W. Patrick, Ralph S. Widrig, Donald R. Johnson, Eugene Hunn, and Helmut Grünberg. Jeffrey S. Marks supplied information on certain birds in the Snake River Birds of Prey Study Area, Idaho.

Especially helpful for his intensive examination of the manuscript has been John W. Weber of Washington State University, a fellow student of eastern Washington and northern Idaho birds and co-author with Larrison of several papers on the birds of that area. Hazel A. Wolf and Grace W. Patrick of the Seattle Audubon Society have offered continuous encouragement as has Donald R. Johnson of the Department of Biological Sciences of the University of Idaho. Richard Knight and his colleagues of the non-game section of the Washington State Game Department have been most helpful in providing information and encouragement. Bob and Elsie Boggs kindly lent the use of a number of their superb nesting bird photos.

The evaluation of distributional information is an extremely difficult process. Practically all range records are now based on sight observations rather than on specimens. This entails a tremendous problem of verifications. Some techniques for screening sight records have been proposed, but even they leave much to be desired and the opportunities for honest error or deliberate fraud are endless. Some persons may find statements in this book which may not represent certain species' ranges as they visualize them, but the author has had to interpret the great mass or records and sightings in the light of judgement based on his own field work and taxonomic studies carried on for half a century in the Pacific Northwest. Only further field work by professionals as well as amateurs will prove him right or wrong.

Earl J. Larrison
Department of Biological Sciences
University Press of Idaho
University of Idaho
Moscow, Idaho
December 15, 1980

INTRODUCTION

This book describes the bird life of the Pacific Northwest, here defined as including the states of Washington, Oregon, and Idaho and the Canadian province of British Columbia ("B. C." in the range summaries). Lesser coverage has been made of the southern Yukon and western Montana. Within this great region occurs a vast variety of geographic and ecologic types, all of this mirrored in a divergent and varied bird life. Nowhere else in the North American continent does the environmental spectrum vary from icy mountain summits to mild heavily-vegetated lowlands, from dripping rain forests to hot arid deserts, from the waters of the ocean to interior plateaus, and from the tundra of the north to the juniper and pinyon pine of the south. Vast wildernesses compete with urban sprawl while idyllic pristine habitats lie within miles of volcanic desolation. Truly, the Pacific Northwest is a wonderful faunal region and it is the purpose of this book to present a picture of its avifauna and how this group of animals is shaped by its environmental diversity. It is well that we know our Northwest birds, for many conservational problems loom on the horizon that we will have to meet with hopefully intelligent value judgments!

Attempts to classify simplistically the great environmental variations in the Pacific Northwest are fraught with difficulties. Almost as many systems for such classification exist as do ecologists! Most of these patterns, however, depend on the use to which they are put. Obviously, for a general book of this kind, a simple system is of most value to its readers. The accompanying map details the major physiographic provinces or geographic regions into which the Northwest can be divided. Study of this map will orient the reader's thinking in a most helpful way. The Cascade Range presents a great barrier separating the moist marine climates and environments to the west from the more arid continentally-contrastive areas to the east. On the extreme east, the Northwest region bucks up against the Rockies. A Coast Range further complicates matters of the "west side" with up-slope depositional areas and rain shadow anomalies. Interpolated mountain systems in the interior further vary the floristics and faunistics of that great region. The physiographic province map and the following ecographic plans are offered not so much for the reader's detailed use (which would require a book-sized description) as to impress him with the myriad details of variation in the region treated by this manual.

A generalized pattern of environmental classification which still has considerable value for groups of habitats and environmental units

7

The Pacific Northwest (Fisher)

is the life zone system devised many years ago by C. Hart Merriam and revised for the Northwest by Charles V. Piper. An outline of this scheme follows:

TRANSITION ZONE

Humid Section The moist heavily-wooded (at least formerly) lowland areas west of the Cascade Mountains and characterized by Douglas fir, western red cedar, lowland hemlock, etc.

Arid Section Timbered: The yellow pine belt east of the Cascade crest. Non-timbered: The grassland belt east of the Cascade crest.

CANADIAN ZONE The montane coniferous forests of the Northwest above the Transition Zone and below the Hudsonian or subalpine zone.

HUDSONIAN ZONE The open semi-forested belt above the dense montane forests in the higher parts of the mountains, where solitary trees or groves of trees are interspersed with meadows of grasses, sedges, and forbs.

ARCTIC-ALPINE ZONE The areas above timberline on the highest mountain peaks characterized by an almost complete absence of higher plants, rocky fields and slopes, and permanent ice and snow.

UPPER SONORAN ZONE The desert of semi-desert areas covered, at least formerly, by sagebrush east of the Cascade Mountains.

Habitats are the smallest and most local ecological units to which distributional patterns can be reduced. A perusal of the following classifications will add to the reader's understanding of the diversity of environments available to the species treated in this book. The discussions of habitats referred to in the accounts which follow will emphasize how these various ecologic types are chosen and utilized by Pacific Northwest birds. In many cases, however, the field birder will find that relatively few species limit themselves to a narrowly specific ecologic type but that most exhibit varying degrees of breadth in their environmental selection.

HABITAT CLASSIFICATION OF THE PACIFIC NORTHWEST DESERT BIOME

1. sagebrush zone
   a. big sagebrush-bluebunch wheatgrass
   b. big sagebrush-barren ground surface
   c. big sagebrush-idaho fescue-forbs
   d. big sagebrush-rye grass

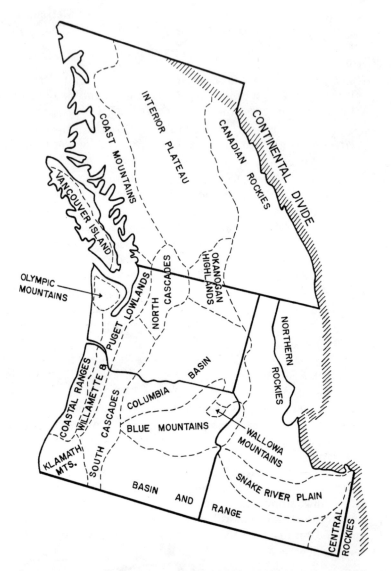

Map. 1. Major geographic regions of the Pacific Northwest. (From *Field Guide to the Butterflies of the Pacific Northwest by James Christensen*)

e. black sage *(Artemisia arbuscula)*
f. scabland sagebrush *(Artemisia rigida)*-Sandberg's bluegrass
2. salt desert shrub zone
   a. shadscale
   b. salt sage
3. grassland zone
   a. bluebunch wheatgrass-Idaho fescue
   b. Idaho fescue-snowberry
   c. sedge-grass
4. sand dune zone
5. greasewood zone
6. bitterbrush zone
7. mountain mahogany zone
8. juniper zone

ALPINE BIOME
1. subalpine fir groves (including Engelmann spruce)
2. white-barked pine
3. meadow (grass-forbs)
4. heather *(Phyllodoce-Cassiope)*
5. sedge meadow
6. barren alpine (low forbs, lichens, mosses)
7. rock (talus, felsenmeer, cliff)
8. snow (ice, glacier)

FOREST BIOME
1. Sitka spruce-hemlock (coastal forest)
2. western hemlock-western red cedar (inner coastal lowlands)
3. Douglas fir-deciduous (alder) (including second growth)
4. alder-maple-dogwood (Puget Sound lowlands)
5. oak-madrona (San Juan and Gulf Islands)
6. deciduous riparian woodland
7. lower subalpine forest (lovely and subalpine firs, yellow cedar, mountain hemlock)
8. pine-larch-fir-interior forest
9. interior oak woodlands
10. western juniper
11. yellow pine (plus Douglas fir) - interior forest
12. lodgepole pine subclimax
13. grand fir
14. silver fir *(Abies concolor)*
15. Shasta fir *(Abies magnifica shastensis)*
16. aspen-lodgepole (Cariboo Parklands)
17. Columbian forest (western hemlock, red cedar, white pine, Douglas fir)

18. boreal forest (closed spruce-hardwood) (white spruce, recent burns, quaking aspen, paper birch, balsam poplar)
19. open spruce (low growing; interspersed with bogs and moss mats)

TUNDRA BIOME
1. treeless bogs (muskegs)
   a. coastal (in coastal forests)
   b. interior (in boreal forests)
2. shrub thicket
   a. coastal alder thicket
   b. floodplain thicket
   c. birch-alder-willow thicket
3. tundra
   a. moist tundra
      1. cottongrass tussocks
      2. dwarf shrub
      3. tall grass meadow
      4. low dense heath shrubs
   b. wet tundra
   c. alpine tundra
4. ice and snow (permanent alpine or arctic areas)

AQUATIC BIOME
1. freshwater
   a. running water (rivers, streams, creeks)
   b. standing water (lakes, ponds, sloughs)
2. salt water
   a. beaches
   b. coastal waters
   c. pelagic waters

MISCELLANEOUS
1. rock desert
2. sand plains
3. bare rock exposures
4. volcanic (lava beds, cinder cones and flats, denuded areas)

A useful project for the amateur birder would be to keep careful notes on the degree of restriction that the various Northwest birds exhibit in reference to the above habitat types.

ARRANGEMENT OF SPECIES

Readers of this book will quickly become aware of the fact that the sequence of species and contents of certain families may differ to a greater or less extent from those of previously published manuals on the birds of North America. The systematic arrangement of species in those works represents the scheme that has been in vogue since the 1930s but no longer represents the most modern views of many ornithologists, particularly those of England and Europe. One of the purposes of this present guide is to present this new system which is based for the most part on the plan used in the REFERENCE LIST OF THE BIRDS OF THE WORLD by John J. Morony, Jr., Walter J. Bock, and John Farrand, Jr. of the Department of Ornithology of the American Museum of Natural History in 1975. For example, readers will find that the seed-eating birds have been divided into several groups, rather than the large family Fringillidae of earlier classifications, while the phylogenetic sequence of orders and families places the highly intelligent corvids at the head, that is, at the end, of the list of families. The exact sequence of the birds in this book, admittedly in any work an attempt to bend a branching reality into a linear sequence of pages, and thus futile from the beginning, seems of somewhat minor importance. Certain current field guides are arranged by illustrative convenience or ecologic types, so this "new" arrangement in this book should not be too traumatic.

The reader will also note that certain species currently lumped together as conspecific in the recent literature are kept separate in this book. The reasons for the author's so doing are two-fold. First, the complexities of the late Ice Age which divided the ranges of many prototypes of certain species of North American birds and their subsequent re-contacts due to the ameliorating influence of post-glacial times plus the environmental alterations of man have produced some occurrences of apparent hybridization in areas of sympatry. We do not believe, however, that the modern concept of species should be based only on reproductive isolation or proclivities, especially in taxa whose evolutionary divergence is relatively recent. Secondly, until these vicars can be more adequately studied and a definition of species more truly representing conditions existing in nature devised (if this is possible), it seems best to retain questionable species as separately-named entities so that we may not lose sight of them and their controversial significance. Ernst Mayr has designated such forms as "semispecies". L.L. Short has recommended considering semispecies taxonomically as species.

CHANGES IN BIRD DISTRIBUTION

The author alluded to the fact of recent range changes on the part of certain birds in the Preface. Some of these relatively recent happenings have been well-nigh startling to old time bird students who can remember when the ranges of Pacific Northwest birds were comfortably "chiseled in stone." The greatly increased number of Northwest birders has indicated that this was really never entirely true, but a number of areas that have been carefully monitored during the years does suggest a number of range changes, not only mass extensions of distributional patterns, but increases in the numbers and occurrences of stragglers. Back in the days when ranges were thought to be rigidly fixed, such stragglers were called "accidentals", a concept of intriguing implication, if nothing else. In the light of recent developments and a realization that change is always with us and perhaps proceeding more rapidly at present (thanks to the environmental perturbations of mankind and the behavioral adaptations of many animals to meet these problems), the term "accidental" is no longer valid. Nor do too closely-defined terms of numerical quantitites seem justified when considered in the light of how thoroughly our sampling of the avifauna really is. It is a theme of this book, then, that the ranges of many birds in the continent are under increased stress and a complete reassessment of them must be made and more adequately monitored. These are truly changing times!

An example of recent range alterations is the number of "eastern" or "northern" species appearing in extreme eastern Washington and northern Idaho. A brief presentation of this event follows.

MIGRATION FLYWAY FOR EASTERN AND NORTHERN BIRDS

The increasing influx of eastern and northern species of birds, as well as the detection of a number of eastern races of Northwestern birds in our area, has revealed the existence of a migrational flyway along the eastern boundary of British Columbia and extending southward along the Washington-Idaho-Oregon border. The numerous spring and fall records of eastern North American subspecies in the western part of Northern Idaho indicate a movement of these individuals that was documented by the late Thomas Burleigh in his recent book on the birds of Idaho, but not appreciated by him as to their actual meaning. A number of species hitherto considered to occur east of the Rockies, such as the Blue Jay, Barred Owl, Philadelphia Vireo, and Tennessee Warbler, and such northern forms as the Hoary Redpoll and Wandering Tattler, have revealed as well the existence of a north-south corridor through the Palouse area.

What are the northern and southern entries (or exits) to this corridor? Why are these exotics showing up now and in continually increasing numbers, as in the case of Barred Owl? While some of the records may be the result of increased activities on the part of bird watchers, this cannot account for all of the sightings of exotics.

Settlement of the areas north of the plains of the Canadian prairie provinces, such as Alberta and Saskatchewan, created a corridor between the spruce forests to the north and the open plains to the south marked by orchards, woodlots, shelter belts, and groves of farm and urban shade trees of the deciduous type to form an access from the northern Middle West and Great Lakes regions westward to the Rocky Mountains. The access route touched the mountain barrier where there are significant breaches, as west of the Peace River country and to the north in what was otherwise a more or less impenetrable barrier. The breaches in the mountains led the birds to expand their ranges into the Rocky Mountain Trench which lies north-south along the western edge of the mountain chain — a great rift-like depression many hundreds of miles long stretching from the interior Arctic regions south to the Coeur d'Alene, Idaho and Flathead, Montana areas. From the southern end of the Purcell and parallel trenches, there is now in the Washington-Idaho border area a mixed and broken interface between the plains of the Columbia Basin to the west and the dense coniferous forests of the Bitterroots to the east along which these eastern birds can move. The increase in deciduous growth along this corridor as the result of urban and farm settlement has enhanced the ecology of the route. Traveling south along the border, these migrants and wanderers meet yet another access route in the form of the Snake River Canyon which takes them to extreme southwestern Idaho and the eastern border area of Oregon. From there, over low passes, the birds can push on to the western part of the Great Basin and into and through the Southwest. Some individuals fan out into various parts of the Northwest, particularly the interior, from this corridor. Apparently, a similar north-south flyway occurs in extreme eastern Idaho where a number of eastern forms have been recorded in recent years.

The following species of eastern or northern birds have used or may use the Idaho-Washington-Oregon migration corridor.

loons	rough-legged hawk
white-fronted goose	gyrfalcon
eiders	yellow rail
white-winged scoter	ivory gull
broad-winged hawk	black-billed cuckoo

PAGE INDEX TO THE BIRDS
OF THE PACIFIC NORTHWEST

18

READING ABOUT BIRDS

Alcorn, G. D. NORTHWEST BIRDS: DISTRIBUTION AND EGGS. Western Media, Tacoma, Washington, 1978. A distributional checklist along traditional lines. Color photos of eggs of Northwest species.

Bruun, B. BIRDS OF EUROPE. Golden Press, New York, 1969. An expanded version in large format of the author's BIRDS OF EUROPE field guide. Places our Pacific Northwest birds in perspective and covers many species that are common to both hemispheres. Very well illustrated.

Burleigh, T. D. BIRDS OF IDAHO. Caxton Printers, Caldwell, Idaho, 1972. An excellently detailed distributional checklist of Idaho birds, but has little other information. Occurrence records up to about 1960.

Campbell, R. W. and H. Hosford. ATTRACTING AND FEEDING BIRDS IN BRITISH COLUMBIA. British Columbia Provincial Museum, Victoria, B.C., 1979. A very excellent manual on the subject for Northwest birds. Highly recommended.

Gabrielson, I. N. and S. G. Jewett. BIRDS OF OREGON. Oregon State College, Corvallis. Detailed coverage of Oregon birds, though many ranges are dated and obsolete.

Godfrey, W. E. THE BIRDS OF CANADA. National Museum of Canada, Ottawa, 1966. A competent, well-illustrated treatment of the birds of Canada. The maps are particularly useful. A valuable book in the Northwest bird student's library. A new edition in preparation.

Guiguet, C. J. THE BIRDS OF BRITISH COLUMBIA. British Columbia Provincial Museum, Victoria, 1965 A series of bulletins (not yet completed) on the birds of the province with illustrations, identifying characters, ranges, and habits.

Harrison, C. J. O (ed.) BIRD FAMILIES OF THE WORLD. Abrams, New York, 1978. A very fine treatment of the families of birds of the world. Gives the advanced field student a survey of the entire bird class. Well illustrated.

Hatler, D. F.; R. W. Campbell; and A. Dorst. BIRDS OF PACIFIC RIM NATIONAL PARK. British Columbia Provincial Museum, Victoria, 1978. Summarizes a mass of field data and the guide to use for birding on the west coast of Vancouver Island.

Hoffmann, R. BIRDS OF THE PACIFIC STATES. Houghton Mifflin, Boston, 1927. Still a very useful manual with its excellent descriptions of ecology and behavior of Pacific coast species.

Jewett, S. G. et al. BIRDS OF WASHINGTON STATE. University of Washington Press, Seattle, 1953. Similar in format to the Oregon book by Gabrielson and Jewett.

Larrison, E. J. and K. G. Sonnenberg. WASHINGTON BIRDS: THEIR LOCATION AND IDENTIFICATION. Seattle Audubon Society, 1968. A detailed discussion of the birds of the state of Washington. Now out of print.

Larrison, E. J.; J. L. Tucker; and M. T. Jollie. GUIDE TO IDAHO BIRDS. Idaho Academy of Science, Ricks College, Rexburg, Idaho, 1967. A field guide to Idaho birds with much information on their ecology and distribution.

Peterson, R. T. A FIELD GUIDE TO WESTERN BIRDS. Houghton Mifflin, Boston, 1961. The standard western field guide for many years. Illustrations and text are very useful. An absolute must for field students. A new edition in preparation.

Peterson, R. T. A FIELD GUIDE TO THE BIRDS. Houghton Mifflin, Boston, 1980. Very valuable for many western birds, particularly eastern species that visit our region. Magnificently illustrated.

Pough, R. H. AUDUBON BIRD GUIDE: EASTERN LAND BIRDS. 1946
AUDUBON WATER BIRD GUIDE: WATER, GAME, AND LARGE LAND BIRDS. 1951
AUDUBON WESTERN BIRD GUIDE: LAND, WATER, AND GAME BIRDS. 1957
Doubleday, New York. An excellent series of books for field use. Many useful details in the various species accounts. Excellent color illustrations of all species treated.

Ramsey, F. L. BIRDING OREGON. Audubon Society of Corvallis, 1978. A very useful guide to birding areas in Oregon, commentaries on identifying difficult groups, and an abundance table checklist of birds of the state.

Robbins, C. S.; B. Bruun; and H. S. Zim. BIRDS OF NORTH AMERICA. Golden Press, New York, 1966. With its excellent color illustrations of all North American species in both sexes and in immature phases, an absolute must for the field student. Text accounts are useful but brief.

Roberson, D. RARE BIRDS OF THE WEST COAST OF NORTH AMERICA. Woodstock Publications, Pacific Grove, California. 1980. Detailed discussion of the rare bird species of the Pacific coast from Alaska south to California. Not only analyzes the distribution of each species treated but considers problems of identification as well. Copiously illustrated. A must for the serious birder.

Snyder, L. L. ARCTIC BIRDS OF CANADA. University of Toronto Press, Toronto, Ontario, 1957. A good account of Arctic birds. Descriptions, ranges, field marks, habitats, and illustrations.

Taverner, P. A. BIRDS OF CANADA. National Museum of Canada, Ottawa, 1934. A very useful manual and well worth having. Long out of print but has been reprinted by the Arno Press, New York.

Terres, J. K. THE AUDUBON SOCIETY ENCYCLOPEDIA OF NORTH AMERICAN BIRDS. Knopf, New York, 1980. The most valuable book a bird student can possess after his field guide. Brilliantly written and illustrated. The best book on birds ever published.

Udvardy, M. D. F. THE AUDUBON SOCIETY FIELD GUIDE TO NORTH AMERICAN BIRDS: WESTERN REGION. Knopf, New York, 1977. Many excellent color photographs of western species. Brief notes on identification and habits.

Wahl, T. R. and D. R. Paulson. A GUIDE TO BIRD FINDING IN WASHINGTON, 1977 ed. T. R. Wahl, 3041 Eldridge, Bellingham, WA 98225. An excellent discussion of good places to look for birds in Washington. Also has a checklist of species. Maps, notes on identification of certain groups, and a list of references to study. Indispensible for Washington birders.

Weber, J. W. and E. J. Larrison. BIRDS OF SOUTHEASTERN WASHINGTON. University Press of Idaho, Moscow, 1977. A detailed distributional list of the birds of much of eastern Washington.

Note: The literature on birds is tremendous and new books constantly appear. The above-listed titles deal wholly or in part with Pacific Northwest birds and the beginning bird student would do well to make them the basis of his ornithological library.

NOTE

The range summaries that follow in the various species' accounts pertain to that part of the bird's distribution in the Pacific Northwest only. Statements regarding the abundance of the species are given in general terms, as the sampling methods employed by birders in the Northwest are crude at best and large areas are still seldom visited. Rather than giving lists of records only, the author has used his judgment in interpreting such data in descriptive terms, for the better understanding of the amateur birder.

E. J. L.

SPECIES ACCOUNTS
LOONS

1. Arctic Loon (Fisher)

Loons are small-goose-sized birds with relatively short necks and long, stout, sharp-pointed bills. The tail is rather short and stiff, while the wings are strong, short, and somewhat pointed. The short legs are located at the end of the body, which makes walking very difficult on land from which flight cannot be attempted. Streamlined body shape, close dense plumage, and ease with which the specific gravity can be altered make these animals capable of expert diving and underwater swimming, which they often do with only the head showing above the water. Loons are birds of open water, being most often found at times other than the breeding season on salt water of the ocean coast, straits, or sounds, and on the larger lakes in the interior. More or less solitary, they are seldom seen in groups of more than two. They feed mostly on fish which are caught by underwater foraging.

There are four World-wide species of loons, all of which occur, commonly or rarely, in the Pacific Northwest. The Common Loon is a rare breeder, but a more numerous migrant and winter resident. While the Red-throated Loon breeds in the northern part of our region, most

23

of us see it, as well as the Arctic Loon and the scarce Yellow-billed Loon as winter visitors. These are primitive birds of great antiquity, yet are relatively poorly known. In fact, some authorities consider the Arctic Loon to represent two species, while the Yellow-billed and Common Loons may be conspecific. All of this points up the need for considering the bird life of any region or continent on a World-wide basis.

PACIFIC NORTHWEST SPECIES

RED-THROATED LOON *Gavia stellata* 24-27 (612-688) Fig. 3

This species is smaller than the Common Loon and has a sharp, thin, up-turned bill; a good field mark when compared to the thick straight bill of the Common Loon. In spring, crown dark gray; hind neck black, streaked with white; sides of head and neck bluish gray; patch on throat red; remainder of upper parts dark brown. Under parts white. In winter, similar to the Arctic and Common Loons, but with the feathers on the back with V-shaped white edges. CALLS. A hoarse grating *kra, kra, kra, kra* or *gr-r-ga, gr-r, gr-r-ga,* etc; also various loon-like cries, but mostly silent. HABITAT. Summer resident in coastal marshes or other open areas near water. Winters on coastal salt water and in estuaries of the larger rivers, particularly in bays along the coast; less commonly on inland freshwater lakes. RANGE. Breeds from the northern Alaskan and Yukon coasts south through the Yukon to the central B.C. coast and Vancouver Island. Winters and migrates along the coast from the Aleutians southward, being most numerous in spring. Rare in the interior east of the Cascades. Some scattered individuals in coastal and inland salt water in summer. Rare spring and fall migrant in Idaho. Has become much more numerous in Puget Sound in recent years.

ARCTIC LOON *Gavia arctica* 27 (688) Figs. 1 and 3

The Arctic Loon is the size of a large duck, but has a loon-like bill and body outline. In spring, the top of the head and the hind neck are bluish gray; remainder of upper parts are black, marked on the back with large white spots; patch on the throat black; under parts white. In winter, hind neck is grayish brown; back blackish, and the throat and under parts are white. The bill appears to be straight or very slightly de-curved and not as heavy as in the Common Loon. The grayish head and black throat are distinctive in spring. CALLS. A harsh crying *kok-kok-kok-kok* and a wailing *oh-h-h* or *ho-ho-oo-ooh,* etc. HABITAT. Breeds on freshwater lakes and ponds in tundra and open taiga; winters mostly in coastal saltwater areas. RANGE. Breeds from the Arctic coasts of Alaska and the Yukon southward to southern Alaska, migrating and wintering mostly in saltwater areas along the ocean coasts of Oregon and Washington, especially in the Gulf Islands of B. C. and in other areas of pronounced tidal passage. Scattered occurrences (mostly in the fall) in the interior east of the Cascades. Nonbreeding birds occasionally seen on salt water in summer. Scarce, but regular, fall migrant in extreme eastern Washington and the western part of northern Idaho along the Washington-Idaho border region.

2. Common Loon (Schultz)

COMMON LOON *Gavia immer* 28-36 (714-918) Figs. 2 and 3

This species is a water bird the size of a goose, but with a heavy sharp-pointed bill. In summer, head, bill, and neck black; collar on neck black; upper parts, checkered with black and white; under parts white. The narrow black collar is bordered above with two half rings of white streaks (below the chin). In winter, crown, nape, and back dark gray with cheeks, throat, and under parts white. The bill is relatively thick and carried more horizontally than that of other loons. CALLS. A tremulous *ho-hah-ah-ah-ho* or *who-oo-oo-oo-oo,* rising in the middle; short barks; various other screams and weird cries. HABITAT. Breeds on secluded mountain and lowland lakes and winters and migrates along coastal bays and inlets as well as adjacent freshwater bodies. Less commonly seen on the larger rivers. A bird of the wild country. RANGE. Breeds throughout Alaska and the Yukon south to Washington, Oregon, and Idaho (scatteringly). Migrates throughout the Northwest, wintering mostly along the Pacific Coast from the Aleutians southward. Non-breeding individuals widely scattered on fresh and salt water during the summer. Fairly common to uncommon migrant through Idaho, wintering irregularly as far north as Lake Coeur d'Alene. Breeds regularly in suitable lakes in Yellowstone National Park and vicinity. Scattered breeder in central Idaho. May be seen any month on the Columbia River in northcentral Washington, especially November through April. Possibly attracted to the increased areas of impounded water in the Northwest.

YELLOW-BILLED LOON *Gavia adamsii* 30-35 (765-892) Fig. 3

This species averages the largest of the loons and frequently stands out among other water birds because of its size and ponderous bulk. The heavy bill has a straight upper edge with a strongly up-turned lower edge and is often carried in an up-tilted position. The line marking the edges of the mandibles is curved, making for a smiling appearance. The eye of this species is smaller and the neck thicker than in the Common Loon. The over-all color of the Yellow-billed Loon is lighter than that of the Common and a dark brown or blackish spot on the head behind the ear is characteristic of the Yellow-billed. A good winter field mark is the brown and white appearance of the bird contrasted with the grayish or blackish and white pattern of the Common Loon. The head and neck are also paler than in the Common Loon. HABITAT. Similar to that of the Common Loon. RANGE. Scattered summer resident in Alaska and the northern Yukon, migrating and wintering southward on salt water along the Pacific coast of southeastern Alaska and B.C., and uncommonly but regularly to the Northwestern states. Records for all season, including summer. Very rare in the interior east of the Cascades, but recorded in southwestern Idaho. Breeds in tundra and marshy areas, but prefers salt water in migration.

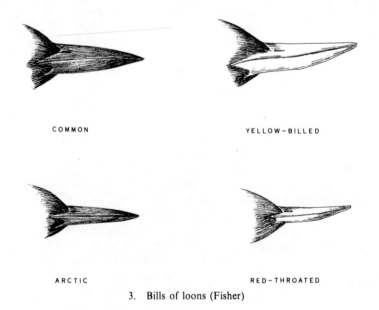

COMMON   YELLOW-BILLED

ARCTIC   RED-THROATED

3. Bills of loons (Fisher)

GREBES

4.   Western Grebe, l.; Pied-billed Grebe, r. (Fisher)

The grebes are duck-sized water birds with slender pointed bills, small heads, and inconspicuous tails. Spending most of their time on water, they are expert divers and swimmers, but fly and walk with difficulty. Instead of pitching over forward in the usual way of surface diving, grebes often sink slowly, till only the head, periscope-wise, projects above the water. The bill may be short, as in the Pied-billed Grebe, or long and pointed as in the Western Grebe. The plumage is dense, smooth, and satiny.

During the summer, these are pond and marsh birds, but in winter, the various Pacific Northwest species may be seen on more or less open waters, mostly singly or in pairs, except the Western Grebe which may congregate on salt water in large flocks. The Pied-billed and Eared Grebes are most commonly found on fresh water in winter (the time when most grebes are observed), while the Red-necked, Horned, and Western are more commonly seen on salt water.

An ancient highly-specialized group, the grebes are adapted for diving from the surface and for underwater swimming. The specially lobed toes propel the birds forward below the water surface with

27

amazing speed. Two basic sub-groups occur in this order, the modestly-colored dabchicks of which our Pied-billed Grebe is a member, and the more ornamented species to which the remainder of the Northwest grebes belong. In all, there are perhaps 19 to 22 species World-wide in this interesting order of waterfowl.

PACIFIC NORTHWEST SPECIES

PIED-BILLED GREBE *Podilymbus podiceps* 12-15 (306-382) Fig. 4
This is a small brown grebe with a round, white, chicken-like bill. Summer birds have black throats and bands on the bill. No white patches in the wing. When swimming, they may show undertail coverts that are white, resulting in an appearance of a "high-riding stern". In winter, the bill is bright brown without a black band, throat dirty white, and under parts unspotted. Extremely rapid ability at diving is characteristic. CALLS. A loud series of *cow-cow-cow* or *cuck-cuck-cuck,* etc., *cow-ugh, cow-ugh, cow-ugh, ka-loooow.* HABITAT. Breeds on freshwater lakes and ponds and sluggish streams with dense shore vegetation; winters on fresh water and on bays and river estuaries in coastal salt water. RANGE. Breeds locally and sometimes commonly from central B.C. southward through the Northwest, wintering through the coastal states from southern B.C. south. Rare straggler to southeastern Alaska. In Idaho, common migrant and uncommon winter resident (especially along the Snake River); fairly common local resident and breeder in Idaho and northeastern Washington.

RED-NECKED GREBE *Podiceps grisegena* 18-20 (459-510)
This species is a large grebe with dark brown upper parts, white throat and sides of head, gray neck, white under parts, and a heavy yellow bill in winter plumage. In summer, upper parts grayish black, under parts white, neck red, hindneck and top of head black, cheeks white. Two white patches in the wing when the bird is in flight. The neck is shorter and thicker than that of the Western Grebe. The triangular-shaped head separates it from the loons. CALLS. A hoarse *ca-wak, ca-wak, ow-ak, cor-rawk,* etc.; various other prolonged, grating, loon-like wailings. HABITAT. Summer resident in marshy or reedy areas on freshwater lakes or sluggish rivers; winters on inshore salt water areas, less commonly in nearby freshwater lakes. RANGE. Breeds from the Arctic coast of Alaska and the Yukon south through B.C. and the Northwest states (uncommonly to rarely), wintering mostly on or near the ocean coast, but also regularly on Puget Sound, and in small numbers on the reservoirs of eastern Washington. Scattered individuals on coastal salt water in summer. Uncommon to rare migrant and summer resident in northern Idaho and northeastern Washington, as well as southern Oregon.

5. Horned Grebe (r., winter) (Schultz)

HORNED GREBE *Podiceps auritus* 13-15 (331-382) Fig. 5

A small grebe. In spring, head black with yellow ear-tufts, neck and sides reddish, back grayish black and under parts white. In winter, difficult to distinguish from the Eared Grebe. However, the Horned has a blackish, somewhat flattened crown sharply separated from the white cheeks, a thicker neck, and a stouter bill. The dark line down the back of the neck is well marked and narrow. The dark color of the crown does not extend below the eye. In flight, one white patch shows on the rear edge of the wing. The bill is deeper than wide. CALLS. A loud nasal *kyark, kyark* or *yark, yark,* etc. HABITAT. Summer resident in marshy areas on freshwater ponds, sloughs, and lakes; winters mostly on coastal salt water and less commonly on larger freshwater bodies. RANGE. Breeds from central Alaska and the northern Yukon southward to the mid Northwest states (breeding in eastern Washington), wintering mainly along the entire Northwest coast. Irregular and less common as a migrant inland. Fairly common, though irregular, migrant and scarce winter and summer visitor and possible breeder in Idaho. Common migrant and winter resident on the Columbia River in central Washington, October through April.

EARED GREBE *Podiceps nigricollis* 12-14 (306-357)

A small grebe, similar to the Horned Grebe in spring, but has a black neck and a black crest on the forehead. In winter, top of head, hindneck, and back dark gray; cheeks, foreneck, and under parts white, closely resembling the Horned Grebe in this plumage, but may be distinguished by the more slender bill and neck and the fact that the white areas of the head are less sharply marked off from the dark areas. The bill appears to be slightly up-turned and is wider than deep. The dark line down the back of the neck is broad. The dark color of the crown extends below the eye. Forehead is high and there is one white patch in the wing. CALLS. An excited *kick, rick-up, kick, rick-up, kick, rick-up;* a mellow *poo-eep, poo-eep,* or *koor-r-r-eep;* a shorter *quer-ip;* and other harsher notes. HABITAT. Breeds in shallower marshy areas of freshwater lakes and ponds in open as well as wooded country; winters on salt water in the north, but more on fresh water in the southern half of the Northwest. RANGE. Breeds from central B.C. south through the region, mostly away from the coastal areas, and winters rarely from southern B.C. southward, mostly in Washington and Oregon. Fairly common spring and fall migrant and summer resident and uncommon winter visitor southerly in Idaho.

WESTERN GREBE *Aechmorphorus occidentalis* 24-29 (612-740)

This is a large grebe with a swan-like neck and a long yellow bill. The top of the head and hindneck are slaty black; the back is dark grayish black; the throat, foreneck, and under parts are silvery white. There is one long white stripe in the wing in flight. CALLS. A shrill *krick, krick-ker-reeeeek* and a long *reek, kerreek-kee-reek* in breeding; also a rapid *kee-kee-kee-kee.* HABITAT. Summer resident on the larger freshwater lakes; winters on fresh water and the bays and river estuaries on salt water. RANGE. Breeds from southcentral B.C. southward, mostly east of the Cascades, through the Northwest, wintering and migrating more commonly in coastal areas and less so in the interior. Fairly common to uncommon migrant and breeder in Idaho. Non-breeding individuals occasionally seen in summer on salt water. *Note.* The Western Grebe may actually consist of two species: a slightly larger more northern taxon with the dark crown on the head including the eye and a dull greenish yellow bill; and a slightly smaller more southern form with the dark crown not including the eye and a bright yellow orange bill.

ALBATROSSES

6. Laysan Albatross (Fisher)

The first sight of an albatross is one never to be forgotten. The bird slowly comes into view, banking and gliding on rigid stiff-set wings over the great swells of the Pacific Ocean. The observer is struck by the appearance of the long narrow wings, the heavy body, and the large hooked bill. Occasionally the bird makes a few wings strokes, but mostly planes through the air displaying its great mastery of gliding. This is the fabled albatross, well known by mariners, which with us is at most only a visitor off the coast in the deep-water offshore zone, some twenty miles or more from land. It frequents particularly the upwelling waters rich in plankton to feed on the abundant squid and fish faunas. Albatrosses commonly follow the fishing boats, often in pairs or small groups, for scraps of fish thrown overboard. Bird students on marine excursions have found considerable success in "chumming" up the birds.

Coming to land only to breed, the albatrosses are the most pelagic of birds, and everything in their anatomy and behavior reflects this fact. They are members of the tube-nosed swimmers, that most interesting of marine groups. The four species that have been found in Northwest waters, rarely to commonly, are usually seen only well off the ocean where special trips by boat must be made.

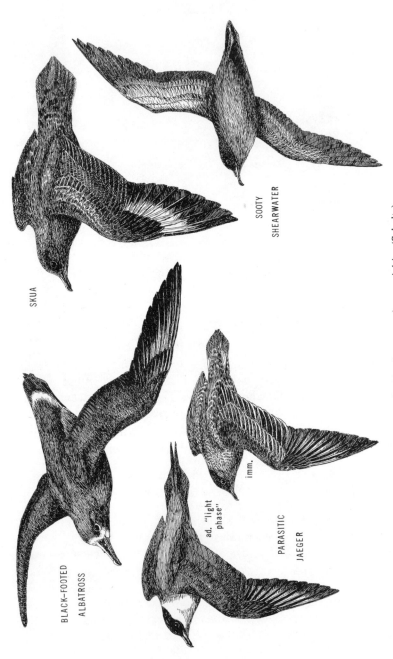

SKUA

SOOTY
SHEARWATER

BLACK-FOOTED
ALBATROSS

ad. "light
phase"

imm.

PARASITIC
JAEGER

7. Four Pacific Northwest marine specialties (Schultz)

PACIFIC NORTHWEST SPECIES

SHORT-TAILED ALBATROSS *Diomedea albatrus* 37 (944)

Adults have a white body with the head and neck tinted with yellowish. The wings and tail are blackish with white patches in the primaries and wing coverts. The bill is yellow and the feet are flesh colored. The short tail is blackish brown. CALLS. A hoarse croak, though mostly silent. HABITAT. In our region, the open expanses of the ocean. RANGE. Very rare offshore spring and fall straggler; formerly common in Northwest marine waters, then completely absent. Current protection on the breeding grounds may account for recent offshore sightings in the Northwest. All albatrosses should be identified with care, as the Laysan and Wandering Albatrosses are somewhat similar and with these birds, and one never knows what may show up. Some doubt has been expressed regarding validity of recent records of the Short-tailed Albatross.

BLACK-FOOTED ALBATROSS *Diomedea nigripes* 28-36 (714-918) Fig. 7

A large dark-colored marine bird looking somewhat like a sea gull but larger and with very long relatively narrow wings. The upper parts are dusky brown with a white face and often a whitish rump. The bill is brownish; the feet black. The under parts are a little lighter. The bird soars and glides like a shearwater. CALLS. Guttural muttering sounds, though usually silent at sea. HABITAT. Offshore ocean areas, usually 20 miles or more from land; often follows fishing boats for handouts of fish scraps. RANGE. Ranges over the open ocean off the coast from the Bering Sea southward, mostly in summer and fall, to out of the Northwest region. Probably the most common albatross in the Northwest marine waters. Rarely to be seen from shore, though this was formerly possible! Occasionally a dead individual floats to shore.

LAYSAN ALBATROSS *Diomedea immutabilis* 32 (816) Fig. 6

A mostly white-bodied albatross similar to the Short-tailed Albatross but with a dark back and wings. The bill and feet are dull flesh colored. The Wandering Albatross is similar, but has the back and all of the wings, except the primaries, white. The bill is yellow to pinkish white. CALLS. Mostly silent. HABITAT. The open ocean. RANGE. Rare irregular visitor off the coast of Washington, Oregon, and B.C., as well as the western and central Aleutians. Mostly in winter; less commonly in summer and fall.

WHITE-CAPPED ALBATROSS; SHY ALBATROSS *Diomedea cauta* 36 (918)

Body mostly white but back and upper surface of wings black. Differs from other dark-backed albatrosses in having the under surface of the wings white except for the extreme tips. Head and neck grayish white. Bill yellowish; feet bluish flesh color. HABITAT. The open ocean. RANGE. Apparently very rare off the Washington coast as a fall straggler.

FULMARS

8. Northern Fulmar (light phase, l.; dark phase, r.) (Fisher)

NORTHERN FULMAR *Fulmarus glacialis* 18 (459) Fig. 8

The Fulmar is a stocky gull-like bird of either whitish or dark-grayish coloration with a stout yellow bill. The back and tail are bluish gray and the wings are light grayish brown. The gliding tilting flight on stiff-set wings near the water is distinctive, together with the color. The wing beat is more rapid than that of the gulls. The dark phase is similar to some of the shearwaters, but the Fulmar's bill is heavier and lighter colored and the legs are whitish. CALLS. Hoarse grunting notes, though usually silent in our area. HABITAT. The open ocean,

34

sometimes in association with shearwaters; in our region, dead, dying, or exhausted birds only to be found near shore. RANGE. Breeds on islands of the Bering Sea, Aleutians, the Alaska Peninsula, and the Gulf of Alaska, wintering (fall, winter, and early spring) mostly off shore from the Bering Sea southward along the Northwest coast, though rarely in the Strait of Juan de Fuca and the northern Puget Sound area. Occasionally seen off the Washington coast in summer. While usually foraging more out to sea, winter storms kill numbers of Fulmars and the well-preserved bodies may be washed ashore along the ocean beaches. Here one may observe the peculiar tube-like arrangement of the external nostrils, typical of this order, which in the Fulmars are fused together. Since the Procellariiformes must drink salt water, the salt is excreted as a concentrated brine by glands in the head and the nostril tubes apparently take care of the "drip".

SHEARWATERS

9. Slender-billed Shearwater (Fisher)

Superficially, these birds resemble gulls, at least in size; but there the resemblance ends. The shearwaters are restricted entirely to salt water and usually that of the open ocean. For the most part, the bills are thin and hooked. Compared with those of gulls, the wings of

35

shearwaters are narrow and the tails smaller. It is the flight of this group that is most characteristic. Instead of flying through the air at some height with beating wings, the shearwaters skim over the waves with a banking gliding flight that is only occasionally interrupted with a few flaps of the wings. The name "shearwater" is truly descriptive, as the birds glide down the hollows between the waves, rising to barely clear the crests of the great combers, often cleaving through the spindrift. One has to go to the ocean beach to see these birds and the best point of vantage is the end of some rocky jetty projecting out to sea from the shore.

Six species of shearwaters pass along our coasts and present an interesting problem in identification. Of these, only one, the Sooty Shearwater, is common, the other five making up minor parts of the shearwater migration. Specific determinations must be carefully made by bird students. Published summaries of ranges and numbers of shearwaters vary considerably, calling for increased observation and greater accuracy in sight identification.

PACIFIC NORTHWEST SPECIES

PINK-FOOTED SHEARWATER *Puffinus creatopus* 19 (484)

A large shearwater with brownish upper parts, black tail coverts, and whitish under parts often somewhat barred with grayish. Bill and feet pinkish. CALLS. Mostly silent. HABITAT. Usually occurs a few miles off our ocean shores. RANGE. Ranges off the coast in spring, summer, and fall, mostly along Oregon and Washington, and less commonly north to B.C. and southeastern Alaska. Most numerous in late summer and early fall.

FLESH-FOOTED SHEARWATER; PALE-FOOTED SHEARWATER *Puffinus carneipes* 19-20 (484-510)

Very similar to the dark-colored Sooty Shearwater in color, but larger. Bill whitish with dark tip, feet pinkish, under wings dark. CALLS. Mostly silent. HABITAT. Coastal waters and the open ocean. RANGE. Rare, but regular, visitor off the coasts of Alaska, B.C., Washington, and Oregon. May be conspecific with the Pink-footed Shearwater.

NEW ZEALAND SHEARWATER *Puffinus bulleri* 16-17 (408-434)

Under parts bright white. Upper parts grayish, except for blackish crown and leading edges and tips of the wings. "M" pattern in the dark of the wings above is distinctive in flight. The bill is bluish, tipped with black. Relatively slow wing beat. CALLS. Mostly silent. HABITAT. The open ocean, but approaching the coastline. RANGE.

Common to uncommon, but irregular, midsummer and fall visitor off the coasts of B.C., Washington, and Oregon; very rare in spring.

SOOTY SHEARWATER *Puffinus griseus* 16-18 (408-459) Fig. 7
This is an all-dark-appearing shearwater with whitish undersurfaces of the wings. Bill and feet are dark. Much the commonest shearwater of our region. CALLS. A nasal *mraah* or *graah-ah* when excited. HABITAT. Often passes close in by the ocean coast, in late summer and early fall, from a few hundred yards off shore to 15 miles out, skimming close over the waves and breakers in vast unending masses. Approaches closer to shore than other shearwaters. RANGE. Ranges commonly both in and off shore in the ocean from Oregon north to the Aleutians. Abundant, but variable, in late summer and early fall, but also in spring, though likely to be found at other times of the year as well. Occasionally enters Puget Sound.

SHORT-TAILED SHEARWATER; SLENDER-BILLED SHEARWATER *Puffinus tenuirostris* 14 (357) Fig. 9
An all-dark-appearing shearwater very similar to the Sooty Shearwater but is slightly smaller in size, and with shorter bill. Under surfaces of wings are dark colored — not grayish white. Not always possible to separate from the Sooty. CALLS. Usually silent. HABITAT. Offshore visitor, often with the Sooty Shearwaters. RANGE. Ranges along the ocean coast in our region from Oregon to the Arctic Ocean, occasionally coming into Puget Sound in the fall and early winter. Very irregular in numbers along the Northwest ocean coast in fall (October and November) and has recently been found there in spring. Abundant in 1977 but absent in 1978.

MANX SHEARWATER *Puffinus puffinus* 13-15 (331-382)
Under parts white with blackish upper parts including the bill. Similar to the Pink-footed Shearwater, but this species is much smaller and has a noticeably faster wing beat. The under surfaces of the wings are much whiter than in the Pink-footed. Upper surfaces of wings much darker than in the New Zealand Shearwater. CALLS. Usually silent. HABITAT. The open ocean. RANGE. Rare visitor in fall along the ocean coast from B.C. south, usually close to shore.

PETRELS

There are several groups of petrels on the oceans of the World, two of which are represented, if only rarely, in our waters. The first, the gadfly petrels of the genus *Pterodroma,* are intermediate in size, flight, and behavior between the true shearwaters and the storm-petrels. Only one species of this group barely gets on our Northwest bird list. The

10. Fork-tailed Petrel (Fisher)

second group, the storm-petrels, is represented by three species. These are small blackish or grayish birds usually seen flitting over the surface of salt water well out to sea. Very often they fly just over the surface with their slender legs and webbed feet dangling below the body. Very commonly, they will follow boats for handouts and thus can be observed at close quarters. It may be surprising to find such small delicate-appearing birds far out from land but these are typically pelagic species coming to shore only for breeding. Some 22 species of storm-petrels roam the seas of the World.

It is said that the name "petrel" refers to St. Peter who walked on the water, in describing the behavior of the birds in hovering or flying just over the surface with their feet often paddling in it. Their flight is a fluttering batlike one and they spend much of their time in the windless friction zone in the few inches above the water's surface. They feed on plankton and small fish and crustaceans that they pick up from the surface and also acquire by diving.

PACIFIC NORTHWEST SPECIES

SCALED PETREL *Pterodroma inexpectata* 11-12 (280-306)

This is a medium-sized petrel with dark upper parts (lighter on proximal halves of wings) and a black crown. Face and throat are white with remainder of under parts dark. The lower surfaces of the wings are whitish with a lengthwise heavy black bar. The bill is dark. CALLS. Mostly silent at sea. HABITAT. The open ocean. RANGE. Rare straggler to the Aleutians, the western Alaskan coast, and the coast of the Northwest states.

WILSON'S STORM-PETREL *Oceanites oceanicus* 6-7 (153-178)
A dark, brownish, sparrow-sized petrel with a white rump and long grayish wing patches. Legs and feet are yellow and the tail is round- or square-tipped. Commonly follows ships. CALLS. Mostly silent at sea. HABITAT. The open ocean. RANGE. Very rare visitor along the ocean coast (Oregon).

LEACH'S STORM-PETREL *Oceanodroma leucorhoa* 8 (204) Fig. 11
This species is a sooty-black petrel with a white rump and silver gray under surfaces of the wings. The bill and feet are black. The tail is

11. Leach's Petrel (Pole)

forked. The flight is very erratic, reminding one of a Nighthawk. CALLS. A low guttural *kick-er-rick-er-oo*, rapidly repeated. Has been also rendered at *petter-retter-rell, petter-retter-rell*. HABITAT. Breeds on rocky islets along the ocean shore; forages over the open ocean. RANGE. Breeds and wanders along the ocean coast from Oregon north to the Aleutians, often nesting in immense colonies. Occasionally straggles to inland marine and fresh waters, as in the Puget Sound area. Prefers warmer waters than the following species. Rarely seen except at night at the breeding colonies or in very small numbers from midsummer pelagic trips.

FORK-TAILED STORM-PETREL *Oceanodroma furcata* 8-9 (204-230) Fig. 10

A little pearl-gray sea bird, slightly smaller than a Robin, usually seen flitting over the ocean surface. The throat is whitish; wing coverts are dusky, edged with white. CALLS. Soft twittering sounds. HABITAT. Breeds on small offshore islets and rocks; forages over water in the offshore zone. RANGE. Breeds in the Aleutians and irregularly along the coast southward, where also an uncommon migrant, to out of the Northwest. Rare winter visitor in southern Alaskan waters. Prefers the deeper offshore waters where it may be common in summer. Breeds in large colonies on the Washington coast.

PELICANS

To the average person, the pelicans must seem to be very bizarre birds, indeed. Yet they are admirably built for their particular mode of existence and use the large bill to great advantage in foraging for food either by diving or scooping up the fishes and other organisms on which they subsist. Briefly, we can characterize pelicans as very large water birds with long flat bills and large extensible throat pouches. The tail is short, but the wings are large with broad wing-spans. The feet are completely webbed. The flight pattern is distinctive and White Pelicans are often observed flying in tight "military" formation, flapping together for a while and then all sailing on outspread wings.

Two species, neither particularly common, visit parts of the Pacific Northwest. The White Pelican is more of an inland bird east of the Cascades, while the Brown Pelican is a sparse visitor along the ocean coast. The wing-spans of the two are immense, about nine feet for the White and six to seven for the Brown.

Another member of this order, the Red-billed Tropic-bird *(Phaethon aethereus)* was recorded off the Washington and Oregon coasts during the 1940s, a single bird for each record. It is the policy of

12. Brown Pelican (Fisher)

this manual not to treat such rarities of more than 30 or 40 years standing, but rather to attempt to depict the birdlife of the Pacific Northwest as it now exists.

PACIFIC NORTHWEST SPECIES

AMERICAN WHITE PELICAN *Pelecanus erythrorhynchos* 60 (1,530) Fig. 13

This is an entirely white pelican, except for the black tips and rear halves of the wings. The bill and feet are yellowish orange. It is the only white bird in the Northwest with such a large yellowish bill. It flies with its head pulled back on the shoulders. CALLS. Mostly silent. HABITAT. Frequents islands in large freshwater lakes for breeding; visitor to large interior lakes at other seasons (though many are non-breeding visitors in summer). Scattered individuals may visit smaller bodies of water. RANGE. Breeds irregularly and locally from B.C. south, east of the Cascades, to the southern border of the Northwest, except in Washington. Non-breeding individuals and groups to be encountered widely in the above area during the summer and migration. Winters mostly south of the region covered in this manual, though a very few in winter as far north as southern B.C. Some straggle irregularly west of the Cascades in the Northwest states. Fairly common

41

13. White Pelican (Schultz)

migrant in southern Idaho; rare north of the Snake River Plains. Summer visitor (non-breeding) to the Potholes, Grant County, Washington, early summer to October.

BROWN PELICAN *Pelecanus occidentalis* 50-54 (1,275-1,377) Fig. 12
This species has grayish upper parts and brownish under parts. The large size, dark color, huge wingspread, and method of alternately flapping and soaring are distinctive. The head and bill are marked with yellow, the gular pouch is brownish, and the legs are black. CALLS. A low *cluck*, though usually silent. HABITAT. In our region, marine and nearby fresh water. RANGE. Sporadic wanderer northward along the ocean coast and inland salt water (straits and sounds) to B.C.; mostly as late summer and fall visitors (very rare in spring) and most numerous on the Oregon coast. Recorded in late December at Boise, Idaho. Numbers apparently increasing in recent years, thanks to elimination of agricultural use of DDT near the breeding grounds.

CORMORANTS

14. Double-crested Cormorant, r.; Ring-billed Gull, l. (Fisher)

Cormorants are goose-sized birds, more or less entirely black of color, often seen sitting upright on posts or pilings (often spreading the wings) or floating in the water where their snake-like necks and upward pointing bills are distinctive. The bill is as long as the head and while the cormorants belong to the same order as the pelicans, the gular pouches of the former are very small. The tail is fan-shaped and often used as a prop while the bird is standing. The feet are webbed and the plumage is glossy and iridescent. Cormorants fish by diving or swimming under water (using the wings in submarine propulsion). Though occasionally seen singly, the birds are strongly gregarious at times, nesting in colonies and migrating in formation.

Of the some 30 World-wide species, three forms occur in the Pacific Northwest and require only a little skill in their identification. While all — the Double-crested, Brandt's, and Pelagic — may be commonly found on salt water, only the Double-crested Cormorant occurs at all regularly on fresh water.

The typical coloration of the cormorants led to the development of the common name from the Latin *corvus marinus* ("sea crow"). These are primarily fish-eating birds and some species use a communal

43

fishing system whereby hundreds or thousands of individuals may herd surface-feeding fishes into dense masses for ease of capture.

PACIFIC NORTHWEST SPECIES

DOUBLE-CRESTED CORMORANT *Phalacrocorax auritus* 30-36 Fig. 14

This is the only cormorant in the region with an orange-yellow bill and face. It is also practically the only cormorant found on both fresh and salt water. It is a large, dark, low-swimming bird which when perched assumes a very upright position. Adults, all black, with long, slender, yellowish bill sharply hooked downward at the tip. Immatures, grayish brown head and neck, light grayish throat and breast, remainder of plumage brownish. In spite of its name, the small crests behind the eyes are not good field marks. CALLS. Silent, except for occasional hoarse grunting croaks when alarmed and various hisses. HABITAT. Breeds on rocks and islets in salt water or in tall trees near water; on large lakes and rivers in the interior. RANGE. Breeds along the coast and nearby marine sounds and straits from the eastern Aleutians and Kodiak area southward and, irregularly, in the interior east of the Cascades from B.C. south. Winters along the coast, mostly on salt water, from southern Alaska southward, though occasionally up the Columbia River as far as the Tri-Cities. Common migrant and summer visitor in southern Idaho where it breeds (at least four nesting colonies). Uncommon to scarce migrant in northern Idaho. Occasional spring and summer visitor and possible breeder in central Washington, as at the Potholes.

BRANDT'S CORMORANT *Phalacrocorax penicillatus* 30-35 (765-892)

A large blackish cormorant with a black bill and dark or bluish gular pouch, surrounded by a buffy patch. Young birds and many adult-sized individuals are brownish. The pouch of the Double-crested Cormorant is yellowish, while that of the Brandt's is dark. CALLS. Low grunts, though usually silent. HABITAT. Breeds on cliffs and rocky islands along salt water; commonly roosts on cliffs; only occasionally seen on fresh water. RANGE. Resident and breeder along salt water from southeastern Alaska (where scattered and uncommon) southward to out of the Northwest. Winters in large numbers in the Gulf Islands waterways in coastal B.C. (most of these individuals probably from breeding colonies along the Oregon coast). Uncommon visitor on nearby fresh water.

PELAGIC CORMORANT *Phalacrocorax pelagicus* 25 (637)

The Pelagic Cormorant is glossy greenish or purplish black in color with a thin narrow bill and white patches on the lower flanks in spring. Small size and thin bills are distinctive. Bill and throat dark. Immatures, dark brownish. CALLS. Low croaks, though usually silent. HABITAT. Nest on rocky slopes and steep cliffs near salt water; forages entirely over salt water; often the commonest cormorant along the ocean coast. RANGE. Breeds from the Bering Sea south along salt water to the coasts of Washington and Oregon in our region. Winters in the Aleutians and along the coasts of B.C., Washington, and Oregon. The commonest nesting cormorant along marine waters.

FRIGATEBIRDS

15. Frigatebird (Fisher)

MAGNIFICENT FRIGATEBIRD *Fregata magnificens* 38-41 (969-1,046) Fig. 15
A large slender, dark-bodied sea bird with very long wings and a long deeply-forked tail. The bill is light colored, long, and strongly hooked. The narrow wings are crooked in flight. The female has a white lower neck and chest. The red throat pouch of the male is greatly expanded during the courtship performance. CALLS. Mostly silent at sea. RANGE. Very rare summer visitor along the ocean coast northward to Oregon and southwestern Washington. Recorded once each in eastern Oregon and eastern Washington.

BITTERNS

16. American Bittern (Fisher)

The bitterns are the marsh birds *par excellence*. They prefer freshwater marshes, swamps, and rush- and cattail-margined sloughs, as well as moist meadows and dense riparian thickets. The various species nest on the ground or on masses of floating vegetation making up hummocks in the swamp or marsh. Bitterns retreat before man, restricting themselves to habitats difficult for him to penetrate. Unfortunately, as civilization continues to "progress", the stake-driving call of the American Bittern is heard less and less. When approached, bitterns have the habit of freezing with the neck upstretched and motionless. Their almost perfect camouflage blends them into the cattails and they are often not detected till they flush.

Twelve species of bitterns occur in the World's bird fauna, being divided into two genera, *Botaurus* and *Ixobrychus*. We are fortunate in the Pacific Northwest in having one representative of each of these two groups, the American Bittern and the Least Bittern.

During the late 1930s and early 1940s, the author of this book, along with Harry Higman and Warren Flock, made a number of canoeing trips through the old Union Bay Marsh on the east edge of the University of Washington Campus. No trip was complete without the sight of an American Bittern and one was usually found before we had turned the bend from the canoe house into the open water of the bay. Many interesting birds were close to the city in those days!

PACIFIC NORTHWEST SPECIES

AMERICAN BITTERN *Botaurus lentiginosus* 24-30 (612-765) Fig. 16
The American Bittern is a large, long-legged, buffy marsh bird, heavily streaked with brown and showing brown wings with blackish tips in flight. The neck has black stripes down the sides which are sometimes concealed. The throat is white with vertical brown stripes. When approached, the bittern often stands motionless with its long heron-like bill pointing upward or flushes with a series of hoarse *quawks.* CALLS. An alarm *quawk;* a muffled *umph-ka-choonk,* given in spring. At a distance, the middle note is loudest and sounds like a stake being driven with a wooden mallet. HABITAT. Freshwater cattail marshes and swamps, as well as moist tall grass meadows. RANGE. Breeds from southeastern Alaska and central B.C. southward through the Northwest, wintering in much of the breeding area. Becoming local and irregular in occurrence with continued "reclaiming" of habitats.

LEAST BITTERN *Ixobrychus exilis* 11-14 (250-357) Fig. 17
The smallest bittern, this little wader is only 11-14 inches long with a 16-18 inch wing span. Males, greenish black above with brownish-yellow under parts; wings with large buffy patches. The sides of the breast are marked with brownish-black patches. There is a long white

17. Least Bittern (Larrison)

stripe on each side of the back. Females, browner above, often with two white streaks (or one buffy line) along the shoulders. CALLS. A low-pitched *coo-coo-coo-coo-coo;* also a harsher *tut-tut-tut.* HABITAT. Freshwater marshes with thick cattails and grasses. RANGE. Breeds in southeastern Oregon; migrant elsewhere in central, southern, and western Oregon and in southern Idaho. Rare as post-nesting straggler northward to B.C.

HERONS

Herons are long-necked, long-legged, wading birds with long pointed bills. Their tails are relatively short, but the wings are long and broad. The toes are long and unwebbed. The plumage is long and loose, and crests and plumes are common, especially during the breeding season. Herons feed by stalking their prey which consists mostly of amphibians, fishes, and large invertebrates such as crayfish. The members of this group are typically marsh and shore birds, and are commonly seen along both fresh and salt water patiently watching for their prey. Water and its immediate environs contain a great variety and quantity of avian foods and it is interesting to observe how nature has adapted a host of birds to avail themselves of this bounty. Small prey is attacked by small waders, the numerous shorebirds and rails, depending on whether the habitat is open or dense. Larger food species attract the herons and cranes, sorting the two groups out according to the availability of water. One of the principal goals of this book is to inform you as to which members of the various environmentally adapted groups of birds make up the Pacific Northwest bird fauna.

PACIFIC NORTHWEST SPECIES

BLACK-CROWNED NIGHT HERON *Nycticorax nycticorax* 23-27 (586-688)
This species is a chunky short-legged heron with a black crown and back, gray wings and tail, and whitish forehead, cheeks, and under parts. The bill is black; the eyes red; and the legs yellow or pink. Immatures, brown, streaked with white; similar to the American Bittern but paler. CALLS. A short, hoarse, high-pitched *quawk* or *wawrk.* HABITAT. Nests in trees in marshy or swampy places or along margins of lakes or rivers; occasionally seen by stock tanks or farm ponds. RANGE. Breeds locally and irregularly from eastern Washington (a large concentration at the Potholes Reservoir) and Idaho southward, wandering after the nesting season north to

18. Snowy Egret (Fisher)

southern B.C. (where rare, but recorded also in spring). Uncommon and erratic winter and migrational straggler in Oregon and Washington (where it winters in small numbers). Fairly common, though irregular, summer resident in southern Idaho, though with eggshell thinning and declining populations; rare in winter. Less numerous and more scattered in northern Idaho.

YELLOW-CROWNED NIGHT HERON *Nycticorax violaceus* 21 (536)
A short-legged, short-necked, stocky, grayish heron with a sharply

49

marked black, white, and yellow head and mottled black and white wings. Bill is short, heavy, and black. The legs are orange. CALLS. A *quawk* similar to that of the Black-crowned Night Heron but higher in pitch. HABITAT. Wooded swamps and wet riparian thickets. RANGE. Rare winter visitor in Oregon.

CATTLE EGRET *Bulbulcus ibis* 19-20 (484-510)
A rather stocky, short-necked, short-legged whitish heron with a yellowish-orange bill, yellowish legs, and light orange crest, breast, and shoulders (in breeding season). Frequently seen in flocks in pastures and crowding around cattle. CALLS. A hoarse croak. HABITAT. Wooded swamps in the nesting season, but forages on dry land and in pastures in close proximity to cattle, feeding on insects flushed up from the grass by the larger animals. RANGE. Scattered summer resident and breeder in southern Idaho. Irregular, but increasing, fall, winter, and spring visitor throughout the region, though most records for west of the Cascades and in southern Idaho. Rare in summer east of the Cascades in Washington. Reported as becoming fairly common in western Washington.

GREEN HERON *Butorides striatus* 17-19 (434-484)
This is a small green-colored heron with a chestnut colored neck and a black crest; back and wing tips are greenish blue. The throat is white and the legs are orange to greenish yellow. Frequently seen perching in trees. CALLS. Various high-pitched squawks and a loud *skyow*. HABITAT. A solitary nester in trees, usually willows, near fresh water. Forages along wooded shores of ponds and sluggish streams. RANGE. Breeds in western Washington, southwestern B.C., and in Oregon, as well as southern Idaho, wandering with increasing regularity after the breeding season north to southern B.C. A few birds winter in western Washington and Oregon and in southern Idaho.

LITTLE BLUE HERON *Florida caerulea* 20-29 (510-740)
A small dark heron with grayish-blue back and under parts and a brownish head and neck. The bill is bluish with a black tip and the legs are bluish green. Immatures of this species are pure white and yearling birds are mottled blue and white. CALLS. A hoarse croak; harsh screams. HABITAT. Wooded swamps, riparian thickets, and moist meadows. RANGE. Very rare fall straggler to northwestern Washington and southwestern B.C.

SNOWY EGRET *Egretta thula* 20-27 (510-688) Fig. 18
This species is a small white heron with yellow feet, contrasting black legs, and a slender black bill. The breeding plumage is similar but with recurved plumes on the back; lores (areas above the eyes) are yellow or

red. CALLS. Ordinarily silent, but will utter a low croak, a grating scold, or an occasional hiss. HABITAT. Nests in wooded swamps; forages in the shallow water of ponds, wet meadows, and sloughs. RANGE. Breeds locally and irregularly in southeastern Oregon, wandering after the breeding season to Washington (rarely), western Oregon, and southern B.C. Uncommon along the ocean coast in spring and (rarely) fall and winter. Fairly common summer resident and breeder in southern Idaho, though currently (1979) experiences some eggshell thinning and population seems to be declining. Rare spring and summer straggler to southeastern Washington and adjacent Idaho.

GREAT EGRET *Egretta alba* 38-40 (969-1,020)
This is a large, entirely white, heron-like water bird with a yellow bill and black legs and feet. There are long white plumes on the back during the breeding season. Almost twice the size of the Snowy Egret. CALLS. Various croaks and a low *cuk, cuk, cuk*. HABITAT. Nests in trees along fresh water; visitor along margins of lakes and in marshes and moist irrigated fields. Also frequents saltwater marshes and lagoons. RANGE. Uncommon breeder in southeastern Oregon and (formerly) in southern Idaho, wandering to west Oregon, Washington, and southern B.C. after the nesting season. Winters uncommonly, but regularly, in southeastern and western Oregon and in Washington. Breeds at the Potholes in central Washington. Rare spring and fall migrational visitor to southern Idaho and rarely to the northern part of that state. Apparently increasing in various parts of the Northwest in almost all seasons.

LOUISIANA HERON *Hydranassa tricolor* 22-26 (561-663)
A medium-sized, long-necked, long-legged heron with bluish upper parts (long plumes in breeding season) and white under parts. CALLS. Various subdued hoarse croaks. HABITAT. Large marshes near salt water. RANGE. Very rare spring and fall straggler to eastern and western Oregon.

GREAT BLUE HERON *Ardea herodias* 42-50 (1,071-1,275) Fig. 19
This is a large, grayish-blue, wading bird with a long bill, neck, and legs. It is practically the only large "crane-like" bird in the region, as the Sandhill Crane is relatively uncommon. It may be distinguished from the latter species by its grayish, rather than brownish, color and the fact that the Great Blue Heron folds its head and neck on its shoulders in flight, while the Sandhill Crane keeps its neck outstretched. CALLS. Vary from hoarse croaks to raucous bellows. HABITAT. Common visitor and forager along shores of rivers, lakes,

19.   Great Blue Heron (Schultz)

20.   Sandhill Crane (Schultz)

and salt water; numerous in marshes and swamps; nests in colonies in tall trees, occasionally some distance from water. RANGE. Breeds fairly commonly throughout the Northwest north to southeastern Alaska and northern B.C. Rare spring visitor to the southern Yukon. Winters irregularly from southern B.C. southward at the lower elevations. The most numerous heron in the region.

STORKS

21. Wood Stork (Pole)

WOOD STORK *Mycteria americana* 35 (892) Fig. 21
A large white bird with a bare dark head and neck, dark bill and legs,
and a light spot on the crown. When flying, the anterior halves of the
wings are white, the posterior halves and tips are black. Legs and neck
are outstretched in flight. CALLS. A hoarse croak. HABITAT.
Wooded swamps and marshy meadows; tide flats along the ocean.
RANGE. Rare straggler to southern Idaho and interior B.C.

IBISES

22. White-faced Ibis (Fisher)

WHITE-FACED IBIS *Plegadis chihi* 19-26 (484-663) Fig. 22
This water bird is a medium-sized wader with a long decurved bill. It is purplish chestnut in color, tinged with iridescent violets, greens, and reds, particularly on the head, wings, and back. The breast is reddish slate-colored. Breeding birds have a border of white feathers at the base of the bill. Tip of the bill, legs, and feet are dull red. Immatures, grayer or browner, lacking the iridescence. CALLS. A low croak or piglike grunting *ka-onk*. HABITAT. Marshes; forages in wet meadows and agricultural lands. RANGE. Uncommon local breeder in southeastern Oregon and southern Idaho. Rare straggler to eastern and southwestern Washington and southern B.C. Fairly common summer resident and breeder (three localities) and migrational straggler in southern Idaho; rare in the northern part of the state. (Includes the "Glossy Ibis")

FLAMINGOS

23.   Greater Flamingo (Pole)

GREATER FLAMINGO *Phoenicopterus ruber* 48 (1,224) Fig. 23
A very large water bird with very long legs and neck and a heavy,
strongly decurved, black and white bill. Coloration pink or reddish.
CALLS. Goose-like honking notes and an accented *huh-HUH-huh*.
HABITAT. Mudflats, shallow bays, and lagoons, mostly along salt
water. RANGE. Visitor to southwestern Washington coast. Two individuals observed May and June, 1975, at Grays Harbor,
Washington. Another in fall of 1980. Most unusual occurrences; possibly escapees from some zoo or bird farms, although the evidence
seems to suggest that they are wild, rather than captive, birds.
However, the status of these occurrences is much in doubt. An apparent escapee observed south of Vancouver, B.C. in 1980.

WHISTLING DUCKS

24.   Fulvous Whistling Duck (Pole)

FULVOUS WHISTLING DUCK *Dendrocygna bicolor* 20-21 (510-536) Fig. 24

A large duck with long stout legs and light brownish head and under parts. The wings and back are mottled darkish. White streaks along the sides and white rump are good field marks, particularly in flight. Somewhat goose-like in appearance and behavior. Neck is longer than in most true ducks. CALLS. A thin, high-pitched, double whistle. HABITAT. Wooded marshes for breeding; forages in open croplands. RANGE. Rare straggler to western Oregon and Washington. One record for eastern Washington. Reported as rare breeder in southwest Idaho. *Note.* The Black-bellied Whistling Duck (*Dendrocygna autumnalis*), characterized by a black belly, has been reported from the Rogue River Valley of Oregon.

SWANS

25. Whistling Swan (Fisher)

The swans are the largest of the water birds. They are completely white with black bills and feet. They are seldom seen away from water and they feed mostly by dipping the head and neck below the surface and by tipping the whole body. Swans might conceivably be confused with snow geese (and sometimes are!), but the much larger size of the former and their long necks should be distinctive.

Fortunate indeed is he who sees a V-formation of these great white birds flying high against a dark blue sky! Their flight is the very apotheosis of grace and dignity as the birds progress in stately manner with ponderous wing beats along their age-old courses. The birds rest on almost any kind of water, large or small, that is mostly fresh, but frequently migrate along the ocean shores. Once thought to be on the verge of extinction, the Trumpeter Swan appears to be making a comeback in the Pacific Northwest.

PACIFIC NORTHWEST SPECIES

MUTE SWAN *Cygnus olor* 58 (1,479)
A large swan with a graceful S-curve in its neck while swimming,

down-pointed bill, and wings partly raised. The bill is orange in color and the prominent black knob on the forehead is distinctive. CALLS. A low grunt, but mostly silent. HABITAT. Lakes, protected saltwater bays, and coves. RANGE. Several feral populations occur in the Pacific Northwest, as on Vancouver Island and southwestern B.C., northern Puget Sound, and in western and eastern Oregon. Increasing in coastal areas.

TRUMPETER SWAN *Cygnus buccinator* 65 (1,658)
This species is very similar to the more common Whistling Swan, but is larger and has an all-black bill. It is best separated from that species by the deeper, louder, more bugle-like voice. The posterior margin of the nostril is more than 2¼ inches from the tip of the bill; the nostril is closer to the tip of the bill in the Whistling Swan. In swimming, this species carries the neck stiffer and straighter than in the Whistling Swan. CALLS. A loud resonant trumpeting that is louder, lower in pitch, and more full-throated than the notes of either the Whistling Swan or the Canada Goose. HABITAT. Breeds by and frequents freshwater ponds, lakes, and rivers, and occasionally fields and wheat stubble (for foraging only); may also be seen in winter in the mouths of rivers by the ocean coast. RANGE. Irregular breeder in southern and southeastern Alaska, the southern Yukon, eastern Idaho, southeastern Montana, eastern Oregon, and eastern Washington (Turnbull NWR). Winters irregularly on open water throughout the Northwest states' part of the breeding range. Becoming more numerous along the ocean coast of Washington and in western Washington in general. Uncommon migrant in Idaho, breeding in the Henry's Lake area. Often found in flocks of the more numerous Whistling Swans, requiring careful examination of the latter wherever found. Stragglers recently found along the ocean coast in summer. Some of the Northwest populations have been introduced.

WHISTLING SWAN *Cygnus columbianus* 48-55 (1,224-1,400) Figs. 25 and 27
This water bird is pure white except for the black bill (often with a yellow spot at the base before the eye) and legs. With its great size, "swan neck", and color, cannot be mistaken for any other wild bird. The domestic and sometimes feral Mute Swan has an orange bill with a black knob near its base and the Trumpeter Swan has a larger all-black bill. CALLS. Similar to those of the Canada Goose, but softer and more musical. HABITAT. Likely to be seen on or near all types of water (mostly fresh), but prefers larger bodies and slow-flowing parts of rivers; occasionally on fields in migration. RANGE. Breeds from the Arctic coast southward to the Alaska Peninsula; wintering and

migrating from southern Alaska southward through the Northwest. Common migrant through eastern Washington. Fairly common spring and fall migrant in Idaho. *Note.* The Bewick's Swan variety *(Cygnus columbianus bewicki)* may be distinguished by the larger amount of yellow on the base of the bill. It may occur very rarely in flocks of Whistling Swans. Has been noted in extreme southern Oregon as rare winter straggler.

GEESE

26.   Black Brant (Fisher)

The geese are large duck-like waterfowl with stocky bodies and long necks. The bill is very similar to that of most ducks. Geese are strongly gregarious, being usually found in flocks. They often assume a V-shaped formation when flying and generally call continuously when in flight. While they do considerable feeding by tipping, most foraging is done on the ground where they graze on green vegetation, grasses and forbs, and search for grain in stubble fields. Geese are among the best known of game birds and the Canada Goose is avidly sought by hunters every fall.

A sure sign of spring or fall is the sight of a formation of Canada Geese flying high over head northward or southward, depending on

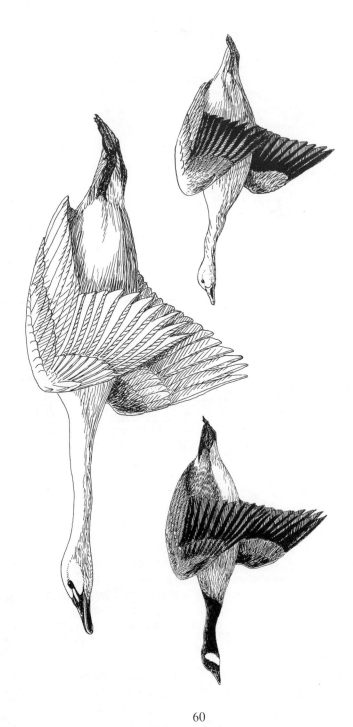

27. Whistling Swan (upper), Canada Goose (lower left), Snow Goose (lower right) (Schultz)

the season. The author once had ample opportunity to study these birds one March when he was camped near Devil's Lake in the Upper Grand Coulee. The geese were migrating northward and would come into the area in the late afternoon, resuming their journey in the morning. Occasionally a flock would arise from the lake and head in the wrong direction (not the proper northeast course in that locality to strike the Columbia River). Soon the stately V would dissolve into a noisy mob, until one of the stronger-flying individuals would turn to the right direction. More birds would form wings on that individual and soon the formation would be reconstituted. To fly strongly in the right direction appeared to be the requirement for leadership in such groups.

PACIFIC NORTHWEST SPECIES

WHITE-FRONTED GOOSE *Anser albifrons* 27-30 (688-765)
A grayish-brown goose with a white band around the base of the bill, black bars on the light under parts, and orange-yellow feet (other geese have black or dark red feet). Immatures, brownish and without white around the bill. CALLS. A throaty, but high-pitched *wah-wah-wah* or *tol-luk, to-lah-luk,* etc. HABITAT. Breeds in open tundra and marshy areas near water; migrates and winters on both fresh and salt water and also visits meadows and stubble fields. RANGE. Breeds in Alaska and the northern Yukon, wintering and migrating from southern B.C. south through the Northwest, particularly along the coasts of Washington and Oregon. Uncommon spring and fall migrant in Idaho.

SNOW GOOSE; BLUE GOOSE *Anser caerulescens* 23-28 (506-714) Fig. 27
A medium-sized white goose with black wing tips and black edges on the sides of the bill; head lacks scabby red skin of the domestic white duck which is occasionally found living in the wild. Birds on the water show a short neck as compared to the long-necked swans. Careful watch should be kept for the rare Ross's Goose which might slip through unnoticed amid large flocks of the Snow Geese. The Ross is slightly smaller than the Snow Goose and a little larger than the Mallard. It is almost identical in color to the Snow Goose, except that the bill is small and lacks the black edging or "lips". "Blue Geese" are thought to be a dark (dark grayish or brownish with black wings) color phase or morph of the Snow Goose, although the evidence is not entirely convincing. What we apparently have here is a case where the birds do not neatly fit into our rigid concepts of binomial and trinomial nomenclature! CALLS. A mellow-discordant, goose-like

honking, as well as shrill cries. HABITAT. Breeds in tundra areas near water; migrates south from the northern Northwest and northeast Asia mostly along the coast and in the interior, stopping both on water and on large moist flats, beach areas, and grain fields. RANGE. Breeds along the Arctic coast of Alaska and the Yukon, migrating southward through the Northwest and wintering in the northern Puget Sound area, and in scattered places elsewhere in the region. Common spring and fall migrant throughout most of the Pacific Northwest. The Skagit Flats' concentration in winter is the largest in the region. A few individuals (nonbreeding?) in summer. The blue color phase is rare in the Northwest; records for southwestern B.C., the Tri-Cities and Puget Sound areas in Washington, and eastern Oregon, as well as the ocean coast.

ROSS'S GOOSE *Anser rossii* 21-25 (536-638)
This goose is slightly smaller than the Snow Goose and a little larger than the Mallard. Almost identical to the Snow Goose in color, but the bill is smaller and lacks the black edging or "lips". A blue phase occurs, as well as blue phase hybrids with the Snow Goose. CALLS. A subdued grunt-like *kug-kug*. HABITAT. Nests in the tundra and winters in the agricultural fields and meadows and waters in central California. RANGE. Sparse migrant through southeastern Alaska, B.C., Idaho, western and eastern Washington, and western and eastern Oregon, wintering mostly south of the Northwest, though a wintering population has been found in southcentral Oregon. Regular in migration at the Malheur NWR. Rare fall visitor in Idaho.

EMPEROR GOOSE *Anser canagicus* 26-28 (663-714)
A small grayish-blue goose extensively marked with black and white scale-like stripes. The head and hind-neck are white while the fore-neck is black. Legs are orange. CALLS. A hoarse *kla-ha, kla-ha, kla-ha,* etc. HABITAT. Breeds in the tundra, but migrates mostly along salt water. RANGE. Breeds along the northwestern Alaskan coast, wintering mainly in the Aleutians, but occasionally wanders south through the coastal Northwest to western and southeastern Oregon.

CANADA GOOSE *Branta canadensis* 23-43 (586-2,000) Fig. 27
This is the common, black-necked, wild goose. The size and colors are variable according to subspecies. Head and neck black with chin (sometimes) black and cheeks white; rest of body brownish gray with white area under the tail. The breast may be gray or brown. The dark-colored race of this species is similar to, but much larger, than the Cackling Goose. The latter (*B. c. minima*) is a small white-cheeked goose not much larger than a Mallard and similar to the larger races

but has dark mouse-gray under parts, a short stubby neck, and occasionally a partial white collar near the base of the black neck. CALLS. A stirring trumpeting series of *qua-honk, ha-lunk, ha-lunk,* etc.; or a high-pitched rapidly uttered *lyuck-lyuck-lyuck-lyuck.* HABITAT. A common resident or breeder in marshy or grassy habitats near fresh water (lakes, ponds, rivers); in migration, frequents larger bodies of water, as well as grassy fields and wheat stubble. RANGE. Breeds and migrates throughout the Northwest, though mostly east of the Cascades. Winters from southern Alaska and southern B.C. southward. Common migrant and uncommon winter visitor in Idaho, breeding commonly in southern Idaho, but irregularly in the northern part of the state. Nests in urban areas in the Puget Sound region.

BRANT *Branta bernicla* 24-26 (612-663) Fig. 26
A small dark goose with a black head, neck, and breast, and a white band around the neck; wings, back, and belly are dark brown; rear under parts and rump are white. May possibly be confused with the Common Loon, but the Brant's head is rounded, the bill shorter, the body heavier, and the back lacks the checkering of the loon. A few birds ("White-bellied" or "American Brant") may have a white, instead of black, belly. A low mellow *kronk, kronk* or *gr-ronk, gr-ronk.* HABITAT. Mostly on salt water in migration; rare on fresh water. RANGE. The Black Brant *(B. b. nigricans)* breeds along the Arctic coast of Alaska and the Yukon, wintering south along salt water, often commonly in certain areas, as at Padilla Bay in western Washington, from southwestern B.C. to out of the Northwest region; rare in the interior of the Northwestern states and B.C. Most numerous as spring migrant (March-April). The American Brant *(B. b. bernicla)* winters sporadically along and near the ocean coast from southwestern B.C. southward; rare inland and in Alaska; very rare fall visitor in northern Idaho and very rare straggler to the Northwest in summer. *Note.* Some authorities consider these two races to be color phases rather than subspecies.

DUCKS

Ducks should be easily identifiable by the obvious neck and tail, "duck-like" bill, usual reliance on flying instead of diving when disturbed, and other familiar duck qualities. Smaller than that of geese or swans, the bill of ducks is broad and flat (though variable as in the "toothed" fish-holding bills of mergansers). The legs are short and placed well back on the body. The feet are webbed. Ducks lay numerous eggs, protecting them with down in the nest. Males have an

28. Mallard (Fisher)

eclipse molt in which they resemble the females for a time after the breeding season and are difficult to identify. To most persons in the Pacific Northwest, ducks are fall and winter birds. Breeding ducks are more scattered and considerably more difficult to observe.

Depending on definition, there are about 116 species of ducks, of which some 37 occur, rarely or commonly, in the Northwest. Our ducks belong to four groups, the dabbling, diving, sea, or stiff-tailed ducks.

These birds are marvelously adapted for their way of life by structure and behavior. Most are beautifully colored and many are world travelers, often covering immense distances in their migratory movements. They are birds of repute not only among the sportsmen but bird lovers as well. Who has not thrilled to their almost magical appearance in the fall on a neighboring pond or lake? Or the sight of their flocks high in the sky? We are reminded of two lines from Pai Ta-shun's poem:

> Dark-flying rune against the western glow—
> It tells the sweep and loneliness of things.

NORTH AMERICAN WOOD DUCK *Aix sponsa* 18-20 (459-510)
Fig. 29
Male, a small beautifully-colored duck, identified by white chin, vertical white streaks on the cheeks, and parallel vertical white and black streaks in front of the wing; a drooping crest is present. In late summer, similar to the female, but with the red and white bill of the winter dress. Females, duller in color with white eyering, white chin, and black bill. CALLS. Males, a mellow whistled *peet, peet, peet,* etc.; females, a sharp *cr-eek, cr-eek,* or *oe-eek, oe-eek,* etc.; various other notes. HABITAT. Nests in holes in large trees in riparian growth near fresh water (lakes, ponds, sluggish streams), particularly in wooded lowland areas; migrates and winters on protected bodies of fresh water. RANGE. Breeds irregularly through the Northwest on both sides of the Cascades from southern B.C. southward, wintering rarely from southwestern B.C. south through the Northwestern states. Rare winter resident in southern Idaho (no breeding).

EURASIAN WIGEON *Anas penelope* 17-20 (434-510)
Similar in general pattern to the American Wigeon, except grayer over

29. Wood Duck (Larrison)

the body and with a reddish head and pale yellow crown. Females, similar to the female American Wigeon, except for the reddish head. CALLS. Males, a wigeon-like whistled *whee-oo;* females, a *quack.* HABITAT. Mostly occurs in bays and marshy areas near fresh water, and rarely along the ocean coast. RANGE. Uncommon, but regular, winter visitor to the Northwest in the coastal areas, but rare in the interior regions. Common spring migrant in the Aleutians, and uncommon and scattered at that season in the interior of the Northwest. Rare migrant in Idaho.

AMERICAN WIGEON: BALDPATE *Anas americana* 18-22 (459-561)
Male, a medium-sized pinkish-brown duck with a grayish two-toned head and white crown (whereby the name "baldpate"); a green patch behind the eye; large white patches in extended wings. Female, light reddish brown with grayish head and neck and white belly. CALLS. Male, a whistled *whew-whew-whew;* female, a soft gutteral note and a loud *kaow-kaow* or *quaw-uk.* HABITAT. Breeds in marshy areas near fresh water; migrates and winters on both fresh and salt water. RANGE. Breeds from northcentral Alaska and northern Yukon southward through the Northwest, east of the Cascades (but at least at one locality, Everett, Washington sewage ponds, west of the mountains). Winters and migrates commonly from southern Alaska and the Aleutians and southern B.C. through our territory, probably most numerous in coastal areas. Rare in summer and as breeder west of the Cascades. Common spring and fall migrant in Idaho, where it is an uncommon summer resident and breeder in the southern part of the state.

FALCATED TEAL *Anas falcata* 20 (510)
Male, a large teal with grayish upper parts, a long drooping crest, elongated wing feathers, greenish head, and a white chin and neck crossed by a narrow black collar. Female, somewhat similar to female Gadwall. HABITAT. Fresh water, but in salt water also in migration. RANGE. Very rare visitor in the Aleutians and Pribilofs in Alaska, in B.C., and in southwestern Washington (record, fall 1978), though the latter bird's status as a wild individual is not certain.

GADWALL *Anas strepera* 18-22 (459-561)
Male, a slender grayish duck with a white belly, black tail coverts, pale brown head, and white speculum on hind wing edge. Female, similar, but browner; bill is yellower than that of the female Mallard and the feet are yellow, not orange; speculum white, not blue. CALLS. A loud *kack-kack,* a deep reedy *queck* or *quok,* and a shrill whistle; female, a

moderate *quack*, like that of hen Mallard, but slightly higher pitched. HABITAT. Breeds in vegetation on dry ground near ponds and shallow lakes; migrates and winters on ponds, lakes, and rivers with considerably shore cover. RANGE. Breeds from southeastern Alaska and central B.C. southward in the Northwest, mostly east of the Cascades; wintering through much of this region (and apparently increasing at this season). Common summer resident in southern Idaho, but uncommon in the northern part of the state.

BAIKAL TEAL *Anas formosa* 16 (408)
Male, a small grayish-sided duck with a white vertical streak between breast and side, elongated wing feathers, and a spectacularly colored green, cream, and black head. Female, similar to female Common Teal but with a white spot at the base of the bill, dark line through eye, and a light line above the eye. CALLS. Male, a clucking *proop* or *wot-wot;* female, a harsh *quack*. RANGE. Very rare winter visitor to the Northwest from B.C. south to western Oregon.

GREEN-WINGED TEAL: COMMON TEAL *Anas crecca* 13-15 (331-382)
Male, a small, gray, reddish-headed duck with a vertical white streak in front of the wing; green patch on side of head, and sooty patch on throat; sides of tail yellowish, bordered with black. Female, similar but head gray-brown without green patch; no blue wing patch (as in female Blue-winged Teal). The Common teal variety has the male similar to the Green-winged Teal but with a horizontal white stripe above the wing and no vertical stripe before the wing. CALLS. Male, a short high-pitched whistle; female, a weak Mallard-like *quack*. HABITAT. Nests on dry ground near, or at some distance from, shallow fresh water (often in wet meadows); winters and migrates on both fresh and salt water. RANGE. Breeds from the central Aleutians and central Alaska south through the Northwest, mostly east of the Cascades; wintering from southcentral Alaska southward. Fairly common spring and fall migrant in Idaho; less numerous as a breeder. The Common Teal *(A. c. crecca)* is resident in the Aleutian Islands, straggling north to the Pribilofs and south to B.C., Washington, and Oregon.

MALLARD *Anas platyrhynchos* 20-25 (510-637) Fig. 28
Male, a large duck with a yellowish bill and feet, green head, white collar, reddish-brown breast, gray sides, and blue or purple speculum (color patch on wing); tail white with black upper "duck tail" coverts. Female, a mottled brown duck with orange bill and feet and blue speculum bordered on sides with white. Domesticated Mallard strains have shorter bills and legs than wild individuals. CALLS. Male, a soft

reedy *yeeb, yeeb, yeeb;* female, a loud insistent *quack.* HABITAT. Breeds wherever there is fresh water; migrates and winters on all kinds of fresh water; less common on salt water. RANGE. Abundant resident, breeder, and migrant throughout the Northwest, wintering mostly from southern Alaska and B.C. southward.

BLACK DUCK *Anas rubripes* 21-24 (536-612)
Male, a mottled dark-colored duck with white wing linings and a blue speculum. Perhaps somewhat similar to dark-colored female Mallard, but the head and neck are much lighter, contrasting strongly with the darker back. CALLS. Similar to those of the Mallard. HABITAT. Visits both fresh and salt water. RANGE. Uncommon to rare migrational straggler and winter visitor in the Northwest. A small breeding colony which began some years ago from released birds is located east of Everett, Washington. Rare in the northern Yukon (Old Crow Flats, June 1, 1977).

NORTHERN PINTAIL *Anas acuta* 26-30 (663-765)
Male, a large, slender, long-necked duck with long central tail feathers, dark head, and white line up the side of the neck and head. Female, similar to hen Mallard, but longer-necked and with a buffy head, bluish-gray bill, and without blue speculum. Bill and head colors are the best marks in the female. CALLS. Male, a low mellow whistle. Female, a quacking note; also a rolling note common to both sexes. HABITAT. Breeds in marsh vegetation near fresh water; migrates on both fresh and salt water. RANGE. Breeds through the Northwest (mostly in more northern half and east of the Cascades), wintering and migrating from southern Alaska southward. Summer resident in southern Idaho; fairly common to common migrant in the northern part of the state.

GARGANEY *Anas querquedula* 15 (382)
Male, a small duck with dark head (a conspicuous, long, white stripe over the eye), neck, breast, and back. A striking white triangle in front of the wing reaching down to the water when swimming. Female, similar to females of other teal and with a long blue stripe in the folded wing. CALLS. Male, a rattling note; female, a low-pitched *quack.* HABITAT. Ponds, lakes, and wet meadows. RANGE. Spring and early summer visitor to the Aleutian Islands. Very rare visitor in Vancouver, B.C. area.

BLUE-WINGED TEAL *Anas discors* 15 (382)
Male, a small dull-colored duck with a large white crescent in front of the eye and a large blue patch on the fore-edge of the wing. Female, similar, but lacking the white facial crescent; head brownish gray; blue

wing patch present. CALLS. Male, a faint lisping or high-pitched whistled peeping; female a faint *quack*. HABITAT. Breeds in well-vegetated marshes and cover by lakes, ponds, and sluggish streams; migrates mostly in fresh water. RANGE. Breeds from southcentral Alaska and the northern Yukon southward in the Northwest, mostly east of the Cascades. Winters very rarely from southern B.C. southward on both sides of the Cascades. Fairly common migrant and uncommon breeder in Idaho.

CINNAMON TEAL *Anas cyanoptera* 15-17 (382-434)
Male, a small brownish-red duck with a large light-blue patch on the fore-edge of the wing. Female, a mottled brown duck with much blue in the wing; difficult to distinguish from the Blue-winged Teal hen, but usually has a buffier breast. CALLS. Male, a low rattling chatter; female, a weak *quack*. HABITAT. Breeds and migrates through freshwater marshes and swamps; often nests in tall grass meadows near or at some distance from water. RANGE. Breeds from the southern Yukon and central B.C. southward through the Northwest, mainly east of the Cascades. Winters very rarely from southern B.C. southward, mostly west of the Cascades. Fairly common, though somewhat irregular, summer resident in Idaho.

NORTHERN SHOVELER *Anas clypeata* 17-21 (434-536)
Male, a medium-sized duck with a long, black, spoon-shaped bill; greenish-black head; white lower neck and breast; red sides and under parts; and bluish patches on the wings. Female, brown-mottled with characteristic spoon-shaped bill. CALLS. Male, a low guttural *took, took, took;* female, a few feeble *quacks*. HABITAT. Nests in suitable cover near freshwater sloughs, ponds, and lakes; migrates and winters on fresh water. RANGE. Breeds from western Alaska and the Yukon south through the Northwest, mostly east of the Cascades; wintering and migrating from southern B.C. and Washington southward. Fairly common migrant in Idaho; less numerous as summer resident; rare in winter.

CANVASBACK *Aythya valisineria* 20-24 (510-612)
Male, a large grayish-white duck with a black breast and tail, brownish-red neck and head, and a long black bill. The flat forehead sloping off in a line with the upper outline of the bill distinctive. The red of the head extends farther down the neck than in the Redhead and the shape of the head is distinctly different from that of the latter species. Female, more grayish, but with the characteristic sloping forehead. CALLS. Male, a harsh guttural croak; female, a *quack* and also a loud *cur-row* when alarmed. HABITAT. Nests in marshy

vegetation along shores of larger bodies of fresh water; migrates and winters mostly on salt water, especially at the mouths of larger rivers. RANGE. Breeds in central Alaska and the Yukon southward east of the Cascades through the Northwest, wintering irregularly from southern B.C. southward. Uncommon spring and fall migrant, uncommon winter visitor and local summer resident in Idaho. One of the commonest diving ducks from the Rock Island Dam to the Chief Joseph Dam on the Columbia River in the winter. Scattered breeder in eastern Washington.

REDHEAD *Aythya americana* 18-20 (459-510)
Male, an uncommon duck, similar to the Canvasback, but is dark grayish, instead of white, on backs and sides, and has a rounded head with a high abrupt forehead and bluish bill with a black band near the tip. Female, with ashy-brown breast, whitish chest, broad gray wing stripe, and a suffused light patch around the base of the bill. CALLS. A deep cat-like *meow* or *keow*. Female, a duck-like *quack*. HABITAT. Nests in marshy freshwater areas; migrates over fresh water. RANGE. Breeds from central B.C. southward locally and irregularly through the Northwest (east of the Cascades), wintering uncommonly through much of the area, except for the northern-most parts. Common breeder in northcentral Washington. Fairly common migrant and uncommon winter visitor in northern Idaho; locally common summer resident and breeder in southern Idaho, less so in northern part of the state. Irregular spring migrant in the southern Yukon.

RING-NECKED DUCK *Aythya collaris* 16-18 (408-459)
Male, a black-headed scaup with a black-tipped bluish bill crossed at the base and near the tip with white rings. Best identified at a distance by the white of the side running up into the black of the back in front of the wing and the characteristic top-knotted silhouette of the head. Female, brownish with characteristic head shape, pied bill, and white eye-ring; similar to female Redhead but darker; the Redhead lacks the rings on the bill. CALLS. Male, a soft resonant *quo, quo, quo,* etc.; female, a sharp *erk, erk, erk,* in alarm. HABITAT. Nests in marshy vegetation on small bodies of fresh water; migrates and winters on rivers and protected bays of lakes; seldom on salt water. RANGE. Breeds from the southern Yukon irregularly southward; especially in northeastern Washington, western Montana, and southern Oregon. Uncommon migrant and rare breeder in southeastern Idaho.

TUFTED DUCK *Aythya fuligula* 17 (434) Fig. 30
Male, a medium-sized scaup-like duck with a black head, breast, and back, and white under parts. A long tuft of feathers hangs down the

30. Tufted Duck (Larrison)

back of the head. Female, dull colored with a shorter tuft and with a white patch at the base of the bill and a white speculum. CALLS. Male, a low whistle; female, a harsh *kurr, kurr.* HABITAT. Vegetation-lined slow-moving or still fresh waters. Fresh or salt (less commonly) waters in winter. RANGE. Rare winter visitor west of the Cascades in the Northwest.

GREATER SCAUP *Aythya marila* 17-20 (434-510)
Male, a medium-sized duck with a blue bill and black head (glossed with greenish; head with purplish in the Lesser Scaup), neck, breast, and tail; remainder of upper and lower parts whitish. Female, brownish; white patch at base of bill. In flight, both sexes show a white stripe on the rear edge of the wing extending about three-fourths the distance from the body to the wing-tip. CALLS. A harsh, discordant, *scawp, scawp,* etc. HABITAT. Nests in marshy vegetation; migrates and winters mostly on salt water and large lakes in coastal areas. RANGE. Breeds from northern Alaska and the Yukon south to northwestern B.C., wintering from southeastern Alaska southward along the coast, mainly on or near salt water. Uncommon to rare east of the Cascades,

71

mostly along the larger rivers. Very rare migrant in Idaho.

LESSER SCAUP *Aythya affinis* 15-18 (382-459)

Both sexes are very similar to those of the Greater Scaup. They are best separated by the length of the white wing stripe which in the Lesser extends about half-way from the body to the wing-tip. The sides and back of the Lesser males are usually a darker gray. CALLS. Male, a low whistle; female, a hoarse guttural purring or muttering. HABITAT. Nests in marshy or sedgy areas near fresh water; migrates and winters mostly on fresh water, preferring smaller bodies of water than the preceding species. RANGE. Breeds from central Alaska and the Yukon south, east of the Cascades, to (sparsely) Oregon and southern Idaho; winters from southern B.C. southward. Rare breeder in western Washington. Mostly seen on fresh water.

COMMON EIDER *Somateria mollissima* 20-26 (510-663)

A large duck. Male, mostly white upper parts and blackish sides and under parts and tail. Head mostly white with a prominent black mask through the eye. Bill is short. Female, light brownish with black mottling. CALLS. Male, a soft *oo-oo-oo*. HABITAT. Nests near salt water; winters primarily on salt water; rarely in fresh water. RANGE. Breeds along the coasts of Alaska from the Arctic to Glacier Bay, wintering southward from the Aleutians to (sparsely) B.C. Very rare migrational visitor in northern Idaho.

KING EIDER *Somateria spectabilis* 20-24 (510-612)

Male, back and sides black with white neck and breast. A prominent orange-yellow patch on the forehead lined narrowly with black. Top and back of head slate-gray. Large white wing patches. Female, similar to female Common Eider, but the brown in the plumage is darker and richer. CALLS. Male, a low cooing *oo-oo-oo*. HABITAT. Breeds along fresh and salt water; winters mainly along salt water. RANGE. Breeds on the Arctic coast of Alaska north of the Seward Peninsula and in the Bering Sea, migrating and wintering from the Bering Sea south along the coast to (sparsely) Washington.

SPECTACLED EIDER *Somateria fischeri* 20-22 (510-561)

Male, upper parts (except head) white; under parts and sides black; head greenish with large buffy (narrowly bordered with black) spectacles. Female, dark mottled brownish but with prominent light brownish spectacles and chin. HABITAT. Similar to that of other eiders. RANGE. Breeds on the northwest coast of Alaska from Barrow to Baird Inlet, wintering in the Aleutians and Pribilofs and southeast to Kodiak and very rarely to B.C.

STELLER'S EIDER *Polysticta stelleri* 18 (459)
Male, a small duck with white head and sides, black back, collar, and chin, as well as small spot in front of wing. Forehead and nape greenish and under parts reddish brown. Female, dark mottled brownish with a blue speculum. CALLS. Male, a low cooing note; female, a harsh *quack;* wings make a whistling sound in flight. HABITAT. Salt water along rocky shores. RANGE. Breeds along the Arctic coasts of Alaska and the Yukon southwestward to the northern part of Bristol Bay. Winters in the Aleutians, Pribilofs, and Kodiak areas; very rarely south as far as southwestern B.C.

HARLEQUIN DUCK *Histrionicus histrionicus* 15-17 (382-434)
Male, a small bluish-black duck with reddish sides and numerous white stripes and spots on the head, neck, and shoulders, the largest being the white patch between the bill and the eye. Female, similar to the female Bufflehead, but has three white spots on the side of the head. CALLS. A short *quack;* a shrill descending whistle. HABITAT. Nests along the rushing streams in the mountains; winters on the wave-washed rocks in turbulent waters along saltwater beaches. Non-breeders congregate in summer about islands in northern Puget Sound, on the Strait of Juan de Fuca, and along the ocean coast. RANGE. Breeds from the Aleutians and westcentral Alaska south along rivers in mountains through the Northwest, wintering in coastal areas, especially along salt water, from the Bering Sea south (also large numbers of non-breeders in summer). A few winter in the lowlands of the interior of the Northwest. Uncommon, irregular, summer resident and breeder in northern and eastern Idaho. From the points of coloration, habitat, and behavior, probably one of the most interesting of all waterfowl.

OLDSQUAW *Clangula hyemalis* 15-16 (382-408)
Male, a small brown and white duck with two very long central tail feathers, a dark spot on the side of the whitish head, and a short stubby bill. In summer, head and neck blackish with white sides of head. In winter, head and neck white with dark spot on side of head. Female, without long tail feathers; dark above and white below with dark spot on side of head; similar in summer but darker. May be told from all but American and Surf Scoters (which are considerably larger) by lack of white or pale gray in the wing speculum. CALLS. A loud twangy or yodeling *ow-ow, ow-ow-ow-ly,* etc. HABITAT. Breeds on open tundra near water; winters and migrates on salt water, rarely on fresh water. RANGE. Breeds from the Arctic coast of Alaska and the Yukon south and west to the Aleutians (including central and southern Yukon and northern B.C.), wintering mostly along the coast from the

73

Aleutians to Oregon; occasionally recorded in the interior east of the Cascades and in north and south Idaho.

BLACK SCOTER *Melanitta nigra* 17-21 (434-536)

Male, an entirely black scoter, except for an orange-yellow knob on the bill; under surface of the wing is silvery, as displayed in flight. Female, sooty brown with light-colored cheeks and black crown. CALLS. A musical, bell-like, wailing whistle, as *koo-lee, koo-lee,* etc. HABITAT. Nest in coastal tundra near water; less commonly in the interior of the North. Winters on salt water along the coast, resting in quiet water off shore and feeding in the surf. More nervous and quicker flying than other scoters. Almost entirely restricted to salt water. RANGE. Breeds along the coasts of Alaska from the Arctic to Bristol Bay and irregularly to Kodiak and Mt. McKinley National Park. Spring and fall migrant and winter visitor along salt water from the Aleutians southward. Regular and fairly common on inland salt water (Puget Sound, etc.) Rare east of the Cascades, both north and south of the Canadian border.

SURF SCOTER *Melanitta perspicillata* 20-22 (510-561)

Male, a large, chunky, black, saltwater duck without white patch in wing (as with White-winged Scoter). Usually with one or more white patches on forehead and back of head. Conspicuous white, black, and red bill is characteristic. Female, dusky brown with dirty white spots on sides of the head; crown and back of head dark blackish brown; no white on wings. CALLS. Low croaking sounds, though usually silent. HABITAT. Nests in open areas near the Arctic coasts. Winters on salt water in heavy surf and breakers areas where small animal food is loosened by wave action; also feeds on shellfish exposed by tides or gathered from the bottom. Occasionally found in inshore areas in sounds and straits. RANGE. Breeds in northern and western Alaska and along the Arctic coast of the Yukon. Many non-breeders, often in large flocks, along the coast in summer from southern Alaska to Oregon. Winters on salt water along the coast from the Aleutians to Oregon. Sparse straggler to the interior east of the Cascades, particularly in the fall. Rare fall visitor to northern Idaho.

WHITE-WINGED SCOTER *Melanitta fusca* 2-23 (510-586)

Male, a large, chunky black saltwater duck with a thick bill and white patch in the wing; head wholly black, except for a white spot below the eye; white speculum showing when at rest and has a white patch in the wing in flight. The bill is orange with a black swelling at the base. Female, lighter, more dusky brown with light facial spots. CALLS. A low throaty *quaark.* HABITAT. Nests in bushy tundra and woodlands near fresh water. Winters mostly on salt water, off shore where the breakers begin to form or in quiet waters (as of Puget Sound and the Straits of Georgia and Juan de Fuca); feeds on shellfish gathered on the sea bottom and swallowed whole; shells are ground to powder in the ducks' strong gizzard according to E. A. Kitchin. Rare on inland fresh water. RANGE. Breeds from northcentral Alaska and the northern Yukon south to southcentral B.C.; winters along the coast from the Aleutians south to out of the territory of this manual. Sparse straggler to the interior of the Northwest, east of the Cascades. Uncommon fall visitor in northern Idaho. Seemingly increasing as a winter visitor east of the Cascades in Washington, probably following the chain of reservoirs on the Columbia and Snake Rivers. Many non-breeders present in summer on salt water in western Washington.

BUFFLEHEAD *Bucephala albeola* 14-16 (357-408)
Male, a small mostly-white duck; part of head in front of eyes, lower cheeks, nape, and back are black; upper cheeks, crown, and rest of under parts are white; wing black with large white patch. Female, a dusky little duck with one white cheek spot. CALLS. Male, a squeaky call; female, a hoarse *quack* or low *kwuk.* HABITAT. Nests in tree holes in wooded growth near freshwater ponds and lakes; winters on both fresh and salt water. RANGE. Breeds from southern Alaska and the Yukon southward to southern B.C. and less commonly farther south to northern Washington. Winters and migrates from southern B.C. and the Aleutians southward throughout territory.

BARROW'S GOLDENEYE *Bucephala islandica* 20-23 (510-586)
Male, similar to the Common Goldeneye, but with a triangular white spot between the eye and the bill on a purplish-black head. Sides of body above wing largely black with small white spots, giving a more "messy" appearance than in the more abundant Common. An excellent field mark is the black of the back in the Barrow's coming almost to the water line in front of the wing unlike the case in the Common, as the shape of the eye-spot is not always easy to determine at a distance. Female, similar to the Common Goldeneye, except the bill in spring is all yellow (bill of the Common is black at the base). CALLS. Rough high-pitched croaks. HABITAT. Nests in tree holes by wooded lakes and ponds, mostly in the mountains; winters on saltwater bays, less commonly on fresh water. RANGE. Breeds from southcentral Alaska and the Yukon southward through the Northwest, mostly in hilly and mountainous terrain. Winters in coastal areas from southern Alaska southward and sparsely in the northern Rockies. Uncommon migrant, winter resident, and scattered breeder in Idaho, especially the eastern part. Common winter resident in northcentral Washington, especially

on the Wenatchee River.

COMMON GOLDENEYE *Bucephala clangula* 17-23 (434-586)
Male, a large chunky duck with a dark greenish-black head, back, and
tail, and a large, round, white spot between the eye and the bill (not
too satisfactory a field mark). Side of body below wings white. Black
of back does not extend to the water line in front of the wings (a good
field character). CALLS. Male, a sharp *cur-r-rew;* female, a hoarse
quack or *keck.* HABITAT. Nests in tree holes by woodland lakes and
swampy or marshy ponds, wintering on both fresh and salt water, especially on more open waters. RANGE. Breeds from central Alaska
and the Yukon south to northeastern Washington (Pend Oreille
County), northern Idaho, and northwestern Montana; winters from
southeastern Alaska and the Aleutians and the Yukon (where
stretches of water in the rivers are open) southward through the
Northwest. Common to fairly common migrant and winter visitor in
Idaho. A few non-breeding birds linger in the southern part of the
range in summer.

HOODED MERGANSER *Mergus cucullatus* 16-20 (408-510) Fig. 31
The mergansers have thin, narrow, rounded bills that are not flat as in
the other ducks. The sides of the mandibles are serrated to hold the
fish upon which they feed. Male, a small black and white duck with
brownish flanks and a large, fan-shaped, white crest, narrowly

31.   Hooded Merganser (Fisher)

76

bordered with black, on the head. On water, the black of the back extends down to form two vertical bars in front of the wing. Female, a small dark-brown merganser with a dark tawny-crested head, dark bill and chest, and a white patch on the wing. CALLS. A hoarse croak or grunt. HABITAT. Nests in tree holes, often in tall cottonwoods, along wooded shores of small isolated lakes and ponds; winters mostly on small freshwater lakes, less commonly on salt water. RANGE. Breeds from southeastern Alaska, southern Yukon, and northern B.C. south to western Oregon, southeastern Washington, and central Idaho, irregularly and locally in suitable habitats. Winters from southern B.C. southward. Uncommon migrant and sparse local breeder in Idaho and southeastern Washington.

SMEW *Mergus albellus* 16 (408)
A small merganser with a very short bill. The male is largely white with a black eyepatch, line around the back of the crown, and two more or less vertical lines in front of the wing. The back is contrastively black and white and the sides are grayish. Female, with a brown forehead and crown and white cheeks; back is brownish and the sides are grayish. HABITAT. Nests in tree cavities along lakes and rivers in the coniferous forests; winters on fresh water and mouths of rivers. RANGE. Rare fall (mostly), winter, and spring visitor to the central and western Aleutian Islands and southward along the coast as far south as extreme southwestern B.C.

RED-BREASTED MERGANSER *Mergus serrator* 20-25 (510-637)
Fig. 32
Male, a large conspicuously-crested merganser with a dark-green head, white collar, and a red neck and breast; sides not white as in the Common Merganser. Female, with pale red head and neck that blends gradually into the white of the throat, instead of being sharply cut off.

32. Red-breasted Merganser (male, l.; female, r.) (Schultz)

CALLS. A loud purring; also a rough croak. HABITAT. Breeds along both fresh and salt water; winters mostly on salt water, less commonly on the larger rivers and lakes. RANGE. Breeds along the coasts of Alaska from the Arctic and southern Yukon to southeastern Alaska and northern B.C., less commonly southward. Winters southward along the coast from southeastern Alaska, rarely in the interior of the Northwest. Apparently breeds somewhat in the interior, as a number of spring and summer records east of the Cascades, but to what extent is unknown (no definite records). Regular migrant in southern Idaho.

COMMON MERGANSER *Mergus merganser* 21-27 (536-688)
Male, a large duck with a long, thin, reddish bill; greenish-black head and blackish upper parts; lower back and tail gray; sides and under parts white; bill and feet red. Female and younger males, gray with dark red-crested head clearly cut off from the body and white throat, a red bill, and white wing-patch. CALLS. A deep throaty *carrk, car-rk, cr-rk,* etc.; often silent. HABITAT. Nests in tree holes, crevices on cliffs, or old hawk nests on lakes and rivers in the mountains. Winters in large flocks (usually) on large lakes or salt water. RANGE. Breeds from southern Alaska and the southern Yukon south to southern B.C. and in the foothills and mountains farther southward in the Northwest. Winters from the southern Yukon and B.C. south. Fairly common, though irregular, resident in northern Idaho. Uncommon migrant and winter visitor in southern Idaho. Uncommon breeder in eastern Idaho.

RUDDY DUCK *Oxyura jamaicensis* 14-17 (357-434)
Male, a small, chunky, neck-less duck with a fan-shaped tail often carried upright and wren-like; in spring, rusty red, with black crown, white cheeks, blue bill, and grayish belly; in winter, similar but upper parts grayish. Female, similar to winter male, but white on cheeks dull and crossed by a dark bar. CALLS. A low, indistinct *chut-chut-chut,* etc.; a squeaky *ticka-ticka-tickity-quack;* a weak *quack;* female, silent. HABITAT. Nests on small ponds; winters on large lakes and saltwater bays. RANGE. Breeds from central B.C. southward through the Northwest, mostly east of the Cascades; winters from southern B.C. south through Washington and Oregon. Fairly common migrant in Idaho, where it breeds sparsely in the northern part of the state, and commonly in the southeastern part.

VULTURES

33. Turkey Vulture (Fisher)

TURKEY VULTURE *Cathartes aura* 26-31 (663-790) Fig. 33
An almost eagle-sized bird, wholly black in color with light or silvery under surfaces of the wings and a naked red head. Characterized by habit of soaring high in the air on up-tilted motionless wings, rocking from side to side. CALLS. Various hisses, grunts, and growls. HABITAT. Open terrain, mostly in arid interior; less numerous on tideflats and adjacent bluffs and cliffs. Nests in rocky brushy places or in crevices on cliffs. RANGE. Summer resident and breeder from southern B.C. south through the Northwest, lingering rarely into early winter in the southern half of the territory. Most numerous in the open arid sections, though found in timbered areas as well.

The New World vultures, of which there are seven species, constitute an ancient group of carrion feeders probably most closely related to the cranes and rails. In Tertiary times, the cathartid vultures lived in both the New and Old Worlds, but now are restricted entirely to the western hemisphere. The Old World vultures developed some 30 million years after the appearance of the cathartids and are similar in general appearance due to their assumption of similar carrion feeding habits. Vultures spend much time soaring on motionless wings, seeking thermals for support, much as does the glider pilot. The habit in these birds provides a means of foraging without the expense of energy in flapping the wings. Since vultures feed on carrion which is often scattered over the countryside, much searching is necessary. Broken and hilly country, bluffs along salt water sounds, and hot desert areas provide the air lifts necessary for soaring.

HAWKS

34. Peregrine Falcon (Fisher)

The hawks are medium-sized, diurnal, raptorial birds generally seen flying through the brush or soaring high in the air in search of prey. The females are usually considerably larger than the males. The bills of these birds are strongly built and hooked at the tip. The wings are long, broad, and round, except in the falcons where the wings are long and pointed. The feet are large and strong and the toes are tipped with sharp claws. For the most part, our hawks feed on live prey, mostly vertebrates, especially mammals and birds.

Of the approximately 280 species of World hawks, some 20 species occur, commonly or rarely, within the territory covered by this manual. Several groups are represented. Ospreys are fish-eating birds and the single species occurs as resident or migrant throughout the

80

World. Kites are graceful fliers that have recently invaded the southern part of the Pacific Northwest. The accipiters are brush and forest foragers and feed largely on birds. The buteos, or "buzzards" as they are known in England, seek their prey while soaring high in the air on their broad wings. One species, the Marsh Hawk, is our representative of the group of harriers, most of which occur in other continents. The falcons are fast-flying raptors that feed largely on birds and mammals, though the tiny Kestrel consumes many insects, such as grasshoppers. The hawks are fascinating in appearance and behavior and have attracted many admirers who, in their common interest, have formed societies for the study of these attractive birds.

PACIFIC NORTHWEST SPECIES

OSPREY *Pandion haliaetus* 21-25 (536-637) Fig. 36
A large white-headed hawk with long pointed wings and a short rounded tail. Black above and white below, with a broad black patch through the cheeks. Usually seen near water into which it dives for fish. Soars with a crook in the wings. CALLS. A rising series of shrill whistles, given singly and in series, as *whew-whew-whi-whi-whi,* etc. HABITAT. Areas containing rivers, lakes, and large ponds, with suitable tall trees, snags, or poles for nesting and waters with an abundance of surface-swimming fish. RANGE. Breeds locally in suitable habitat from northern Alaska and the Yukon south through the Northwest, wintering mostly south of our territory, but a number of winter records west of the Cascades and a few east of that range. Irregular, though locally common, breeder in northern and eastern Idaho and southwestern Oregon.

WHITE-TAILED KITE *Elanus leucurus* 15-17 (382-434)
A small hawk, almost gull-like in its color pattern of white under parts and grayish upper parts, though it has a prominent black patch on each shoulder. The wings are long and pointed and in flight are held upward with downward-pointing tips. The feet are often dangled and much hovering is engaged in. Meadow mice make up most of the diet. CALLS. Various whistled notes, often like those of the Osprey. HABITAT. Open meadows, hay fields, and marshes are preferred. Nests are placed in trees near water or marshes. RANGE. Numbers of this hawk increased rapidly during the 1970s in Oregon, both sides of state, and in southwestern Washington, mostly as a straggler at all times of the year from farther south, and sparse as a breeder in the former state. Recorded from northern Idaho. A good example of a species which first appeared in the Northwest as a straggler, mostly in

81

TURKEY VULTURE

BALD EAGLE

GOLDEN EAGLE

ad.

imm.

ad.

imm.

35. Left to right: Turkey Vulture, Bald Eagle, Golden Eagle (Schultz)

the fall and winter, and then increased during the spring and summer, and finally became a breeder.

BALD EAGLE *Haliaeetus leucocephalus* 33-43 (842-1,096) Fig. 35
A very large black hawk with white head and tail. The immatures are entirely dark colored with irregular whitish areas in the wing linings. The legs and toes of this species are yellow and unfeathered. The large size of the wings in flying birds is unmistakable, the leading edges of which are almost straight and at right angles to the body. CALLS. A high-pitched, twittering, metallic *kweek, kweek,* etc. HABITAT. Resident and visitor along salt water and large bodies of fresh water in the interior (lakes and rivers). Requires tall trees for nesting and gulls or ospreys for robbing of fish or tideflats and beaches to scavenge for dead fish. Will catch live fish in the water with backward "grab" of the feet. Occurs mostly in the lowlands, but occasionally in the subalpine areas of the mountains. RANGE. Breeds from northwestern Alaska and the Yukon south through the Northwest, though mostly along the coasts of Alaska and B.C. Many northern individuals migrate southward to Washington and northern Idaho in winter and increasingly to northwestern Oregon. Uncommon breeder in eastern Idaho along rivers.

MARSH HAWK; NORTHERN HARRIER *Circus cyaneus* 19-24 (484-612) Fig. 36
A medium-sized hawk with long, blunt, black-tipped wings and a long rounded tail. Color is uniformly gray (male) or brown (female and immature), with a white rump patch (best field mark). In flying, the wings are held arched above the horizontal. The legs are yellow, long, and unfeathered. CALLS. A very rapid shrill *kee-kee-kee* or *chek-chek-chek.* HABITAT. Open areas, such as prairies, sagebrush plains, damp meadows, grain fields, marshes, tideflats, and subalpine country. Foraging done near the ground. RANGE. Breeds from northern Alaska and the Yukon south in proper habitat through the Northwest. Winters from southern B.C. southward, more commonly west of the Cascades; rarely northward. More numerous in winter in the Northwest.

NORTHERN GOSHAWK *Accipiter gentilis* 20-26 (510-663)
A large dark-grayish hawk with short rounded wings and a long rounded tail. Back dark bluish gray; under parts light marbled gray, and a white line over the eye. Immature, brownish streaked below, with a line over the eye (unlike the similar Cooper's Hawk immature which lacks a white line over eye). Flies with an alternate flapping and gliding flight pattern. CALLS. A piercing high-pitched staccato *cac-cac-cac-cac,* etc. HABITAT. Prefers dense and coniferous forests;

36. Left to right: Osprey, Red-tailed Hawk, Marsh Hawk (adult male above, immature, below) (Schultz)

wandering to edges of clearings, snag areas in lowlands, and nearby open places in winter. Forages often below the tree tops and is commonly met flying a few feet above the ground along a trail or mountain road. RANGE. Resident and breeder from central Alaska and the Yukon south through the Northwest, wintering and migrating from B.C. southward. *Note.* This and the following two species are difficult to tell in the field and are probably best identified by size even though there is overlapping in this character. A rule of thumb that might help: Sharp-shin is slightly larger than the Kestrel; Cooper's is crow-size; and the Goshawk is like a Red-tailed Hawk in size.

SHARP-SHINNED HAWK *Accipiter striatus* 1-14 (255-357) Fig. 37
A small bluish-gray hawk with short rounded wings and a long square-tipped tail. Under parts white, streaked or barred with reddish. In flying, the bird alternates several quick wing-strokes with a glide. Immature, brown above, brown and white streaked below. Can be separated from other small hawks, such as the Kestrel and Merlin, on the basis of the wing shape and length and from small male Cooper's and immature Goshawks by the tail shape. CALLS. A strident high-pitched *kik-kik-kik,* etc. HABITAT. Mixed broken woods and brush from lowlands to subalpine areas (especially in the latter zone in the fall). RANGE. Breeds from northern Alaska and the Yukon south through the Northwest, wintering and migrating from B.C. southward.

COOPER'S HAWK *Accipiter cooperii* 14-20 (357-510)
A medium-sized bluish-gray hawk with short rounded wings and a long rounded tail. Under parts rusty barred. Immature, brown, streaked below; similar to immature Goshawk, but lacking white stripe over the eye. Tail longer and rounder at tip than in the Sharp-shinned. Has the accipitrine flight habit of alternately flapping and gliding. CALLS. A rapid, metallic, cackling *kak-kak-kak-kak,* etc., or a high-pitched *pee-a, pee-a, pee-a.* HABITAT. Broken semi-open areas in both coniferous and deciduous woods. Seen more often in the open than is the Sharp-shinned Hawk. RANGE. Breeds from central B.C. south through the Northwest, wintering through most of the breeding range, except the northernmost parts. Many birds descend to lower, more open, areas in winter, as do many forest species.

RED-SHOULDERED HAWK *Buteo lineatus* 18-24 (459-612)
A slender medium-sized buteo with reddish under parts and anterior halves of wings, heavily-barred tail, and light posterior halves of under surface of wings. From above, the posterior halves of the wings are heavily barred. Shoulders are reddish and the bases of the wing primaries appear translucent. CALLS. A loud ringing *kee-you.*

37. Sharp-shinned Hawk (l.), Kestrel (r.) (Schultz)

HABITAT. Prefers river bottoms, marshes, moist woods, and woodlots. Forages commonly over farmland. RANGE. Rare fall, winter, and early spring visitor to western Oregon, Washington, and B.C. Formerly bred in Oregon (19th century) and may now breed at Harbor, Oregon.

BROAD-WINGED HAWK *Buteo platypterus* 14-18 (357-459)
A small, chunky, short-tailed buteo with white, very finely marked under surfaces of wings, light brownish-marked belly, black wing tips, and a heavily barred tail. Wings appear relatively short and broad. Barred tail and thin whistled call are distinctive. CALLS. A shrill, thin, whistled *kwee-e-e-e-e.* HABITAT. Wooded areas. RANGE. Very rare spring (May) straggler to southern Idaho and very rare in late summer (August and September) in northeastern Washington (records for several years). Recorded also from B.C.

SWAINSON'S HAWK *Buteo swainsoni* 19-22 (484-561)
Similar in size to the Red-tailed Hawk, but has longer, more pointed wings. The broad dark breast band is distinctive. The forward half of the under surface of the wing is light colored (buffy) and unmarked, contrasting with the dark rear half of the wing. The tail is grayish below. The upper parts are immaculately dark colored. The white chin contrasts with the dark head and neck. Melanistic individuals are best told by the light face and tail. CALLS. A shrill squealing whistle. HABITAT. Hot, dry, open country of the interior with a few scattered trees for nesting; rare, mostly as fall visitor, in dry "rain shadow" areas west of the Cascades. RANGE. Breeds and migrates from northeastern Alaska and the northern Yukon south through the Northwest, except rarely (mostly as a migrational straggler) in the area west of the Cascades.

RED-TAILED HAWK *Buteo jamaicensis* 19-24 (484-612) Fig. 36
A large, broad-winged, fan-tailed buteo with dark brown upper parts, light to dark (depending on color phase) under parts, and red tail. Immatures are similar, but have a dark gray tail barred with black and dark midbelly area and a light-colored breast. The red tail is the best field mark. The underwing pattern is the reverse of that of the Swainson's Hawk — the flight feathers are lighter than the wing linings. CALLS. A hoarse, gull-like, screaming *pee-er,* descending in pitch. Frequently imitated by jays. HABITAT. Mixed open or broken woods, burns, logged-over land, alpine regions, and open interior prairies where scattered trees or cliff ledges furnish nesting sites. RANGE. Summer resident and breeder from central Alaska and the Yukon south through the Northwest, wintering from southwestern B.C. southward (commonly in western Washington). Uncommon to

rare, or even absent, in winter in the northcentral and northeastern parts of Washington and in Idaho.

HARLAN'S HAWK *Buteo harlani* 20-22 (510-561)
A somewhat variably-colored buteo with a mottled-white terminally-banded tail. Under parts may be whitish (light phase) or anterior darkish (wings) with black belly (dark phase). Most individuals seen are entirely dark (with light spots above) and have a light-colored tail. Shape, size, and call similar to those of the Red-tailed Hawk. Some workers consider this hawk to be a color phase of the latter species. HABITAT. Primarily wooded areas or open places with patchy woods. RANGE. Summer resident and breeder in northern B.C., the southern Yukon (where the most common buteo in some areas), and Alaska. Uncommon late fall and winter visitor (apparently increasing in numbers) and rare spring visitor elsewhere in the Northwest (southern B.C., Washington, and northern Oregon).

ROUGH-LEGGED HAWK *Buteo lagopus* 20-24 (510-612)
This species is a broad-winged long-tailed hawk with a black back, top of tail, and (usually) a black belly; head and breast are buffy, streaked with blackish; under surface of tail is whitish with a broad dark tip; pantaloons are buffy, streaked or barred with black. Best identified by black belly and black patch at "wrist" on otherwise light-appearing under surface of wings. Often seen hovering in the air in search of prey and is the only buteo in the region with this habit. The other rough-legged hawk (the Ferruginous Hawk) hovers somewhat less commonly and for shorter periods of time. CALLS. Various high-pitched descending screams. HABITAT. Open country, such as fields, prairies, marshes, and tideflats. RANGE. Breeds from northern Alaska and the Yukon south to the Aleutians and southern Alaska, wintering from southern B.C. southward, mostly east of the Cascades. Fairly common winter resident in Idaho and eastern Washington. Regular visitor in Puget Sound (Skagit and Samish Flats areas) and southwest Washington in winter. Very rare non-breeder in the Northwest states in summer.

FERRUGINOUS HAWK; FERRUGINOUS ROUGHLEG *Buteo regalis* 23 (586)
A large broad-winged hawk characterized by white under parts and reddish brown upper parts and pantaloons. A white patch near the tip of the upper wing. The less common black phase may be recognized by the white wing-patches and light un-banded tail. CALLS. High-pitched squealing cries. HABITAT. Open prairies of grass or sagebrush, lowlands to foothills. RANGE. Summer resident and

breeder from southeastern Washington, where rare, south to eastern Oregon, southern Idaho, and beyond. Winters rarely north to eastern Oregon and southern Idaho. A few straggle west of the Cascades.

GOLDEN EAGLE *Aquila chrysaetos* 30-40 (765-1,020) Fig. 35
A very large blackish hawk with golden-brown crown and hind-neck. Greater size and length of wings easily separates the Golden Eagle from the buteos. The legs are feathered down to the toes. Immatures, similar to adults except that the tail is white with a broad dark band at the tip. CALLS. Shrill screams. HABITAT. Rough open areas in the lowlands, foothills, and mountains with proper supply of rabbits and ground squirrels for forage and cliffs to nest on. RANGE. Resident and breeder from northern Alaska and the Yukon south in preferred habitat throughout the Northwest, but most numerous in the arid interior.

AMERICAN KESTREL; SPARROW HAWK *Falco sparverius* 9-12 (230-306) Figs. 37 and 38
This species is a small hawk with long pointed wings and a long square-tipped tail. It flies in typical falcon manner or hovers in midair. Wings are bluish-gray (female brownish); back red, barred with black; tail red with black bar at tip; under parts light (male, with spots; female, with buffy streaks). Face is strongly marked with black and white (including the black falcon mustaches). The tail is rounded when soaring, square when more folded in direct flight. CALLS. A rapid high-pitched series of *ki-wee, ki-wee* or *killy-killy-killy,* etc. HABITAT. Open country throughout, ranging from subalpine areas to ocean beaches, but probably most numerous in grain fields, grasslands, and sagebrush of the arid interior. RANGE. Breeds from central Alaska and the Yukon south through the Northwest, wintering from southern B.C., northern Idaho, and Montana southward.

MERLIN; PIGEON HAWK *Falco columbarius* 10-14 (255-357)
A small pigeon-sized hawk with long pointed wings and a long square-tipped tail. Back is dark brown, blue-gray, or black (depending on subspecies). Tail is heavily barred. Under parts light brown, streaked with dark brown or black. A small dark-colored falcon. CALLS. A shrill, rapid, high-pitched *ki-ki-ki-ki,* etc. HABITAT. Nests in open woodland and forages over ocean beaches where it is particularly fond of shorebirds, but inland as well over marshes, fields, open woodlands, and suburban areas. RANGE. Breeds from northwestern Alaska and northern Yukon south through the Northwest, wintering commonly from southern B.C. southward. In Idaho, mostly a rare migrant and winter visitor; rare breeder in the southeastern part of the state.

38. Kestrel at nest hole (Boggs)

PRAIRIE FALCON *Falco mexicanus* 17 (434)

A medium-sized long-winged falcon with light brown upper parts, dark brown mustaches, pale brown tail, and white under parts (immaculate on throat, but streaked on breast and belly). Dark "wing-pits" may be seen from below while bird is in flight. CALLS. A high-pitched cackling scream. HABITAT. Hot, dry, open terrain in the interior with rocky buttes or rim-rock for nesting sites; a few may visit the saltwater tideflats west of the Cascades in winter. RANGE. Resident and breeder from central B.C. south through the Northwest, mostly east of the Cascades. Mainly a casual to rare fall and winter visitor west of the Cascades. Permanent resident in southern Idaho. Uncommon winter visitor in Idaho and eastern Washington.

GYRFALCON *Falco rusticolus* 20-25 (510-637)

The largest of the falcons in our region, it has the typical pointed wings of the group. Its overall appearance is generally grayish or whitish. It is similar to the Peregrine Falcon, but is larger, longer-tailed, more uniformly colored, and lacks the heavy mustache marks. Top of head is heavily streaked with white. Upper parts gray to grayish brown, mottled with dark gray. Under parts white, spotted on belly and flanks with blackish brown. A white phase may occur which is all white with fine dark spots. CALLS. A shrill rattling scream. HABITAT. Nests in open tundra areas, wintering along the ocean beaches and on the broad open areas in the arid interior. RANGE. Breeds in northern and central Alaska and the Aleutians, as well as the northern and southern Yukon, wintering irregularly and rarely to Oregon, Washington, and northern and southern (very rarely) Idaho. Several spring and fall records.

PEREGRINE FALCON; DUCK HAWK *Falco peregrinus* 16-20 (408-510) Fig. 34

A large hawk with the typical quick deep wing-beat of a falcon, long pointed wings, and long narrow tail. Dark blue-black above; buffy white below, marked with fine spots and barrings. Broad black mustache marks of the falcon on the sides of the head below the eyes. Much darker with facial markings more emphasized than in the Prairie Falcon. CALLS. A harsh *kek-kek-kek-kek,* etc. HABITAT. Nests on cliffs, particularly along the ocean coast and less commonly inland, foraging over adjacent tideflats and beaches, as well as marshes and prairies in the interior. Mainly in open country at other times of the year. RANGE. Breeds locally and very irregularly from northern Alaska and the Yukon south through the Northwest, wintering and migrating from B.C. southward, mostly west of the Cascades. Currently showing a low reproductive rate.

39. Turkey (Fisher)

TURKEY *Meleagris gallopavo* Males, 48 (1,224); females, 36 (918)
Fig. 39

This introduced species is very similar to the domestic turkey but is more slender. It cannot be confused with any other avian species, what with the bronzy cast to the plumage and the naked head and neck of the male. The female is smaller and less iridescent, but still "turkey-ish". CALLS. Typical gobble of the male; also an alarm *pit-pit* and a flocking call of *keow-keow.* HABITAT. Prefers open woods and forests where there are frequent clearings with proper brush food species. RANGE. Introduced or spreading into various parts of the arid and semi-arid Northwest, such as the Yakima Indian Reservation; Columbia River near Lyle, Washington; Umptanum Ridge, north of Yakima, and also San Juan, Stevens, Okanogan, and Klickitat Counties of Washington; southwestern and southeastern Oregon; Snake River Canyon, Idaho-Washington-Oregon; St. Maries, Idaho area; and the Penticton, B.C. region, where a few have straggled north from northeastern Washington into southeastern B.C.

This interesting species, which Benjamin Franklin considered a better choice for our national bird than the war-like eagle, has been in-

troduced into a number of places in the Pacific Northwest with vary-
ing degrees of success. The past history of the Turkey in the eastern
U.S. is excellently reviewed in the account of this species in Richard H.
Pough's AUDUBON WATER BIRD GUIDE, pp. 188-190 (1951).

This is the first species of the Order Galliformes to be treated in
this manual. The order is World-wide and is comprised of approximately 210 species. There are two species of turkeys, one of which occurs in North America.

GROUSE

40. Spruce Grouse (Fisher)

The grouse are small to large, fast-flying, chicken-like game birds,
the bills of which are short and decurved; the tails and wings, short.
The toes are sometimes feathered and are used to scratch food from
the soil and for running, as these birds spend much of their time on the
ground, foraging and moving from place to place. As recognized in
this book, some nine species occur in the Pacific Northwest.

The Blue Grouse, currently considered a single species by many ornithologists, is here returned to two species on the basis of
morphological and behavioral characters and the fact that their
origins are a complicated evolutionary matter peculiar to the Pacific

Northwest. This is a part of the great problem of a number of forms whose ranges were divided by recent continental glaciations and have been newly reunited, distribution-wise at least. Examples are to be found not only among several species of grouse, but in certain jays, woodpeckers, orioles, juncos, flycatchers, warblers, etc., which have been "solved" in a number of inconsistent ways. The crux of the matter is that taxonomists have not faced the fact that only those characters should be used to define species which have adapted those taxa to their particular ways of life. Names should be used to emphasize the existence of forms and their unique qualities. Problems such as these cannot be handled by irresponsible lumping. This book treats the matter in a conservative manner until a more satisfactory solution can be worked out and eschews the blind following of certain "experts" which is hardly the scientific way.

Perhaps the matter is well expressed by George B. Schaller in the following quotation from his recent book, STONES OF SILENCE, published in 1980:

> Biologists like to have all species neatly classified and arranged into discrete categories based on the degree of relationship. Nature refuses to abide by such strictures, and to the chagrin of taxonomists there are many species which cannot be tidily stuffed into pigeonholes.

PACIFIC NORTHWEST SPECIES

SPRUCE GROUSE; FRANKLIN'S GROUSE *Dendragapus canadensis* 16 (408) Fig. 40
A small dark-colored grouse of the upper forest which has brown upper parts heavily barred with black; black throat, breast, and tail with white spots at base; orange patch of skin over the eye; and black sides strikingly barred with white. Female is brownish, barred with blackish brown. Noted for its extreme tameness. CALLS. "Drumming" sound is more like a flutter than the tight roll of the Ruffed Grouse; a clucking *kruk, kruk* or rolled *kr-r-r-r-uk*. HABITAT. Open to semi-open coniferous woodlands of the mountains, particularly in the upper parts of the dense montane forests where they begin to open up under increasing subalpine influence. RANGE. Resident from northern Alaska and northern Yukon south in the mountains to northeastern Oregon and central and eastern Idaho, occurring mostly east of the Cascade crest.

DUSKY GROUSE; BLUE GROUSE *Dendragapus obscurus* 18-21 (459-536)
A large grouse of the upper mountain forests, appearing larger than the Ruffed Grouse. Male, dark grayish in color with a well-defined terminal gray band in the tip of the tail. Female, smaller and more mottled with brown and with a dull grayish belly. Perhaps best identified in the field on the basis of distribution. CALLS. A series of five or six low subdued hoots given while the bird is on the ground and audible for perhaps a hundred yards only. HABITAT. Prefers semi-open country, particularly on ridge tops, subalpine areas in mountains, as well as burns and cut-over timber land. Mostly a bird of the hilly and mountainous terrain, showing considerable seasonal movement (in search of lower areas for breeding, moving to higher elevations in late summer for insects and seeds, and working down again in the late winter and early spring for buds and needles for food). Most commonly seen in the subalpine or Hudsonian zone. RANGE. Resident from the southern Yukon and northern B.C. south through B.C. (excepting the coastal region) to northeastern and northcentral Washington, northeastern Oregon, and Idaho. Fairly common, if scattered, breeder on mountain tops in southern Idaho. Basically an interior species.

SOOTY GROUSE; BLUE GROUSE *Dendragapus fuliginosus* 18-23 (459-586)
Similar to the preceding species except that the tip of the tail has little or no grayish band. Female, very similar to that of the preceding species. CALLS. Five or six loud, low-pitched, booming hoots given from treetops and audible to over a mile. HABITAT. Very similar to that of the preceding species, essentially a bird of the subalpine country. RANGE. Resident from the southwestern Yukon south through the Alaska Panhandle, extreme northwestern and coastal B.C., and western Washington and western Oregon, including the east slope of the Cascades from central Washington south through eastern Oregon into California. Basically a coastal species.

WILLOW PTARMIGAN *Lagopus lagopus* 14-17 (357-434)
Male, (winter) pure white with a black bill and outer tail feathers; no black streak between bill and eye; (summer) mostly reddish with fine dark barring; wings and feathered legs white. Female, (winter) white as in male; (summer) mottled brownish. CALLS. A sharp rattling call; a cackling gobble by the male; various clucking notes. HABITAT. Prefers willow clumps and willow-spruce growths in river bottoms, hillsides, and alpine areas. RANGE. Resident and breeder from northern Alaska, the Aleutians, and northern Yukon south in suitable habitat

41. Nest and eggs of Ruffed Grouse (Boggs)

42. Sage Grouse (Fisher)

to central and southeastern B.C. Rare straggler to northwestern Montana.

ROCK PTARMIGAN *Lagopus mutus* 13-15½ (331-395)
Male and female (winter) similar to the Willow Ptarmigan but with a black streak between the eye and the bill and projecting behind the eye as an eye line. The white plumage in the species is pink-tinged, unlike the yellow-tinged phase of the Willow. The summer male is similar to that of the Willow, but slightly lighter brown and with a light chin. Females are very similar in summer in the two species. CALLS. A rolling two-part call; a pheasant-like cackling note; various purrs and clucks. HABITAT. Bare, rocky, alpine areas; barren mountain tops in the more southern parts of the range. RANGE. Resident and breeder from northern Alaska and the northern Yukon south to northern B.C. and less commonly in the coastal mountains south through the province to the U.S.-Canada border.

43. White-tailed Ptarmigan (winter, l.; summer, r.) (Schultz)

WHITE-TAILED PTARMIGAN *Lagopus leucurus* 12-13 (306-331)
Fig. 43
A small grouse of the open alpine areas of the mountains. Brown, with white belly, wings, and tail in summer and wholly white, except for black eyes and bill, in winter. No black in tail in this species. Summer males and females similar. Calls. A soft low clucking; a soft hooting note. HABITAT. The high heather and rock fields of the highest montane areas above timberline, rarely dropping down to the subalpine meadows and groves, except in winter. RANGE. Resident and breeder from southcentral Alaska and the northern Yukon south to Vancouver Island, the southern Cascades of Washington (Mt. St. Helens,

at least formerly!), the Wallowas of Oregon, and the mountains of northern and central Idaho. Locally irregular in distribution.

RUFFED GROUSE *Bonasa umbellus* 16-19 (408-484) Fig. 41
A reddish-brown small-chicken-sized bird with a black band at the end of the tail. Small crest and a black ruff on either side of the neck. Belly whitish and strongly barred with black. Grayish phase (more common in the interior); brown colors variously replaced by gray, especially on the tail. Usually not seen till flushed. CALLS. A drum-like series of sounds beginning slowly and accelerating into a rapid whir. A short *quit-quit* in alarm. Various chirps and clucks. HABITAT. Prefers dense shady stands of coniferous and deciduous trees, particularly in canyon bottoms and other protected places, from the lowlands to intermediate elevations in the mountains, but commonly visiting the forest edges of clearings and old logging roads in twilight hours of early morning and late afternoon. RANGE. Resident, often common, from western Alaska and central Yukon south through the Northwest.

SHARP-TAILED GROUSE *Tympanuchus phasianellus* 17 (434)
A medium-sized, pale, gray-and-brown grouse of the arid grass-covered areas with generally heavily spotted color pattern and short pointed tail. Breast is dirty white with dark v-shaped marks; belly more unmarked. No ruffs on neck. CALLS. Owl-like hoots, followed by low, rolling, muttered notes; various cacklings and gobbles. HABITAT. Grassland and grain and hay fields in the open arid interior, as well as prairies and parklands in or near coniferous or deciduous woodlands. RANGE. Irregular local resident and breeder from northcentral Alaska and the Yukon south through the Northwest in the arid interior east of the Cascades. Less common than formerly, especially in the more southern and eastern parts of the range in our region.

SAGE GROUSE *Centrocercus urophasianus* Male, 28 (714); female, 22 (561) Fig. 42
A grouse of the open sagebrush areas as large as a small turkey. Male, speckled grayish brown with whitish throat and breast (all variously barred) and black belly; long spike-like tail feathers. Female, smaller, with shorter tail; similar to the female Ring-necked Pheasant and female Ruffed Grouse, but tail shorter than pheasant's and not fan-shaped as in the Ruffed Grouse hen. CALLS. A low *kuk-kuk-kuk* when flushed; various other sounds when strutting. HABITAT. Primarily sagebrush plains; unfortunately strongly reduced in numbers as the sage deserts are "developed" for agriculture. RANGE. Local irregular resident from southern B.C. (formerly) southward through the

Northwest in suitable habitat east of the Cascades. In Idaho, now mostly in the southern part of the state. Extirpated from many parts of its former range, especially in Washington and B.C.

QUAILS

44. Bobwhite (Fisher)

These are small to medium-sized, plump, gallinaceous "game birds" with much gray and brown in the plumage. They are usually found in brushy or open wooded areas and are strongly gregarious, generally occurring in small flocks.

The quails, along with the pheasants and peafowl, constitute the great family Phasianidae of which there are about 166 species in the World. They are closely related to the grouse.

The entire order of the Galliformes is extensively used for food by many peoples around the globe and makes up a very important group of game birds in the Pacific Northwest. The native species were much more numerous in past times than they are now. The author remembers talking to "old timers" who never failed to be amazed by the numbers of Ruffed Grouse in the forests and the great quantities of Sharp-tailed Grouse in the grassy prairies. In fact, one of them remembered that when he and his brothers went hunting "sharp-tails", they would bring back a wagon load of these birds to the ranch house — perhaps one of the reasons they are not so common anymore! Of course, we must remember the great amount of environmental alteration that has taken place in the ranges of many of our game birds. All or most of the species described here are not native to the Northwest, having been introduced for hunting purposes. Common habitats for quail are the brushy gullies that intersect farmlands.

PACIFIC NORTHWEST SPECIES

MOUNTAIN QUAIL *Oreortyx pictus* 11 (280)
Somewhat similar to the much more numerous California Quail but characterized by a long, straight, backward-pointing plume on the head and a bright brownish-red throat. A single white stripe extends from the eye down each side of the throat. The back and tail are greenish brown. CALLS. A tremulous *tr-r-r-r;* a loud mellow *too-look, too-look, too-look;* a loud *quork* given by the male; other clucking notes. HABITAT. Brushy hill and mountain sides, burns, brush patches on canyon walls, and logged-off land. RANGE. Irregular local resident in reduced numbers from northern Washington and northern Idaho (south from the Clearwater River) southward. Introduced into Vancouver Island. Most numerous in Oregon. Scattered in the Puget Sound region; uncommon, but regular, resident in Kitsap and Mason Counties, Washington.

SCALED QUAIL *Callipepla squamata* 10-12 (255-306) Fig. 45
This is a grayish-colored quail heavily scaled or barred on the under parts, neck, and upper back, and with a white crest. CALLS. A loud call of *pay-cos;* a barking *kuck-yer.* HABITAT. Prefers the dry desert places, often far from water. Often found in gullies and dry washes. RANGE. Introduced into several areas in eastern Washington, as in Grant and Kittitas Counties, and Eltopia and the Juniper Forest, Franklin County. Also the Yakima Firing Range, Yakima County.

CALIFORNIA QUAIL *Lophortyx californicus* 9-11 (230-280)
A grayish-brown quail with a short plume curving forward over the face from the crown. The plume is shorter in the female. Throat is black in the male; light brown in the female. The back is brownish and the tail grayish. A white line over the eye extends down the cheek and along each side of the throat. The belly is strongly scaled, with a rufous patch. CALLS. An insistent *kuk-wher-go;* a soft *pit-pit-pit* in flocking; a sharp *turk* in alarm. HABITAT. Brush patches and adjacent open ground, hedgerows, fields, truck gardens, city parks, and suburban areas; mostly at lower elevations. RANGE. Introduced successfully

45.   Scaled Quail (Fisher)

into suitable areas in southern B.C., Washington, Oregon, and western Idaho. Probably native in southwestern Oregon. Numbers vary from place to place; seems to suffer severely from harsh winters. Tends to be very spotty in occurrence.

GAMBEL'S QUAIL *Lophortyx gambelii* 10-11½ (255-293)
A desert quail similar to the California Quail but the male lacks the ventral scaling and has a black patch on the buffy belly. Forward-pointing plume and black white-margined chin as in the California Quail. The female lacks the scaled pattern. CALLS. An increasing *kway-er, kway-er, kway-er* and a rhythmical series of *kuk-wek, kuk-wek, kuk-wek,* etc.; various other notes. HABITAT. Shrubby areas along desert streams. RANGE. Introduced to several localities in the Northwest states with varying success. In Idaho, occurs only in the area of the junction of the Lemhi and Salmon Rivers.

BOBWHITE *Colinus virginianus* 9-11 (230-280) Fig. 44
A small light-brownish quail with white (male) or tan-colored (female) throat and line over the eye; reddish-brown upper parts and breast; white belly, finely-marked with dark-brown barrings; flanks streaked with reddish brown. The tail is gray. CALLS. A loud whistled *oh, bob-whoit;* a softer *quoi-ee.* HABITAT. Agricultural cropland, as well as

46. Gray Partridge (Fisher)

47. Chukar (Pole)

adjacent weed patches and roadsides. RANGE. Introduced at various times in different local areas in the Northwest with generally varying success. A few scattered individuals remain, particularly in the Palouse Country and southwestern Idaho. Resident in good numbers in southern Pierce County, Washington, as in burns in the Horn Creek area. Reported regularly in the Sequim-Dungeness area of Washington.

OLD WORLD PARTRIDGES

CHUKAR *Alectoris chukar* 13 (331) Fig. 47
A large, light-colored, grayish-brown, quail-like game bird with a tan throat bordered by a black band which passes also through the eye and across the forehead, grayish breast, buffy belly, and whitish flanks heavily barred with black. The back and tail are pale grayish brown. The legs and bill are bright red. CALLS. A sharp *whee-too;* a soft series of *chuck, chuck, chuck,* slowly accelerating to a whir. HABITAT. Open, barren, rocky hillsides and canyon walls, particularly in the arid interior; rarely to subalpine areas. RANGE. Successfully introduced to suitable habitat in numerous places in southern B.C. and southward through the Northwest, preferring rocky arid terrain, primarily east of the Cascades. Not successful west of that range in Washington.

RED-LEGGED PARTRIDGE *Alectoris rufa* 13-14 (332-357)
Similar to the Chukar, but has black streaks on the breast and a bright red bill and legs. Sides are more heavily barred. CALLS. *chuck, chuck-or.* HABITAT. Mostly farmed fields in the its new range. RANGE. Introduced and established for some years (beginning 1967) in the Kittitas Valley of Washington. *Note.* Several other game bird species have been liberated in the Northwest from time to time, with varying degrees of success. Many have either failed or not spread beyond their original points of introduction. Most of these have not been treated in this book.

GRAY PARTRIDGE; HUNGARIAN PARTRIDGE *Perdix perdix* 11-13 (280-331) Fig. 46
A medium-sized quail-like bird with a reddish-brown un-marked head, brownish back, gray breast, and white belly separated from the breast by a broad sooty-brown bar. Sides and flanks are barred with chestnut. The tail shows reddish in flight, unlike those of other quails and partridges in the region. CALLS. A low-pitched rolling *churr;* a single high-pitched *whit* or *ker-whit* given in flight; a hoarse *kee-ah.* HABITAT. Open habitats with some scattered cover, as croplands,

grainfields, meadows, old orchards, sagebrush, desert rimrock areas, etc. RANGE. Successfully introduced and now local resident in suitable habitat from southern B.C. (Okanagan Valley, lower Fraser River area, and the vicinity of Victoria) southward. Most numerous in open areas east of the Cascades. Has not "taken" well west of the Cascades.

PHEASANTS

48.   Ring-necked Pheasant (female, 1.; male, r.) (Schultz)

RING-NECKED PHEASANT *Phasianus colchicus* Male, 33-36 (842-918); female, 20-24 (510-612) Fig. 48
The introduced "Chinese Pheasant". A large, long-tailed, chicken-like bird. Male, highly colored with a greenish-black head and neck, scarlet wattles (skin patches) on sides of the head, white collar, and a long sweeping tail. Female, smaller and grouse-like, but with a longer pointed tail than in those birds. CALLS. The crow of the male is a double-noted *cu-cuck* or *koor-kuk*. HABITAT. Open fields, grass-lands, and weedy areas with adjacent brush or groves of trees. RANGE. Successfully introduced and now resident from southern B.C. south through the Northwest. Probably more numerous in open, arid, and semi-arid areas east of the Cascades. Various other species of pheasants have been introduced in the Northwest at times, without their becoming successfully established. The Japanese Pheasant still occurs on Fox Island, southern Puget Sound.

CRANES

49. Sandhill Crane (Fisher)

These are large, long-legged, long-necked birds that are most likely to be confused with herons, but the crane's lack of plumes and the habit of keeping the neck outstretched in flight separate these birds.

The great size of the Sandhill Crane, particularly the Greater Sandhill race, the stately demeanor of the bird, its stentorian voice, and its courtship performance make this one of the most interesting of birds. Its comparative scarceness and preference for wild places and moor-like meadows increase the romance of the species. Although accused, rightly or wrongly, of being an injurious species in some parts of North America, it certainly is harmless in the Northwest and needs to be strictly protected. Its large size, however, makes it a possible target for gun-happy youths. Fortunately, it is a shy bird and does not permit close approach in the open habitats it prefers. In migration, it forages over grasslands and grainfields and along the shores, marshes, and shallow edges of freshwater lakes, ponds, and rivers. Occasionally migrates southward over the mountains.

The cranes belong to the great order Gruiformes which contains some of the most peculiar of birds. Many show reluctance or inability to fly and are either distantly related to the shorebirds or represent a parallel line of development as large and small "shore birds".

PACIFIC NORTHWEST SPECIES

SANDHILL CRANE *Grus canadensis* 34-48 (867-1,224) Figs. 20 and 49

A large, gray, heron-like bird with a bald red forehead. The crane flies with its head and neck out-stretched (not folded with head on shoulders as in the Great Blue Heron). CALLS. A deep rolling *k-r-r-oo*. HABITAT. Open tundra, grasslands, wet meadows, marshes, grainfields, and margins of lakes and rivers. RANGE. Breeds from the Arctic coasts locally and irregularly southward (at least formerly) through the Northwest (east of the Cascade mountains), migrating in often large flocks through the interior of the northwest states, and in lesser quantities along the ocean coast (though large flocks stop at Sauvie Island, Portland), to winter to the south of our territory. A few have been found during the winter just west of the Cascades in the Sauvie Island and Ridgefield Refuge areas. In Idaho, migrates throughout but now breeds only in the central (Stanley Basin) and southeastern parts of the state; uncommon as scattered winter visitor. The "Greater Sandhill Crane" breeds in southern Oregon and southern and eastern Idaho.

WHOOPING CRANE *Grus americana* 50-56 (1,275-1,428)

An immense white bird with a long neck and black primaries showing in flight. The face, chin, and crown are red. CALLS. Rolling trumpeting notes that carry for very long distances. HABITAT. Open prairies and marshes. RANGE. Introduced into southeastern Idaho (Grays Lake) by cross-fostering with Sandhill Cranes. May rarely be found migrating through that part of the Northwest.

RAILS

Rails are small, quail-sized, chicken-like swamp or marsh birds with exceedingly shy habits. They are much more frequently heard than seen, but are irregularly and sparsely distributed in the Northwest and not often found by the average bird student. The flight of these birds is very weak and their voices are cackle-like.

These are among the most mysterious of birds. As shy in the north as tinamous are in the south, we often suspect that they are present in the marshes we are exploring, but we very seldom see them. All we hear is the whinnying or cackling notes emanating from the watery, muddy, usually impenetrable swamp. Here are species that seem to have life styles similar to the charadriform shorebirds but prefer to forage in densely vegetated aquatic margins in closed-cover marshes, swamps, and wet meadows, rather than the open sandy or muddy, but

50. Yellow Rail (Fisher)

not heavily inclosed, shores that are preferred by the sandpiper clan. Dillon Ripley's recent monograph on the rails of the World is an excellent introduction to this group and well worth study by any student of marsh birds. While we obviously have specialists in certain bird groups among the professional ornithologists, we should have more specialization among the lay group. Their studies, directed toward particular genera or families, could well increase our knowledge of many of the lesser known birds of the Northwest.

PACIFIC NORTHWEST SPECIES

VIRGINIA RAIL *Rallus limicola* 9-10 (230-255) Fig. 51
A rail with a long slightly-decurved bill, white chin, reddish throat and breast, gray cheeks, blackish upper parts (streaked with brown), up-turned tail, blackish flanks (barred with white), and brownish-red bill and legs. The extremely long toes of the rails help to identify them in comparison with sandpipers of similar size. CALLS. A vibrant metallic *kid-ick, kid-ick, kid-ick,* etc., or *kik-kik-kik-kik-kik,* etc.; also a sharp *cut-cut* or *cutah, cutah.* HABITAT. Freshwater, as well as saltwater, marshes and wet meadows and pastures. RANGE. Local summer resident and breeder from western Washington and central and southern B.C. south in suitable habitat through the Northwest.

51. Virginia (top) and Sora Rails (immature, l.) (Schultz)

Winters through much of the breeding range where climate is not too severe; less common east of the Cascades. Locally common summer resident and breeder in northern and southern Idaho.

SORA *Porzana carolina* 8-9 (204-230) Fig. 51
A small marsh bird with a short chicken-like bill, black lores and throat, gray fore-neck and breast, and an up-turned tail; under parts heavily barred; back mottled brownish. CALLS. A querulous *sor-ee;* a sharp *keel;* a descending whinny-like series; a *cut-ah, cut-ah, cut-ah,* etc. HABITAT. Freshwater and, in migration and winter, saltwater marshes, wet meadows, and grassy patches bordering sloughs, lakes, and beaver ponds. RANGE. Local summer resident and breeder from

B.C. and the Yukon south through the Northwest. Rare in southeastern Alaska. Winters mostly south of the Northwest, though a few remain in the Puget Sound area and along the ocean coast, as well as in the interior during mild winters.

BLACK RAIL *Laterallus jamaicensis* 5-6 (128-153)
A very tiny all-black rail with a very short black bill, yellow legs, and a white-spotted back and flanks. Check for the spotted back and flanks to separate this species from the black chicks of larger rails. CALLS. A sharp *kik, kik, kik, kik;* also a softer *croo-croo-croo.* HABITAT. The grassy upper borders of freshwater marshes and the grassy *Salicornia* meadows above high tide along the ocean coasts. RANGE. Recorded in eastern Oregon. A few unverified sight records elsewhere in the Northwest.

YELLOW RAIL *Coturnicops noveboracensis* 6½-7½ (166-191) Fig. 50
A small yellowish rail with a white wing-patch showing mainly in flight. The bill is short, and yellow. Legs yellow. The upper parts are strongly striped. An extremely shy bird, even for a rail. CALLS. A patterned series of ticking notes, as *tic-tic, tic-tic-tic;* or *kuk-kuk-kuk-kuk-kuk-kuk-kuk.* HABITAT. Wet meadows, shallow freshwater marshes, saltwater meadows, where there is mainly grass. RANGE. A rare spring and fall visitor in Washington, Oregon, and southern B.C. Rare migrant in eastern Idaho.

COMMON GALLINULE *Gallinula chloropus* 12-15 (306-382)
Somewhat similar to the American Coot, but with a reddish bill and forehead plate, white spots along the sides and under surface of the tail, and long yellow legs and toes. CALLS. A variety of loud, harsh, chicken-like squawks and clucks. HABITAT. Freshwater marshes. RANGE. Very rare spring visitor to eastern Oregon. One record, May 1972.

COOTS

52. American Coot (Fisher)

AMERICAN COOT *Fulica americana* 13-16 (331-408) Fig. 52
A duck-sized blackish-gray bird with a black head and neck and a
white bill; moves head back and forth while swimming. Conspicuous
long legs and unwebbed feet (having instead round discs on bottoms of
toes). CALLS. A grating *kuk* or *keck* and a *pult-a, pult-a, pult-a,* etc.
HABITAT. Freshwater marshes, ponds, and lakes and occasionally
on salt water in winter; often forages on nearby grassy shores.
RANGE. Resident and breeder, often commonly, through much of
the Northwest from the southern Yukon and northern B.C.
southward. Common local summer resident and breeder, as well as
migrant, in Idaho; less common in winter in northern part of state.

SHOREBIRDS

53. Sanderling (Fisher)

These are small- to medium-sized, compact, wading birds that frequent saltwater shores, river and lake margins, and wet meadows. The term for the group, "shorebirds" is excellent because, with few exceptions, this is where you find them, foraging, often in flocks, near the edge of fresh or salt water.

The shorebird assemblage in the Pacific Northwest, with its variety of waters, is quite large, numbering some 52 species more or less regularly visiting our region. Some, of course, are quite rare, having been detected only once or a few times. Others, like the ubiquitous Killdeer, are very common and well known to all bird students. Obviously, such a great series of birds presents challenges and frustrations to the amateur ornithologist. Many species are very similar and must be identified with great care. The scenes in which the shorebirds occur are often very romantic, ranging from rocks and reefs amidst the crashing surf of the outer coast to the quiet margins of some interior pond or lake. To many of us, these forms are among the most fascinating of all Northwest birds.

This great group, approximately 160 species strong, are internationalists, many of them. When you see them along some ocean shore, you are looking at birds that know no national or continental boundaries. Their ranges and their habitats are cosmopolitan ones. They are true citizens of the World. How much we have to learn from our lesser brothers!

PACIFIC NORTHWEST SPECIES

BLACK OYSTERCATCHER *Haematopus bachmani* 17 (434)
This is a large stocky shorebird, completely black in color, except for the flat, heavy, red bill and flesh-colored legs. CALLS. A loud *wheep, wheep;* a soft *phee-a.* HABITAT. Rocky ocean shores, generally on the outer coast; favors areas of heavy breaking surf. RANGE. Resident, breeder, and migrant along the Aleutians and the coast of Alaska south along the outer ocean coast, including the San Juans, the straits, and Protection Island, through the Northwest to out of our territory.

BLACK-NECKED STILT *Himantopus himantopus* 15 (382)
A large black and white shorebird with an almost straight bill. Somewhat similar to the Avocet, but with wholly black upper parts, white face and breast, shorter bill (2½ to 3¾ inches), and reddish legs. The wings are unpatterned. CALLS. A rapid *yep-yep-yep-yip-yip-yip,* etc., and a harsh tern-like *kark, kark, kark,* etc. HABITAT. Open marshlands and wet meadows as well as shallow fresh water; often found in irrigated pasture land. RANGE. Local summer resident and breeder in southern Oregon, southern Idaho, and the Columbia Basin of Washington, straggling rarely in spring (mostly) to southwestern B.C. and Montana, as well as to the Willamette Valley of Oregon. Recent breeding records from southcentral Washington, as near George and Moses Lake (1973), Grant County.

AMERICAN AVOCET *Recurvirostra americana* 17 (434)
A large black and white shorebird with a long (3½ to 4 inches) upward-curving bill and bluish legs. Head, neck, and chest are pale cinnamon. Fall adults and immatures lack the cinnamon tinge, having the head, neck, and breast washed with grayish. CALLS. A loud rapid *wheep, wheep, wheep.* HABITAT. Alkaline sloughs and mudflats bordering lakes and ponds in the arid interior prairie country. Mudflats and shallow water for wading are necessities. RANGE. Summer resident, breeder, and migrant from eastern Washington and northern Idaho southward through the Northwest, mostly east of the Cascades. A few to southern B.C. Rare west of the Cascades. Rare in summer in northern Idaho, though sometimes locally common in late summer and fall; common, though local, in the southern part of the state.

112

BLACK-BELLIED PLOVER *Pluvialis squatarola* 10-12 (235-306)
A large, short-billed, chunky shorebird. In spring, upper parts grayish white, mottled with black; face, throat, breast, and belly black; rear under parts white. A broad white stripe over the eye extends down the neck. In winter, mostly grayish white with fine brown mottlings on back and breast. A black "arm-pit" patch shows when wing is raised; also a conspicuous white stripe evident in the wing when the bird is in flight. Snow-white rump in all plumages. CALLS. A plaintive, mellow, whistled *hee-er-ee* or *purr-reel*. HABITAT. Tideflats and muddy and sandy margins of both salt and fresh water. RANGE. Breeds along the northern Arctic coast and south along western Alaska to the mouth of the Yukon River. Winters along the ocean coast from southwestern B.C. southward where common migrant and uncommon summer visitor. A migrant only in the interior east of the Cascades. Rare spring and uncommon fall migrant in Idaho.

LESSER GOLDEN PLOVER *Pluvialis dominica* 10-11 (255-280)
A plover larger than a Killdeer with dark-brown upper parts mottled with golden-brown spots and solidly-black under parts. The tail is brownish — not whitish as in the Black-bellied Plover. A broad white stripe over the eye extends down the neck during the breeding season. In winter, a dark brownish-looking plover without conspicuous black and white markings. No white stripe in wing or black "arm-pits". CALLS. A harsh rolled *quee-e-e-a* or *quee-del-ee.* HABITAT. Open habitats (tundra, ocean beaches, tideflats, grasslands, cultivated fields, etc.) RANGE. Breeds along the Arctic coasts of Alaska and the Yukon south to northern B.C., migrating through southern Alaska and regularly and commonly southward through the remainder of the Northwest (mostly along the coast). Very rare winter visitor and rare summer straggler in the Northwest states. Rare spring and uncommon fall migrant in Idaho.

SEMIPALMATED PLOVER *Charadrius semipalmatus* 6-8 (153-204)
A small Killdeer-like bird, gray or gray-brown above and white below; crown and cheeks blackish; chin, throat, and collar around neck white; white line across forehead and through the eye; one black breast band or collar; bill orange with black tip (spring) or completely black (winter); legs orange yellow. Somewhat smaller than the Killdeer, the Semipalmated Plover lacks the orange rump of its cousin. Black colors are replaced by gray-browns in fall adults and immatures. CALLS. A crying whistled *chee-wee* or *too-lee.* HABITAT. Sandy beaches and mudflats along salt water; margins of larger lakes in the interior. RANGE. Breeds from northern Alaska and the northern Yukon south to southern Alaska and central B.C., and irregularly to the

54. Killdeer (upper), Common Snipe (lower) (Schultz)

southern Washington coast. Migrates and occasionally winters and summers along the coast of the Northwest to south of our territory. Numerous migrational records for the interior east of the Cascades. Uncommon spring and common fall migrant in northern Idaho; rare in fall (late summer) and spring in southern Idaho.

KILLDEER *Charadrius vociferus* 10-11 (255-280) Figs. 54 and 57
The familiar robin-sized plover of open places; shows two black bands across the throat and a light red or orange tail. Dark above, light below; white forehead with black bar across fore-crown; white patch behind the eye; lores and cheeks dark; chin and throat white. Plumage of adults and immatures similar the year around. CALLS. A high-pitched *kee-dee-ah, kee-dee-ah,* etc.; also a plaintive *cry-babee, cry-babee,* etc. HABITAT. Found in a great variety of open places, usually, but not always, near fresh water. Not common on saltwater beaches or marshes. RANGE. Common summer resident and breeder from the southern Yukon south through the Northwest, wintering from central B.C., northern Idaho, and western Montana southward.

SNOWY PLOVER *Charadrius alexandrinus* 6-7 (153-178)
A small pale-gray shorebird with white under parts, face, and sides of head; black bar over fore-part of crown, spot behind eye, and distinctive incomplete black collar. Female, black markings of male are brownish. In winter, markings are the same color as the back. Legs and bill are dark. CALLS. A soft whistled *koo-whee-ah;* also a *tee-teet* or *koo-wheet.* HABITAT. Dry sandy beaches above high tide lines along the ocean coast; rarely on alkali flats and lake shores in the arid interior. RANGE. Breeds along the ocean coast from southwestern Washington (Leadbetter Point) southward and locally in eastern Oregon, wintering and migrating along the Washington coast and southward. Rare elsewhere in the interior and western B.C. Rare in spring in southern Idaho where it may rarely breed.

MONGOLIAN PLOVER *Charadrius mongolus* 8 (204)
A medium-sized plover characterized by a reddish buff breast (topped by a thin black line), white throat and forehead, black line through eye and a thin black line from eye to bill, brownish-red crown, and dark back. In winter, blacks largely replaced by grays; reddish breast absent, with a grayish collar, and upper parts lighter; white line over eye. CALLS. A clear, whistled, single or double note. HABITAT. Mostly along saltwater beaches. RANGE. Very rare fall visitor along the ocean coast of the Northwest. Two records, northwestern Oregon.

MOUNTAIN PLOVER *Charadrius montanus* 9 (230)
A light-colored medium-sized plover with clear, un-mottled, light brownish upper parts; black crown and line from eye to bill; and white forehead and line over eye. The white-bordered black band on the hind edge of the wing in flight is distinctive. Winter plumage is dull and drab, but not spotted or speckled; the wing linings are pure white, contrasting with the drabness of the rest of the body. CALLS. Short

shrill whistles. HABITAT. Dry, open, sparsely-grassed prairies and fields where it prefers to run, rather than fly, if bothered. RANGE. Rare late fall and winter visitor west of the Cascades in Washington and Oregon and very rare spring straggler in southeastern Idaho and eastern Washington. May breed in the high valleys of central Idaho.

DOTTEREL *Eudromias morinellus* 8½ (217)
A medium-sized shorebird with a mottled grayish back, head, and breast, with the latter crossed with a distinct narrow white collar. A white stripe over the eye. The deep red belly, white collar bordered with black, and prominent white line over the eye distinguish the spring plumage of this species. CALLS. A twittering whistled *wit-e-wee.* HABITAT. In migration, prefers grassy meadows, fields, and saltwater marshes and flats. RANGE. Very rare fall visitor to the ocean coast. One recent record, Ocean Shores, Washington, September 8, 1979.

HUDSONIAN GODWIT *Limosa haemastica* 14-16 (357-408)
This species has a long, up-turned, godwit bill; rusty finely-barred breast; brownish-gray back; and a broad white ring near the black tail. A white wing stripe and blackish under wings seen in flight aid in its identification. Non-breeding birds are less brown and more whitish. The crown is dark brownish. The white rump and black tail (narrowly tipped with white) are good marks. CALLS. A *godwit, whit,* or *te-wit* given in flight; though often silent. HABITAT. Marshes, meadows, and seashore areas; prefers to feed in shallow water. RANGE. Breeds sparsely in the Yukon and Alaska, straggling very rarely south in migration to B.C., eastern Washington, and Idaho, and along the Pacific coast to western Oregon.

BAR-TAILED GODWIT *Limosa lapponica* 15-17 (382-434)
Similar to the Hudsonian Godwit but with unmarked, clear, pinkish cinnamon under parts and heavily spotted upper parts. Light line over eye and dark brown line through eye. Up-turned bill. Tail is white, crossed with a number of narrow black bars. In winter, much lighter, but the barred tail is distinctive. CALLS. A low barking *ter-rek, ter-rek, ter-rek* in flight. HABITAT. Mudflats and beaches along the ocean coast. RANGE. Breeds along the northern and western coasts of Alaska, migrating along the Aleutians. Rare southward along the Northwest coast as migrational straggler, especially in late summer and early fall and very rarely in the spring.

MARBLED GODWIT *Limosa fedoa* 18 (459)
A large shorebird with a long straight or slightly up-turned bill and uniform buffy-brown coloration marked with blackish-brown spots and

bars; cinnamon wing-linings. Similar in size and color to the curlews, but the bill of this species is not down-curved. CALLS. A harsh *kerk* or *ker-reek, ker-whit* or *godwit.* HABITAT. Mudflats on both salt and fresh water, as also the shores and adjacent grasslands of inland sloughs and ponds. RANGE. Straggler, uncommon migrant, and rare winter visitor to various parts of the Northwest, mostly along the coast.

WHIMBREL; HUDSONIAN CURLEW *Numenius phaeopus* 16-18 (408-459)
A large, brown, long-legged shorebird with a long down-curved bill (usually less than four inches long); crown black with a white line through the center and over each eye. Similar to the Long-billed Curlew, but smaller, grayer, and more striped (especially on the head). CALLS. A soft whistled *cur-lew, cur-lew;* a series of four to seven short whistles given in flight, as *tee-tee-tee-tee-tee-tee.* HABITAT. Breeds on open tundra near water; migrates mostly over saltwater shores, wet meadows, and tidal flats. RANGE. Breeds in northern Alaska from the Arctic coast south to the mouth of the Yukon River and in the central Yukon. Migrates southward mostly along the coast where also uncommon summer visitor; less commonly inland (east of the Cascades). Winters mostly south of the Northwest, though a few to be noted in our region at that season. Rare in northern Idaho and extreme eastern Washington in spring.

BRISTLE-THIGHED CURLEW *Numenius tahitiensis* 17-18 (434-459)
Similar to the Whimbrel, but more reddish. The barbless thigh feathers are of no value in sight identification. The rump is clear, unbarred, reddish brown. CALLS. A drawn-out *aw-oo-wit.* HABITAT. In our region, probably mostly saltwater beaches. RANGE. Very rare migrational straggler to the Northwest coast. One record, Vancouver Island, May 31, 1969.

LONG-BILLED CURLEW *Numenius americanus* 20-26 (510-663)
A very large brown shorebird with an unstriped head and a long downward-curving bill more than four inches long. The body is cinnamon brown in color, speckled with blackish dorsally and on the throat and sides of the breast. The wing linings are cinnamon. The size and bill are distinctive. CALLS. A shrill ringing *pill-will* or *curl-e-e-oo;* a rapidly-uttered *cur-lee, cur-lee, cur-lee,* etc. HABITAT. Nests on high grassy hillslopes in the arid interior; migrates along both fresh and salt water. RANGE. Summer resident and breeder from southern B.C. south through the Northwest, east of the Cascade Mountains, in

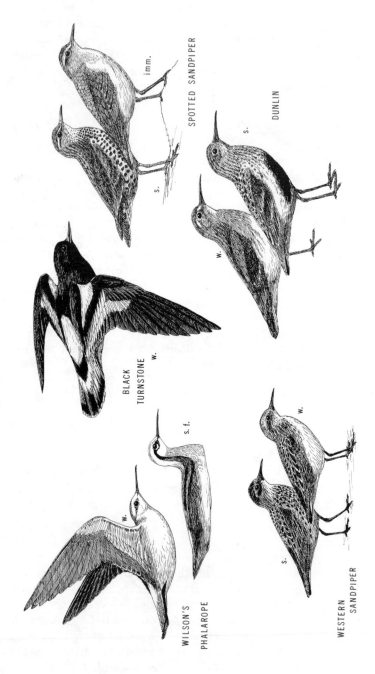

SPOTTED SANDPIPER

imm.

s.

DUNLIN

s.

w.

BLACK
TURNSTONE

w.

WILSON'S
PHALAROPE

w.

s. f.

WESTERN
SANDPIPER

s.

w.

55. Five Pacific Northwest Shorebirds (Schultz)

118

suitable habitat. Winters mostly south of the region covered by this book. Uncommon migrant and winter visitor along the ocean coast. In Idaho, uncommon migrant in northern part of the state, but fairly common, though irregular, summer resident and breeder in the southern part.

UPLAND SANDPIPER; UPLAND PLOVER *Bartramia longicauda* 11-12 (280-306)

A medium-sized buffy-white shorebird with a short straight bill about as long as the head. Upper parts heavily mottled; under parts whitish, with dark brown mottlings on the lower throat and dark "V's" on breast; buffy wash on wings and sides of tail. The tail is long for a sandpiper. Presents a short-legged, round-headed, long-necked appearance. Often holds wings stretched up above the back momentarily upon alighting. Frequently perches on fence posts. CALLS. A whistled *whip-whip-whee-ee-ee-oo,* rapidly repeated; a soft weird *whooooleeee* or *wheeeeloooooo.* HABITAT. Open wet grasslands and hay meadows in upland areas and mountain valleys. RANGE. Irregular local summer resident and breeder from northern Alaska and the northern Yukon (fairly common on open upland and forest tundra) south through the Northwest to eastern Washington (Spokane County where one or two pairs breed, but where the habitat may yield to the bulldozer), northern Idaho (Kootenai County), and northeastern Oregon, east of the Cascades. Rare migrant in northern Idaho. Rare west of the Cascades as a migrational straggler along the coast.

SPOTTED REDSHANK *Tringa erythropus* 11 (280)

In spring and summer, a long-billed dark sooty sandpiper with numerous white markings over the body. The bright orange-red bill and legs and white rump are distinctive. Uniformly gray in color in the fall and winter, but the bill and legs are distinctive. CALLS. A drawn-out whistled *too-it.* HABITAT. Aquatic shores and margins, both of fresh and salt water. RANGE. Rare spring and fall migrational straggler along the ocean coast from Oregon northward.

GREATER YELLOWLEGS *Tringa melanoleuca* 12-15 (306-382)

A large gray and white shorebird with long orange-yellow legs and a slightly upturned black bill; shows dark wings and white rump and tail in flight. CALLS. In flight, three ringing whistled notes, as *whee, whee, whoo.* HABITAT. Open areas along water (both fresh and salt); frequently seen wading in shallow water; widespread and adaptable in foraging from lowlands to subalpine areas. RANGE. Summer resident and breeder from central Alaska south to central B.C., migrating through much of the Northwest, and wintering from southwestern B.C. southward along the coast. Regular in summer as non-breeder along coastal salt water.

LESSER YELLOWLEGS *Tringa flavipes* 9-11 (230-280)
This species is almost identical in color to the Greater Yellowlegs, but the bill is shorter and perfectly straight. The Lesser is small and appears to have half the bulk of the Greater. Legs are lemon yellow. Breast appears considerably browner than in the Greater. CALLS. In flight, a ringing *whee-oo* uttered singly or in pairs; also a rolling series of notes. HABITAT. Very similar in ecology to the Greater Yellowlegs. RANGE. Summer resident and breeder from northern Alaska and northern Yukon south to central B.C. (east of the Cascades), migrating through the remainder of the Northwest. In Idaho, uncommon spring migrant in the northern parts, but fairly common and regular in fall throughout the state. Very rare winter straggler in the Northwest states. Regular in summer as non-breeder along coastal salt water.

SOLITARY SANDPIPER *Tringa solitaria* 7-9 (178-230)
This is a dark-colored sandpiper with a white belly; legs are dark green. Best field marks are the white tail strongly barred with black and the white eye-ring. CALLS. A sharp *peep-peep-weep* or *peep-weep,* especially given when flushed; a short sharp *pit* or *pit-pit-pit.* HABITAT. Margins of isolated lakes, ponds, woodland pools, as well as secluded streams from low to intermediate elevations; most commonly seen as singles along out-of-way waters in late summer and early fall (from lowlands to subalpine country), hence the common name. RANGE. Local resident and breeder from central Alaska and the northern Yukon south to northern B.C., migrating through the remainder of the Northwest. Common migrant in northern Idaho and uncommon to rare migrant in southern Idaho and west of the Cascades.

WOOD SANDPIPER *Tringa glareola* 8 (204)
A medium-sized sandpiper, like a miniature yellowlegs, but at least 2 inches shorter than the Lesser Yellowlegs and only lightly spotted on neck, breast, and sides. A prominent white rump and light under wings. Tail barred like that of the Solitary Sandpiper, but the yellow legs in this species are distinctive. CALLS. A musical *whee-whee-whee* in flight and a sharp *chip-chip-chip* in alarm. HABITAT. Probably the usual sandpiper haunts in our area in migration. RANGE. Very rare fall migrational visitor: one record, near Vancouver, B.C., September 13, 1979.

WILLET *Catoptrophorus semipalmatus* 15-17 (382-434)
A large gray and white shorebird with a relatively long straight bill and blue legs. Uniform grayish color when at rest and flashing black and white wing pattern in flight are distinctive. Spring adults often have a U-shaped brown barring on the light brownish-gray breast. Slightly larger than the yellowlegs. CALLS. A loud musical *pill-will-willet;* a whistling *whee-ee* or *whee-wee-wee.* HABITAT. Breeds in wet meadows and grassy margins of ponds in the arid interior, migrating along saltwater beaches and marshes. RANGE. Summer resident and breeder in southeastern Oregon and southern Idaho. Spring and fall migrant and occasional winter visitor along salt water from Puget Sound and the Washington ocean coast southward. Rare in eastern Washington and B.C.

SPOTTED SANDPIPER *Actitis macularia* 7-8 (178-204) Figs. 55 and 56
The familiar shorebird of stream and river margins. Upper parts brown; lower parts white, covered with large, round, black spots; fall plumage similar, but without the spots and with a white line over the eye and dark smudge on each side of upper breast. Teetering and stiff-winged flying behavior are distinctive. CALLS. A sharp *peet-weet, pee-er-wee,* or *weet, weet, weet,* etc. HABITAT. Breeds and migrates along the margins of streams and lakes from lowlands to subalpine areas; forages in the open on exposed rocks, floating logs, etc. RANGE. Summer resident and breeder, often common and widespread, from northern Alaska and the northern Yukon south through the Northwest, wintering uncommonly from southern B.C. southward, mostly along the coastal sections.

WANDERING TATTLER *Heteroscelus incanus* 11 (280)
A medium-sized shorebird. Solid gray above; white below, heavily barred with black. White line over eye; yellow legs. Under parts solid gray and unbarred in fall. White eye-ring distinct in fall. CALLS. A whistled *whee-wee-wee-wee-wee-wee-wee.* HABITAT. Rocky shores and reefs exposed by the tides along the ocean coast, as well as rock jetties; at high tide, forages along the drift line. RANGE. Breeds from central Alaska and northern Yukon south to northwestern B.C., migrating through the Northwest commonly along the ocean coast and very rarely in the interior (northeastern Washington, northern Idaho, and Upper Klamath Lake, Oregon). A few in winter.

RUDDY TURNSTONE *Arenaria interpres* 8-10 (204-255)
A short, stocky, plover-like bird with orange legs and conspicuous face pattern. Breeding male, head mostly white with gray stripes on crown;

three broad black lines on side of head and one across the forehead. Chin and throat white; breast black with white from shoulder meeting it; belly white. Back blackish with large patches of reddish brown. White patch on shoulder and middle of back. Spring female, similar but duller. Winter adults and immatures are brownish above with a gray breast. CALLS. An alarmed *tiwu-tiwu-titi* (repeated), a conversational *kek-kek, kek-kek,* etc., and a shrill *kewk.* HABITAT. Sandy pebble or shell strewn beaches along salt water; aquatic margins in the interior. RANGE. Breeds along the Arctic coast southwestward to the mouth of the Yukon River, migrating south mainly along the coast and in Puget Sound; rare in the interior east of the Cascades. Uncommon winter visitor along the ocean coast. Often observed on the Washington coast in spring and summer. Occasionally in southern Yukon and extreme northern B.C. in interior (Atlin).

BLACK TURNSTONE *Arenaria melanocephala* 9 (230) Fig. 55
This turnstone is similar in size to the Killdeer. Head, neck, throat, and back are black, spotted with white in spring; belly, lower back, rump, and basal half of tail white; tail coverts and terminal band black; bill is black, short, and slightly upturned. Black and white wing and tail pattern distinctive in any plumage. CALLS. A rattling kingfisher-like cry; also a loud *weet, weet, to-wheet.* HABITAT. Rocky or pebbly beaches along salt water, particularly those uncovered at low tide; also exposed surf-washed reefs. RANGE. Breeds along the western and southern coasts of Alaska and winters in coastal areas from southeastern Alaska southward through the Northwest. Very common spring and fall migrant and winter visitor along salt water in Washington and Oregon.

WILSON'S PHALAROPE *Phalaropus tricolor* 9-10 (230-255) Fig. 55
Spring females are characterized by broad neck stripes of red blending into black from shoulder to eye on a light reddish neck. Top of head gray; throat white. Wings and back grayish, streaked with dark red. Breast and under parts white. Bill black; legs greenish. Shows no white in wing when in flight. Male, similar, but duller, with white spots on nape of neck. Upper parts dark brown, spotted with grayish. Under parts whitish, faintly washed on neck and upper breast with pale reddish. CALLS. Grunting notes, as *wheck, wheck, wheck,* and a low *wah-hoo.* HABITAT. Freshwater marshes or pond or slough areas where food may be obtained, "sandpiper-like", by foraging on mud and wet grass flats and shores, as well as by the more usual phalarope method of surface gleaning on open water. RANGE. Breeds from the southern Yukon south through the interior east of the Cascades in the Northwest, migrating through the region covered by this manual

mostly south of Canada, uncommonly in the coastal areas, and commonly east of the Cascades, in late summer and fall and also in the spring. In Idaho, fairly common migrant, uncommon local summer resident in northern Idaho and somewhat more numerous in the southern part of the state. Recent breeding records for southern Vancouver Island and the northern Olympic Peninsula.

NORTHERN PHALAROPE *Phalaropus lobatus* 6-8 (153-204)
A small-sized shorebird usually seen swimming in water where its peculiar spinning action while feeding is distinctive. In summer, female is sooty-gray above, white below, with dark-gray collar across the breast and red patches on sides of the neck. Head gray; throat white. In fall and winter, black crown and bar through eye, back streaked with black and tan, and white under parts. Sharp needle-like bill. In any season, a white wing-bar is distinctive. The male is much duller. CALLS. A sharp *kit* or low *kut;* a grunting chatter while feeding. HABITAT. Coastal and inland salt water, as well as bodies of fresh water in the interior of the Northwest. RANGE. Breeds along the northern, western, and southern coasts of Alaska and the Yukon and in the interior, migrating northward (commonly) and southward through the Northwest, both to sea off the ocean coast and in the interior. Very rare along the coast and in the inland salt waters in winter. Uncommon migrant in Idaho. The Red Phalarope is the coastal phalarope after November.

RED PHALAROPE *Phalaropus fulicarius* 8-9 (204-230)
A long-necked sandpiper-like bird most likely to be seen swimming in the water, particularly off shore. In spring, neck and under parts red; crown black; face white; back brownish striped; broad white wing bar. Male, somewhat duller than female. In fall, bluegray above, white below with belly often sprinkled with rusty brown; dark line through eye. Similar at this time to the Northern Phalarope, but can be identified by the stouter bill, unstreaked blue-gray back, and white crown. CALLS. A sharp whistled *tseet* or *weet;* various other notes. HABITAT. Offshore oceanic waters during migrations and wintering, but occasionally forced to inshore areas or rarely to the interior of the Northwest by storms. Often seen near whales. RANGE. Breeds along the Arctic coasts of the Yukon and Alaska southwest to the Yukon Delta. Migrates southward in winter, mainly well off shore, along the Northwest coast. A few straggle to the interior, including northern Idaho.

COMMON SNIPE *Gallinago gallinago* 10-11 (255-280) Fig. 54
The familiar, long-billed, brown-striped "jack snipe"; similar to the

56. Spotted Sandpiper on nest (Boggs)

57. Nest and eggs of Killdeer (Boggs)

dowitchers but lacks white back and rump found in those species and has a red tail. Zig-zag flight is characteristic. CALLS. A series of harsh *scapes* uttered when flushed. A peculiar winnowing sound, like *huhuhuhuhuhuhu,* given mechanically in spring nuptial flight. HABITAT. Prefers fresh and saltwater marshes and wet meadows of low to moderate elevations. RANGE. Summer resident and breeder from northwestern Alaska and the northern Yukon south through the Northwest, wintering from southern B.C. southward. Common summer resident in Idaho; less numerous, depending on weather conditions, in winter.

SHORT-BILLED DOWITCHER *Limnodromus griseus* 10-11 (255-280)
A long-billed, brownish, snipe-like bird with a white lower back and rump. White stripe down middle of back in flight separates this species from the similar appearing Common Snipe. Breast is pale cinnamon in spring; pale gray in fall. Bill approximately 2½ inches long. CALLS. A rapid *pit-pit-pit* or mellow rolling *tew, tew, tew,* etc. HABITAT. Soft mudflats and margins of both fresh and salt water. RANGE. Breeds along the coast of southern Alaska and in the southern Yukon and northeastern B.C. areas, migrating and summering along the coasts of the Northwest. Less common spring and fall migrant in the interior east of the Cascades.

LONG-BILLED DOWITCHER *Limnodromus scolopaceus* 12 (306)
This species is very similar to the Short-billed Dowitcher, but has a longer bill (close to 3 inches in length). Upper parts more reddish in summer and darker in winter plumage than in the Short-billed. Spots on under parts in band across chest, rather than scattered as in the other species. Sides, barred rather than spotted. Not always to be satisfactorily separated from the Short-billed in poor light or at any considerable distance. CALLS. A single to triple *keek* (as *keek, keek, keek).* HABITAT. Mudflats, mostly along fresh water. RANGE. Breeds along the Arctic coasts of Alaska and the Yukon south to the north of the Yukon River, migrating through the remainder of the Northwest. Uncommon winter visitor west of the Cascades (a few records east of the range). Common irregular fall migrant and fairly common spring migrant in Idaho.

SURFBIRD *Aphriza virgata* 10 (255)
This is a stocky bird of Robin size with a stout bill that is shorter than the head and colored black above and yellow below and with yellow feet. In spring, head and neck streaked with black and white; back mottled brown and black; spread wing showing white stripe; rump and

basal half of tail white, with black terminal band; under parts white with crescent-shaped spots. In fall, upper parts brownish gray; breast, gray; belly white. CALLS. A sharp *kee-week* or *kee-wee-ah.* HABITAT. The surf-swept and intertidal rocks and reefs; breeds on gravel bars in open tundra areas. RANGE. Breeds in the Mt. McKinley area, in western Alaska, and in the central and northern Yukon mountains. Winters and migrates from southeastern Alaska southward through the coastal region of the Northwest. In spring and summer as non-breeder in Washington coastal salt water.

RED KNOT *Calidris canutus* 10-11 (255-280)
A chunky medium-sized shorebird with a relatively short bill and greenish legs. In spring, has pale reddish face, breast, and belly and mottled gray and black back. Similar to the dowitchers but has larger body, shorter bill, and white on rump does not extend onto back. In fall, white breast with light gray upper parts and whitish rump. Similar to the Black-bellied Plover but with shorter legs and lacking the thick plover beak. Shows narrow white line in wing during flight. CALLS. A low-pitched *knut* and a harsh *wu-quoit* ending in a roll. HABITAT. Sandy beaches, mudflats, and less commonly rocks along salt and fresh water. RANGE. Uncommon breeder in northwestern Alaska; migrates commonly (spring) and uncommonly (fall) along the coasts of the Northwest; rarely inland as spring and fall straggler; rare in winter west of the Cascades.

SANDERLING *Calidris alba* 7-8 (178-204) Fig. 53
In winter, whitest of the sandpipers; pale gray above and white below, with a dark patch at the bend of the wing, much white in the spread wing, black legs, and short, stout, black bill. In spring, head, back, throat, and breast speckled with rusty, black, and white. Frequently hops on one leg. CALLS. A sharp *kip* or *twick-twick;* a soft rolling twitter. HABITAT. Sandy beaches near the surf along the ocean; less common on margins or larger lakes in the interior and on tidal mudflats. RANGE. Breeds along the Arctic coast, migrating south along the Pacific coast of the Northwest, to winter from southern B.C. southward along salt water. Common as summer visitor along coastal salt water. Regular, though uncommon, spring and fall migrant in the interior east of the Cascades. In northern Idaho, rare in spring and uncommon in fall as migrant; rare in southern part of the state.

SEMIPALMATED SANDPIPER *Calidris pusilla* 6 (153)
A small "peep" very similar to the Least and Western Sandpipers in fall. May be separated from the Least by slightly larger size, black instead of yellow legs, stouter bill, grayer color, and relatively un-

speckled breast. Distinguished from the Western by the slightly smaller size, shorter straighter bill, and grayer shoulders (not splotched with rusty color). Unlike both Western and Least in that the white of the sides comes up in front of the bend of the wing. CALLS. A hoarse *cherk;* also a rapid staccato series of notes; a sharp *ki-i-ip.* HABITAT. Mudflats, sandy beaches, and aquatic margins of both fresh and salt water; occasional late summer visitor in subalpine areas in the mountains. RANGE. Breeds on the Arctic coast south along western Alaska to the mouth of the Yukon River, migrating sparsely through the Northwest (less commonly in the Pacific coastal areas). Rare spring and fairly common fall migrant in Idaho.

WESTERN SANDPIPER *Calidris mauri* 6-7 (153-178) Fig. 55
Very similar to the Least Sandpiper but is slightly larger and has black bill and legs. The bill is decurved and slightly longer than that of the Least. Considerable rufous on shoulders, crown, and ear patches. In fall, breast white with pale buffy wash on sides. CALLS. A plaintive *kreep* given in flight; a short *surp* when flushed. HABITAT. Various kinds of open aquatic margins, both salt and fresh, particularly tidal mudflats and adjacent sand beaches. More numerous on ocean coast than on inland marine waters. RANGE. Breeds along the northern and western coasts of Alaska south to Nunivak Island, migrating southward through the Northwest and wintering and summering (as non-breeder) fairly commonly from B.C. south, mostly along the coast. As migrant in Idaho, common in fall and rare in spring.

RUFOUS-NECKED SANDPIPER *Calidris ruficollis* 6-7 (153-178)
A small peep characterized by a rusty-red chin, throat, and fore part of neck and by the black bill and short black legs. Remainder of the under parts are white. In winter, the red replaced by grayish and the species too closely resembles the Semipalmated Sandpiper to be indentified with certainty. CALLS. A high-pitched *chit-chit* or *pit-pit-pit;* a single *pit.* HABITAT. Mostly saltwater beaches. RANGE. Very rare summer and early fall visitor to southwestern B.C. Early fall record for Oregon coast.

LEAST SANDPIPER *Calidris minutilla* 5-6 (128-153)
A small sparrow-sized sandpiper, brown-and-black streaked above, whitish below; breast buffy, streaked with dark brown. Identified by yellow-green legs and short black bill. In fall, breast is brownish, finely streaked with darker brown. CALLS. A loud *kreep* or *sreet* given in flight; a rapid series of *kwees* when flushed. HABITAT. Various open moist places bordering salt or fresh water; mudflats and sandy beaches preferred. RANGE. Breeds in coastal areas of Alaska and the Yukon,

more commonly in southern Alaska, migrating throughout the Northwest and wintering and summering sparsely on the Washington and Oregon coasts. Fairly common spring and fall migrant throughout Idaho. A recent Oregon record of the Temminck's or Long-toed Stint is probably this species.

WHITE-RUMPED SANDPIPER *Calidris fuscicollis* 7-8 (178-204)

A gray-brown sandpiper with whitish under parts; distinct black-brown streaking on breast and sides; white unmarked rump; black central tail feathers; white line over eye. Grayer in fall with darker upper parts and less distinctly marked under parts. CALLS. A thin scraping *jee-jeet* or sharp *tzeet* when flushed. HABITAT. Mudflats and beaches along fresh and salt water, as well as wet meadows and river margins. RANGE. Breeds along the Arctic coasts of Alaska and the Yukon, migrating southward sparsely and irregularly to the Northwest states. Very rare in the interior.

BAIRD'S SANDPIPER *Calidris bairdii* 7-8 (178-204)

Similar to, but slightly larger than, a Western Sandpiper, with a finely streaked buffy wash on the head and across the breast and a buffy-brown back with white feather edgings like scales. Closely resembles a Semipalmated Sandpiper, but this species is larger and has a darker face than the Semipalmated; also may be separated from it and others by Baird's black legs and bill. Wings, when at rest, extend noticeably behind the tip of the tail. CALLS. A harsh rolling *kree-ee-ee-ee.* HABITAT. Prefers the upper drier parts of aquatic margins, both fresh and salt, though probably more common in the interior and preferring fresh water. RANGE. Breeds along the Arctic coasts of the Yukon (and also mountains of the interior) and Alaska, south to western Alaska, migrating along the coast and through the interior of the Northwest; more numerous in fall. Occasionally recorded in the mountains in the late summer migration.

PECTORAL SANDPIPER *Calidris melanotos* 8-9 (204-230)

A slender, streaked, brownish sandpiper. Back rusty, streaked with black; neck and breast streaked with brown, sharply separated from white throat and belly (forming a neat "bib"); neck more slender than in other sandpipers; legs greenish yellow. Similar to the Baird's Sandpiper but legs yellowish, rather than black. Lacks the fast-moving behavior of most peeps. CALLS. A reedy *keer* or short *tchep;* a harsh *crrrik* or *kirk* when flushed. HABITAT. Wet grassy flats and meadows near fresh and salt water. RANGE. Breeds along the Arctic coasts of Alaska and the Yukon south along the western Alaskan coast to Bristol Bay and probably to the central Yukon. Common fall migrant through the Northwest, mostly west of the Cascades. Rare in spring west of that range. In Idaho, fairly common fall migrant in the northern parts of the state but rare in spring; less numerous in southern Idaho.

SHARP-TAILED SANDPIPER *Calidris acuminata* 8 (204)
Similar to the Pectoral Sandpiper, but upper parts and (particularly) breast washed with buffy. Breast appears spotted instead of streaked, the pattern not being sharply separated from the white belly as in the Pectoral. Bright chestnut crown is distinctive. CALLS. A soft *keek* or *pleep, pleep.* HABITAT. Grassy margins of tideflats and tidal pools. RANGE. Occasional fall and rare spring migrant and winter visitor along the coast of the Northwest from northern Alaska southward; very rare in the interior east of the Cascades.

ROCK SANDPIPER *Calidris ptilocnemis* 8-9 (204-230)
This is a stocky, dark, bluish-gray sandpiper with marbled gray and white breast and sides and a white belly. The combination of dark rump and white wing-stripes separates this species from the Black Turnstone and Surfbird. In spring, the under parts are lighter, but with a large dark patch on the breast which is distinctive. CALLS. A rapid series of *clu-clu-clu-clu,* etc. HABITAT. Prefers rocky shores near salt water. RANGE. Breeds along the central western coast of Alaska and on islands of the Bering Sea, Aleutians, etc. Winters and migrates (mostly in spring) from the Alaska Peninsula south along the coast of the Northwest.

DUNLIN; RED-BACKED SANDPIPER *Calidris alpina* 8-9 (204-230) Fig. 55
In spring, reddish above, black patch on belly, and streaked white breast. In winter, dark gray above and white below with gray breast. Identified also by relatively long stout bill which curves downward near the tip. CALLS. A whistled *chruu* in flight; a *tweet-tul-ut* when flushed; also a rapid staccato series of notes. HABITAT. Sandy beaches and mudflats along salt water, as well as the shores of large freshwater lakes. RANGE. Breeds along the northern and western coasts of Alaska, wintering abundantly from B.C. southward, and migrating through the Northwest (mostly along the coastal areas; rare in the interior). Uncommon summer visitor along the ocean coast. In Idaho, rare migrant.

CURLEW SANDPIPER *Calidris ferruginea* 7-9 (178-230)
A medium-sized sandpiper with a long de-curved bill, solid reddish brown head, neck, and under parts in spring and a grayish back with white under parts (lightly barred on sides of breast) in fall. Similar to

the Dunlin in fall, but this species has a white rump. CALLS. A soft mellow *chirrup.* HABITAT. Mudflats and sandy beaches, often with Dunlins. RANGE. Rare late summer and early fall and very rare spring migrant along the ocean coast of the Northwest. Very rare spring migrant east of the Cascades.

SPOON-BILLED SANDPIPER *Eurynorhynchus pygmeus* 6½ (166)
A small sandpiper (peep) with a distinctive spoon-shaped broadening to the tip of the bill. Light brownish above in spring with spotted breast and sides. Grayish above and white below in winter, but the bill and relatively dark back are characteristic. CALLS. A high-pitched trill. HABITAT. Ocean beaches and mudflats, especially in seaweed washed up on the beach. RANGE. Very rare late summer and fall migrational wanderer along the coast of the Northwest.

STILT SANDPIPER *Micropalama himantopus*
A medium-sized, long-legged, relatively long-billed shorebird. In spring, upper parts mottled brown, black, and white. Under parts whitish, heavily barred with dark brown. Head streaked with white and black with brownish-red stripes along margins of crown and through the eyes. Bill tapered and turned down slightly at tip. In fall, very similar to the Lesser Yellowlegs, but is smaller, with greenish, rather than yellow, legs and has a conspicuous white stripe over the eye. Also somewhat resembles a dowitcher, but has shorter bill, longer legs, and paler under parts. CALLS. A soft *whu* or rolled *whree.* HABITAT. Moist open flats along both fresh and salt water. RANGE. Breeds along the Arctic coast. Rare migrant (mostly in the fall) from the southern Yukon southward through the Northwest. Rare in the interior east of the Cascades.

BUFF-BREASTED SANDPIPER *Tryngites subruficollis* 8 (204)
Similar to the Baird's Sandpiper, but buffier. This tame little sandpiper's brown back feathers are "scaled" with buff, all under parts (except under tail coverts) are buff and the legs are bright yellow. No other small sandpiper is so evenly buffy below. Bright gray wing linings are seen in flight. The bill is relatively quite short. CALLS. A low trilling *pr-r-r-reet* and a sharp *tik* or *tik-tik-tik-tik-tik.* HABITAT. Grassy flats and wet meadows near water; sometimes found on drier short-grass prairies, as well as fields and wheat stubble. RANGE. Breeds along the Arctic coast of Alaska and the Yukon, migrating sparsely through the Northwest in late August and early September, mostly along the ocean coast, as at Ocean Shores, Washington. Rare as fall migrant in Idaho.

RUFF (female is "reeve") *Philomachus pugnax* 8½-11½ (217-293)

A medium-sized shorebird in which the spring male has elongated ear tufts and long breast feathers that may be white, brown, or black and sometimes barred. The female is grayish. The male is similar to the female in winter. CALLS. A low *tu-whit* when flushed; though usually silent; an occasional *too-ee* in flight. HABITAT. Saltwater beaches and occasionally mudflats in the interior. RANGE. Rare but seemingly regular fall migrational wanderer in the Northwest, mostly along salt water. Appears to be increasing in our region.

JAEGERS AND SKUAS

58.   Long-tailed Jaeger (Fisher)

Birds of this group are often spoken of as "parasitic" in the broad sense in that they derive much of their living during migration and winter by harrying food-laden gulls and terns, causing these birds to drop their food, usually fish, and using it for the jaegers' sustenance. On the tundra breeding grounds of the far North, the jaegers prey on the young of ground nesting birds and on lemmings and other rodents. The word *jaeger* means "hunter" in German and these species seem very well named. Mt. McKinley National Park is a good place to see jaegers in summer action and the author has found Sable Pass a particularly good place to watch them. In migration, however, one

131

generally has to go off the Pacific coast. Here, one may see the jaegers following the offshore flocks of gulls and terns. When a school of herring is found and the gulls are feeding, the jaeger watches till one catches and swallows a fish, then it pursues the gull and forces it to disgorge the fish which the jaeger catches before it falls to the water. This is the standard marine method of feeding for all three jaegers.

Though looking somewhat like a stocky dark-colored gull, the Skua has habits much the same as those of the jaegers. Nesting mostly in the extreme southern parts of the oceans and continents, the bird wanders widely around the World and is only a rare visitor to our shores. It is perhaps the most dread of marine bird predators, along with the Great Black-backed Gull.

PACIFIC NORTHWEST SPECIES

SKUA *Catharacta skua* 22 (561) Fig. 7
A large, dark brown, hawk-like sea bird with a hooked bill and webbed sharp-clawed feet. White patches in the wings; a short square tail. Predatory hawk-like habits and swift flight are distinctive. CALLS. A shrill, strident, gull-like scream, from which the name "skua" is derived; a duck-like quacking note. HABITAT. The open ocean, usually well off shore, and seldom coming within sight of land. RANGE. Uncommon, but regular, visitor to the ocean coasts of the Northwest, mostly well off shore, but occasionally seen working along the ocean beaches. Most records for late summer and fall. Some recent workers consider most Northwest birds to be the South Polar Skua *(C. maccormicki)* which is lighter in color with shorter bill. There is the possibility that all skuas may belong to one World-wide species *(Catharacta skua)*.

POMARINE JAEGER *Stercorarius pomarinus* 22 (561)
Jaegers are gull-like birds with elongated central tail feathers and beaks with a hook or tooth at the end. They have a falcon-like flight. This species appears larger and heavier than most jaegers and is usually barred on the under parts with a broad dark breast band and white in the wing primaries. Best identified by the blunt-tipped, broad, and twisted projecting black central tail feathers. The breast band is prominent in the light phase. Flight is heavy and gull-like. The dark phases in jaegers are mostly all grayish, but the characteristic tail feathers are the field marks of significance. CALLS. Various squealing hawk-like cries. HABITAT. Offshore marine waters, where feeding gulls and terns may be robbed of their prey. RANGE. Breeds along the Arctic coasts of the Yukon and Alaska, south in western Alaska to the mouth of the Yukon River and to the northcentral B.C. coast, migrating

southward on salt water, mostly off shore (where common), to along the Northwest coast, rarely wandering inland and to the interior east of the Cascades. Most records for late summer and fall. Recorded in southwest Idaho.

PARASITIC JAEGER *Stercorarius parasiticus* 17 (434) Fig. 7
Top of head and rest of upper parts of this marine predator are mostly dark; under parts and neck are white-immaculate (light phase) or heavily barred (dark phase). Best identified by the length of the projecting tail feathers, 2½ to 3½ inches and pointed in this species. The legs are black and there is a yellowish wash on the neck and breast. The flight is similar to that of a small gull. CALLS. A dry *tick-tick,* or *cher-reck, cher-reck,* or *tuck-tuck;* a mewing *ka-aaow.* HABITAT. Inshore as well as offshore marine areas; especially visiting inland salt water regions during spring and fall migrations. RANGE. Breeds from the Arctic coasts of Alaska and the Yukon south to the Aleutians and Kodiak along the coast and in the interior to central Alaska, migrating along salt water through the Northwest. Rare visitor to the interior east of the Cascades in Washington and Oregon. Commonly seen along salt water in September and October and occasionally in May.

LONG-TAILED JAEGER *Stercorarius longicaudus* 21 (536) Fig. 58
Similar to the more common Parasitic Jaeger, but larger, solid white below, back noticeably lighter than the clearly defined black cap, and legs bluish gray. The projecting central tail feathers may be as long as 10 inches (usually 4-6 inches), while those of the Parasitic seldom reach 4 inches. The flight is rapid and tern-like. CALLS. A shrill harsh *cree-oo,* though mostly silent in our area. HABITAT. The open ocean, usually fairly well away from land. RANGE. Breeds in northern and central Alaska (and along the coasts of the northern and western parts of the state) and the Yukon, migrating uncommonly and irregularly off shore along the Northwest coast. Rare in the interior of the Pacific states, in northern and southern Idaho, and in coastal and interior B.C., mostly in the fall (rare in the spring).

GULLS

59.   Gulls (Fisher)

Gulls are stout, long-winged, grayish-white birds with graceful tireless flight. Because of their close similarity, some of our gulls are difficult to identify. Bill markings and leg colors are good field characters but can be seen satisfactorily only on birds close in under good light conditions. Size, flight characteristics, and general coloration are usually the only clues available in separating distant birds. Descriptions in this manual apply to adults. Many immatures cannot be satisfactorily distinguished in the field. Several excellent identification summaries by expert field persons have recently been published. In the species accounts that follow, the material in quotation marks is by Harry Nehls, master Portland, Oregon field ornithologist and longtime student of bird distribution in the Oregon region, as published in the AUDUBON WARBLER, newsletter of the Audubon Society of Portland.

PACIFIC NORTHWEST SPECIES

"Among the most conspicuous wintering birds in the Pacific Northwest are the gulls. Although many species have distinctive field marks that immediately identify them, the 8 'Herring' type gulls that winter in this area are very closely related and are similar in appearance. In the breeding season the identifying marks used to separate the species become bright and conspicuous but in winter these colors and patterns fade and dull. Most field guides give good descriptions of the birds but confuse the birder with details not always consistent enough to be of any help. Each species has one or more points that can quickly identify it but the birder must take care and give attention to details, even then some birds will give trouble. Most adult gulls, however, can be identified.

"Several steps should be taken in order to quickly and easily identify any gull you observe; select an individual, do not try to work on the whole flock at the same time; note the color of its legs; check the degree of grayness of the back; and the color and pattern on the wing tips (primaries). Such things as the size and shape of the bird, color of the eyes, and the color and shape of the bill are secondary field marks and should be used only after some experience and practice. If your bird has pink or flesh-colored legs, it will be either a Glaucous, Glaucous-winged, Western, Herring, or Thayer's Gull. If the legs are greenish, yellowish or bluish-gray, it will either be a California, Ring-billed, or Mew Gull."

IVORY GULL *Pagophila alba* 16-19 (408-484)
A small gull, pure white in color with black legs. CALLS. Harsh, shrill, tern-like notes. HABITAT. Mostly on salt water, though in our region as straggler likely to occur on any type of aquatic habitat. RANGE. Winters along the coasts of Alaska and the Yukon and very rarely southward in the Northwest to B.C. and Washington.

HEERMANN'S GULL *Larus heermanni* 18-21 (459-536)
A medium-sized gull with a dark gray body, whitish head and neck, red bill, and black feet and tail (tipped with white). Base of tail and under parts are light gray. CALLS. Low, short, cackling or muttering notes; also a short, high-pitched gull-like *whee-ee;* often silent. HABITAT. Salt water; common in August when the smelt come in to spawn along the ocean beaches; the gulls hover over the breakers to catch the silvery fish from the crests of the waves (Kitchin). Often parasitizes the larger gulls. RANGE. Late summer and fall (postbreeding) visitor along the Northwest coast to Puget Sound and southern Vancouver Island. Less numerous as spring visitor and winter straggler along salt water in the region, mostly along the sea coast.

RING-BILLED GULL *Larus delawarensis* 18-20 (459-510) Fig. 14
"One of the lightest and cleanest looking gulls. The light gray back

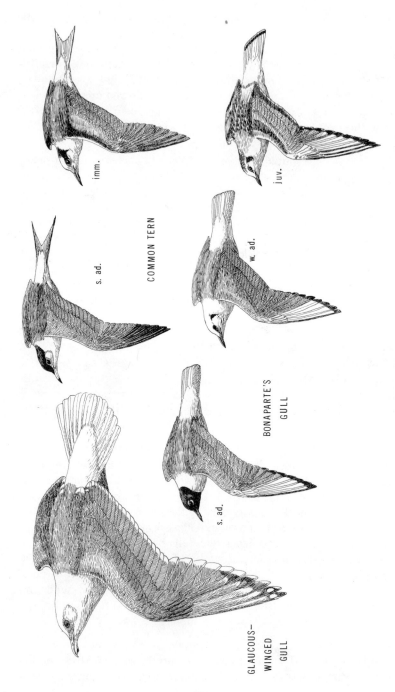

imm.

juv.

COMMON TERN

s. ad.

w. ad.

BONAPARTE'S
GULL

s. ad.

GLAUCOUS—
WINGED
GULL

60. Left to right: Glaucous-winged Gull, Bonaparte's Gull, Common Tern (Schultz)

136

and white body remain fairly clean looking all year. This gives considerable contrast to the deep black wing tips. Although the black tip has some white in it, it doesn't show well and many Ring-bills have been mis-identified as Kittiwakes as they fly in the distance. The best field mark, of course, is the well-defined black ring about the light-colored bill near the tip. The legs remain yellowish all year." CALLS. A shrill piercing *kree* and a subdued *kow-kow-kow,* etc. HABITAT. Nests on small islands on interior freshwater lakes; winters in a variety of habitats (docks, tideflats, beaches, garbage dumps, sewer outlets, etc.). Often the most abundant gull species in the arid interior. RANGE. Breeds from southwestern and central Washington, southern B.C., northern Alberta, northern Saskatchewan, and central Manitoba southward, migrating through the Northwest in fall to B.C., and wintering through the lower Northwest from Washington south. Late summer visitor in southeastern Alaska (Stikine River Flats). Recent breeding records at Willapa Bay and Grays Harbor in western Washington. Records for Idaho for every month, though more numerous in summer than in winter.

MEW GULL; SHORT-BILLED GULL *Larus canus* 16-18 (408-459)
"This species gets quite dingy and muddy looking in winter and there is much variation in the depth of the gray of the back. Fortunately, its small size and small dull greenish-yellow bill easily identify this species. There is no regular bill markings but in winter there is often an irregular dark band near the tip looking more like a patch of dirt than a color marking. In flight, it is most easily identified by the large white patch in the black wing tips. This species, and the Ring-billed Gull, are often seen walking over plowed farm fields. The smaller size and dingier-looking plumage, along with its bobbing plover-like head and bill will usually be enough to identify this species." CALLS. A sharp, shrill, querulous *kwew, kwew, kwew,* etc. HABITAT. A common gull in the interior of the northland, being frequently seen along fresh water. In the southern part of the Northwest, regular in all the usual gull haunts and habitats. RANGE. Breeds from northern Alaska and the northern Yukon south along the coast to B.C. and in the interior to northeastern Alberta, wintering and migrating commonly along the coast from southwestern B.C. and nearby fresh waters southward to California. Rare but regular migrant (April and May; October and November) to the interior of the Northwest east of the Cascades.

HERRING GULL *Larus argentatus* 22-26 (561-663)
"In size, shape, and coloration, Herring Gulls look quite a bit like Glaucous-winged Gulls. They even get dingy looking in winter like them, but there is always a sharp contrast with its pale gray back and

black wing tips. This is especially noticeable on the underwing patterns where the very black wing tips contrast with the silvery wash of the rest of the underwing. Under some conditions, it is often difficult to separate this species from the Western Gull. The underwing pattern is the key point at this time. The glaring white eye of this species is seldom of use in identification." CALLS. A loud shrill *quee-ah, kee-arr-r-r,* or *kyow-kyow-kyow;* also a gutteral *ha-ha, ha-ha-ha,* etc. HABITAT. Visits both fresh and salt water, adjacent garbage dumps, canneries, and open fields (for resting); regular, though not common, around seaports. RANGE. Breeds from central Alaska and the Yukon to southern Alaska and B.C., wintering from southern Alaska south uncommonly along the Northwest coast and east of the Cascades in Washington and northern Idaho. Apparently quite rare in eastern Oregon.

CALIFORNIA GULL *Larus californicus* 20-23 (510-586)
"The gray of the back is somewhat darker than most of the other 'Herring' type gulls and is noticeable, even in flight. The legs in this species, although yellowish in summer, often become bluish-gray during the winter months. The bill shows a reddish patch near the tip, and in winter, a dark patch above it." CALLS. A shrill piercing cry; a soft *kuck* or *kuck-kuck-kuck,* more or less similar to notes of the Herring Gull. HABITAT. A variety of aquatic sites, favoring fresh water as well as saltwater areas; nests in colonies on small islands on larger lakes in the arid interior. RANGE. Breeds on fresh water (mostly locally on lakes) mainly east of the Cascades in the Northwest, but winters along the north coast from southern B.C. southward. Less common in southeastern Alaska as a late summer and fall visitor. Several breeding colonies in central Washington. Populations in the interior of the Northwest are increasing with extensive irrigated agriculture, canals, ponds, and human settlements. In Idaho, fairly common summer resident in the northern part of the state, but common as a summer resident and breeder in the southern part. Sparse and irregular east of the Cascades in winter. Increasing as breeder in eastern Washington.

WESTERN GULL *Larus occidentalis* 24-27 (612-688) Fig. 61
"In sharp contrast to the above species, Western Gulls have deep slaty backs with extensive black wing-tips. The underwings are very dark — black at the tips and washed with deep gray over much of the rest of the wing. This species remains fairly clean looking all year. Hybrid Western X Glaucous-winged Gulls are fairly common in some areas. Usually under close scrutiny it is fairly easy to identify the parentage, but many superficially look like Herring Gulls and can often cause

61. Western Gull (Fisher)

confusion." CALLS. A high-pitched cry, such as *kee-a, kee-a, kee-a,* etc.; also a guttural *kuck-kuck-kuck* or *kak, kak-kak-kak.* HABITAT. Breeds on exposed rocky islets along the ocean coast; winters mostly along the coast; penetrates neither offshore nor inland areas. RANGE. Resident and breeder along the Northwest coast from northwest Washington south, wintering north to southwestern B.C. along the ocean coast and Puget Sound. Mostly to be found along salt water. The few records east of the Cascades are dubious. Glaucous-winged and Western Gull hybrids with characters intermediate between the two species are increasing in numbers in the coastal areas, giving some credence to the current belief among certain European ornithologists that a number of our large gulls are conspecific.

SLATY-BACKED GULL *Larus schistisagus* 24-27 (612-688)
A large dark-backed gull slightly larger than a Western Gull with a yellowish-instead of dark, iris; reddish, instead of yellow, eye-ring; and more white on the wing-tips. Probably should be identified by specimen only. The legs are reddish flesh color. CALLS. A high-pitched *kee-kee-kee,* etc.; a deep *kyaww, kyaww, kyaww,* etc. RANGE. Very rare spring visitor to the Northwest coast. One record, Victoria, B.C., March 1, 1974.

GLAUCOUS-WINGED GULL *Larus glaucescens* 24-28 (612-714)
Figs. 59 and 60
"This pale-backed species gets quite dingy looking in winter and all colors dull down quite a bit. The wing-tips on a standing bird show quite slaty at times but never look black; in flight, the wing-tips are definitely grayish. The undersides of the wings show little or no pigment, even at the tips." CALLS. A ringing screaming *klee-e-er;* a low-pitched *kowk, kowk;* also various other notes. HABITAT. Breeds on islands and rocks along the ocean coast and in the San Juan Islands; at other times common along salt and fresh water, particularly at land fills, sewer outlets, and wharf areas; not penetrating very far up rivers. RANGE. Breeds along the western Alaska coast from the Bering Sea south to northwestern Oregon, wintering from southeastern Alaska to south of the Northwest along salt water and adjacent inland waters. Uncommon in winter near the confluence of the Columbia and Snake Rivers in eastern Washington. Rare fall visitor to Idaho. Occasionally hybridizes with the Herring Gull.

GLAUCOUS GULL *Larus hyperboreus* 28 (714)
A large, pale, gray-mantled gull with white — not dark-colored — wing-tips. Bill yellow with red spot on lower mandible. Legs are flesh colored; eyes yellow. Second-year birds are almost wholly creamy white with a whitish bill. "Seldom is an adult Glaucous seen this far south. The clear unpatterned white wing-tips are a dead give-away. Check the tip of the bill for a reddish mark or a black tip. If neither is present, check for a possible albinistic bird." CALLS. Hoarse raven-like croaks and gull-like screams. HABITAT. In migration and winter, mostly on the open ocean beaches. RANGE. Breeds on the Arctic coasts south along western Alaska to Bristol Bay, wintering and migrating uncommonly along the Northwest coast from the Bering Sea to California. Straggles rarely into the interior east of the Cascades as winter visitor. Becoming somewhat more numerous in the interior with the conversion of the free-flowing Columbia and Snake Rivers to chains of dead-water reservoirs. Rare winter and spring visitor to northern Idaho (numbers are few, but it is conspicuous in a mixed flock of gulls).

ICELAND GULL *Larus glaucoides* 23-25 (526-637)
Characterized by medium size (slightly smaller than the Herring Gull) and pure white wing-tips. Somewhat similar in the various plumages to the Glaucous Gull, but much smaller. Long wings extend beyond the tail when the bird is at rest. CALLS. Similar to those of the Glaucous Gull. HABITAT. In the vicinity of salt (usually) or fresh

water. RANGE. Very rare winter and spring and fall migratory wanderer in the Northwest, mostly along the salt waters, though several records in northern Idaho in the Coeur d'Alene Lake and Spokane areas. Some records in doubt, due to difficulty of identification and perhaps were immature Thayer's Gulls.

THAYER'S GULL *Larus thayeri* 21-24 (536-612)
Very similar to the Herring, but slightly smaller (only a little larger than a California Gull). The mantle is very pale gray, usually somewhat lighter than in the Herring Gull. The feet are pink, the eyelids red or blackish, never orange or yellow, as in the Herring Gull; the iris of the eyes is brown or mottled, as in the Glaucous-winged Gull, but not yellow or white as in the Herring Gull. The bill is slender, usually a greenish or pale yellow color. The wing-tips are dark gray or black, with the 10th (outer) primary with a large mirror, the 9th primary with a mirror and a white tongue that runs up into it, making primary number 9 almost white with just a little black. Often primary number 10 also shows this long white tongue. There is much less black in the Thayer's Gull than in the Herring. In fact, the amount of black on white wing-tips is even less than in the Mew Gull.

"While on the ground this species looks very much like a Herring Gull, but with a little practice, subtle differences can often be recognized (dark eyes, a rather thin mottled bill, somewhat smaller size and more delicate build). Although the wing-tips appear black much of the time, the color varies from very deep slate to deep black. However, when the bird flushes, the dark tips seem to disappear; only a small band of black can be noticed in the whitish tips. The under-wings are almost completely without pigment. As the plumage brightens in the spring, the dark eyes and reddish-purple eye-ring are quite different from the white eyes and yellow-orange eye-ring of the Herring Gull. Thayer's Gulls are much easier to identify than many birders believe. The wing pattern is unique and with practice and patience, this species can be identified standing along a mixed flock or by itself."
CALLS. Similar to those of the Herring Gull. HABITAT. Similar to that of the Herring Gull. RANGE. Spring and fall migrant and winter resident along the Pacific coast of the Northwest, mostly along salt water and the lower stretches of the larger rivers; rare in the interior east of the Cascades. *Note.* Species status doubtful. Considered by some specialists to be conspecific with the Iceland Gull.

LAUGHING GULL *Larus atricilla* 16-17 (408-434)
A small gull with dark-gray wings and mantle (the wings with a white hind margin), dark red legs and bill, and black head in summer and

white head (dark gray ear-patches and nape) in winter. No mirrors or white spots in wings, only the black wing-tips. The all-dark wings separate this species from the Bonaparte's and Sabine's Gulls and the lack of white mirrors from the Franklin's Gull. CALLS. A high-pitched laughing *ha-ha-ha-ha,* etc. HABITAT. Similar to that of other gulls in our area. RANGE. Very rare late summer and early fall visitor along the Oregon coast north to the mouth of the Columbia River. Also recorded in eastern Oregon (Malheur) in spring.

FRANKLIN'S GULL *Larus pipixcan* 14-16 (357-408)
A small, gray-backed, black-headed gull with a dark red bill and feet, black wing-tips (margined at feather tips with white) separated from the gray of the wing by a white band, and (in winter) a white head and dark patch extending around the nape from eye to eye. The black head in summer plumage is distinctive in its interior range. CALLS. A soft mewing or clucking note and a shrill mournful *week-a* or *po-lee.* HABITAT. Breeds on freshwater marshes, foraging on nearby meadows and fields, often following the plow where they do in-estimable service to the farmer for which they are too often repaid by having their breeding sites "reclaimed". RANGE. Breeds in eastern Oregon (large numbers at Malheur Refuge) and southern Idaho, wandering in migration (late summer and fall) and winter to B.C. and through the Northwest states on both sides of the Cascades. Uncommon along the ocean coast, though regular and not uncommon in the Vancouver-Victoria-Bellingham area in late summer and fall. In Idaho, rare late summer visitor in northern part and fairly common local summer resident in the southern part.

BLACK-HEADED GULL *Larus ridibundus* 15 (382)
A small dark-headed gull with a reddish-brown head in summer, grayish wings and mantle, black wing-tips, and red bill and legs. In winter, adults are white-headed with a gray nape and a white spot behind the eye. The leading edge of the outer half of the wing is white, the first primaries totally white with narrow black tips. CALLS. A harsh short *kwup* or *kwur-ir-ip.* RANGE. Very rare late summer and fall visitor along the coast and inland salt waters.

BONAPARTE'S GULL *Larus philadelphia* 12-14 (306-357) Fig. 60
A small red-footed gull with the outer half of the wing white, edged with black; head black in summer, white in winter with a black spot behind the eye; bill black. CALLS. Deep nasal sounds resembling the twangs of a jew's harp; rather silent in winter, but very noisy in spring. HABITAT. Coastal areas on salt water, as well as the larger lakes and . rivers in the adjacent interior. RANGE. Breeds from western and central Alaska and southern Yukon south in the Northwest to central

142

B.C., migrating through the Northwest, and wintering mostly along the coast from southern B.C. southward. Uncommon as non-breeding summer resident. Irregular occurrence along rivers and large lakes in the interior has been noted. In Idaho, rare spring and uncommon fall migrant.

LITTLE GULL *Larus minutus* 11 (280)
A small robin-sized gull with a black head and blackish under surfaces of the wings. CALLS. A tern-like *kek-kek-kek-kek* or a high-pitched *ka-ka-ka-ka,* etc. RANGE. Rare but regular fall migrational visitor in the coastal regions, mostly on salt water. Most records for the late summer and fall, though a few for winter and spring.

ROSS'S GULL *Rhodostethia rosea* 12½-14 (319-357)
A small pure-white (tinged with pinkish) gull with a narrow black collar and grayish wings and mantle in summer. Adults in winter similar but without the collar and with a gray nape. There is no black in the wings — entirely gray in color. The tail is pointed. CALLS. High-pitched musical notes. RANGE. Very rare migrational straggler; one record, Victoria, B.C.

BLACK-LEGGED KITTIWAKE *Rissa tridactyla* 14-16 (408-459)
A small gray-headed gull with a yellowish bill, black feet, and solid black wing-tips cut squarely across as if the tip had been dipped in black ink. CALLS. A soft *keet-wake, kee-ee-wake;* a series of harsh shrill notes. HABITAT. Mostly off shore over the open ocean; occasionally blown in to land by storms where they may rest on logs stranded above the high tide line. RANGE. Breeds on islands from northwestern Alaska south to the Aleutians and the Kodiak areas, wintering mostly off shore, where common, from the Aleutians south to California but often commonly to the ocean coast during that season. May visit inland salt waters (sounds, straits). Recorded rarely in the Puget Sound area and twice in eastern Washington (O'Sullivan Reservoir; Clarkston) which it may have reached by following the large impounded rivers; also recorded in summer in eastern Oregon. Non-breeders regularly present along the coast in summer.

RED-LEGGED KITTIWAKE *Rissa brevirostris* 14-16 (357-408) Fig. 62
Similar to the Black-legged Kittiwake but with a darker gray mantle, grayish under-wings, and red legs which are not visible in flight. Bill yellowish, but shorter than in the other kittiwake. CALLS. Similar to those of the Black-legged Kittiwake. RANGE. Breeds and winters in the Bering Sea, occasionally straggling to other parts of the northeast Pacific as the Aleutians, the Yukon, and the coasts of Washington and northwestern Oregon.

62. Red-legged Kittiwake (Fisher)

63. Sabine's Gull (Fisher)

144

SABINE'S GULL *Xema sabini* 13-14 (331-357) Fig. 63

A small black-footed gull with a forked tail. Outer half of wing black, large white patch at center of after-edge of the wing, rest of mantle grayish; head slate-gray in summer, but white in winter with grayish on hind-neck; bill black with a yellow tip. CALLS. A single, harsh, grating croak or short scream. HABITAT. Mostly on the open ocean well off shore, coming to inshore waters only during late summer and early fall. RANGE. Breeds along the Arctic coasts of the Yukon and Alaska south in western Alaska to Bristol Bay, migrating along the Northwest Coast, mostly off shore, but occasionally on inland marine waters. Has been recorded in eastern Oregon and Washington, mostly as a fall migrant, and occurs rarely in Idaho (recorded from southwest part of state).

TERNS

64. Caspian Tern (Fisher)

The terns are similar to and closely related to the gulls, but are more slender in body and more graceful in flight (whence the name "sea swallows"), and having pointed more slender bills and often deeply-forked tails. They are far less numerous and more irregularly distributed than are the gulls, apparently preferring somewhat more

145

protected areas disdained by their larger cousins. Terns frequently breed on inland waters, often in small colonies, and are best studied in such places. They wander more widely in migration and winter and a few can then be seen on some of the larger lakes and on salt water. Unlike the gulls, much of the feeding of terns is done by diving into the water for small fish near the surface. Fly-catching for insects is also practiced.

There are approximately 36 species of terns around the World, of which six have been recorded in the Pacific Northwest. With the exception of the Black Tern, a member of the marsh tern group, the remainder are colored very much alike with the typical gull pattern of gray wing and gray mantled upper parts and white under parts. To determine some species, careful attention must be given to details.

PACIFIC NORTHWEST SPECIES

BLACK TERN *Chlidonias nigra* 9-10 (230-255)

A graceful little tern with a short slightly-forked tail. In spring, has black head and under parts, dark gray back and wings, and white under surface of the tail. Lighter in fall and winter with head (except for dark markings around the eye, ear, and nape) and under parts whitish, and wings and back dark gray. CALLS. A sharp *kik, ki-dip,* or *ki-dik;* a *keep* given in a rapid series; a descending *kleearr.* HABITAT. Nests on shores and islands in freshwater lakes and adjacent marshy areas; spring and fall visitor over both fresh and salt water. RANGE. Summer resident and breeder from central B.C. (and rarely the southern Yukon) south through the Northwest east of the Cascades (rarely to southeastern Alaska). Wanders in migration throughout the Northwest region, though most numerous in the interior. Rare west of the Cascades in fall and very rare in winter. Fairly common, though irregular, summer resident in Idaho.

CASPIAN TERN *Hydroprogne caspia* 21 (536) Fig. 64

A gull-sized tern with a black cap, grayish upper parts, and white under parts. Forehead black, streaked with white in winter. Bill large and red. Under surface of wing-tips shows considerable black color. Tail slightly forked, not deeply so as with Forster's and Common Terns. CALLS. A very harsh *ka-ow, carr,* or *kaa-ap.* HABITAT. Nests, scatteringly and irregularly, by freshwater lakes and ponds in the interior east of the Cascades. Migratory visitor in certain areas along the ocean coast, as at Grays Harbor, Washington where the birds commonly forage the shallow waters at high tide (Kitchin). RANGE. Local irregular breeder in the Northwest, mostly in the arid interior, though in large numbers more recently in Grays Harbor and Willapa Bay,

Washington; uncommon (though occasionally common and widespread) migrant on both sides of the Cascades (coastal from B.C. to Oregon). Regularly seen along the ocean coast, as at Leadbetter Point and Ocean Shores, Washington. Uncommon, though irregular, in winter. Uncommon summer breeder in southern Idaho, but rare in the northern part of the state.

COMMON TERN *Sterna hirundo* 13-16 (331-408) Fig. 60
This is a grayish-white tern with red feet and bill (tipped with black); black cap in summer, but with white forehead in winter; in flight, bill usually is held downward. Wing-tips are broadly and not sharply dark bordered. See also the Forster's Tern. CALLS. A short sharp *kik-kik-kik-kik;* a high-pitched raspy *kee-yaar.* HABITAT. Protected bays and covers on both salt and fresh water; migrates over open ocean. RANGE. Migrates south through the Northwest from B.C., mainly west of the Cascades, though a few east of that range. In Idaho, rare spring and uncommon fall migrant.

ARCTIC TERN *Sterna paradisaea* 14-17 (357-434)
Very similar to the Common Tern, but slightly grayer below. Face appears to have a white streak below the black cap. Outer tail feathers are longer than the wing-tips when the bird is at rest. Wing-tips are narrowly and sharply dark bordered. In spring, the bill is deep red for its entire length; solid black in fall. Feet red. The legs are shorter than in the Common Tern, so that the Arctic stands lower than the Common when the two are at rest together. It is questionable whether fall adults of the two species can be separated in the field. CALLS. Whistled *kee-wee* or *kee-er-er;* other notes similar to those of the Common Tern. HABITAT. Migrates mostly off shore over the open ocean. RANGE. Breeds from the Arctic coasts of the Yukon and Alaska south to southern Alaska and northern B.C. (recorded nesting at Everett, Washington), migrating off shore and along the ocean coast of the Northwest but also rarely through eastern Washington and northern Idaho. Seemingly more numerous than originally thought to be. All terns deserve careful scrutiny.

FORSTER'S TERN *Sterna forsteri* 14-15 (357-382)
A grayish-white tern very similar to the Common Tern but with wing primaries that are lighter than, or as light as, the rest of the wing, rather than darker as in the Common. The Forster's Tern has a grayish rump; whitish in the Common. In fall adults and immatures, the dark patch on the head of the Forster's extends as a spot from eye to eye only; while in the Common, it extends completely around the back part of the head. CALLS. A sharp *kit;* a nasal *kyarr* or *zree-arr.*

HABITAT. Breeds on freshwater marshes in the arid interior; less common than formerly as these areas are "developed". Along inland rivers and lakes in migration. RANGE. Summer resident and breeder from eastern Washington south through the interior of the Northwest. In Idaho, fairly common, though local, summer resident and breeder in the southern part of the state.

LEAST TERN *Sterna albifrons* 8½-10 (217-255)
A very small robin-sized tern with grayish upper parts and white under parts. The white forehead is enclosed by black lines running forward through the eyes to the bill from the black crown, a distinctive pattern. The bill is yellow, tipped with black while the feet are orange-yellow. CALLS. A sharp *kit, kit, kit* or accented *kit-tick, kit-tik, kit-tik,* etc. HABITAT. Prefers the sand dune areas along the ocean coast, foraging in saltwater lagoons or the ocean itself. RANGE. Rare spring and summer straggler in both coastal and interior (southern Idaho) regions of the Northwest.

ALCIDS

65. Horned Puffin (Fisher)

These are small, chunky, duck-like birds with short necks, small rapidly-beating wings, and straight bills. Entirely marine and habitual divers, they come only rarely to fresh water. The bill is often compressed with the covering deciduous in many species and frequently has horny processes. The wings are pointed but short and the legs are attached far back on the body, so that the birds walk in an upright position and poorly at that. The plumage, often crested, is compact. The alcids feed on marine fishes and invertebrates and often nest on sea cliffs in dense colonies or in burrows. Most individuals of this family are to be seen along the ocean coast, with a lesser number in inland salt waters.

Some 21 species of this group, the family Alcidae, occur around the World. Though bizarre in appearance and behavior when compared with more familiar species of birds, they are highly successful and widely distributed. They would seem to take the place in the Northern Hemisphere of the penguins of the Southern, or vice versa. One species, the extinct Great Auk, was even flightless, resembling the

149

66. Common Murre (upper), Pigeon Guillemot (center), Tufted Puffin (lower) (Schultz)

penguins very closely. Flightless birds have always been at a disadvantage with man and many are either extinct or endangered. The potential threat to the alcids lies mainly in destruction or curtailment of breeding sites, since these birds must have a particular kind of habitat for nesting. Setting aside of the preserve on Protection Island, Washington for the nesting of certain alcids and other birds that was dedicated to the late Zella M. Schultz is a necessary step if we are to preserve these interesting birds in good numbers.

PACIFIC NORTHWEST SPECIES

THICK-BILLED MURRE; PALLAS'S MURRE *Uria lomvia* 17-19 (434-484)
In summer, similar to the more numerous Common Murre, but with a noticeably thicker and shorter bill. In winter, this species has a white chin and cheeks with a broken black collar, unlike the great amount of white on the head of the Common Murre. CALLS. A sheep-like bleating; other murre-like purrings and croakings. HABITAT. As with most alcids, breeds on cliffs and ledges and forages in the open sea. RANGE. Breeds from Point Barrow south to the Pribilof and Aleutian Islands and the Kodiak area. Winters from southeastern Alaska north to the southern limit of sea ice. Occurs rarely in the Yukon and in the marine waters of B.C., Washington, and Oregon as a migrational straggler and winter visitor.

THIN-BILLED MURRE; COMMON MURRE; BRIDLED MURRE *Uria aalge* 16-18 (408-459) Fig. 66
A large alcid with white under parts and a dark head, neck, back, and wings in spring and summer. Winter plumage is similar, but with white on sides of neck and face divided by a black line behind the eye. The bill is long and pointed. Some individuals, the "bridled murres", have a white eye-ring and line running backward along the side of the head like an eyeglass temple. This latter phase may be a valid species, as several authorities believe. CALLS. A purring *mur-r-r-r;* a hoarse *arrh-ha;* various other squawks and rolled growls. HABITAT. Nests in colonies on steep-sided islands off the ocean coast; widespread on salt water in spring, fall, and winter. RANGE. Breeds on islands and along the coast from northwestern Alaska south to California, wintering on salt water north along the coast to the limit of open water.

PIGEON GUILLEMOT *Cepphus columba* 12-14 (306-357) Fig. 66
In summer; a small, black, duck-like bird with large white wing patches; in winter, mostly white, except for black back and wings (white wing patches present as in summer plumage). CALLS. A faint, low, piping whistle, as *whit-whit-zeeeee-zeeeee,* repeated fairly rapidly; also a single *zeeeee.* HABITAT. Nests in burrows (original or borrowed) in perpendicular banks, in rock crevices, or on level ground; common at other seasons on inland salt water areas. RANGE. Resident and breeder on rocks, islands, and cliffs along salt water from the Bering Sea and Aleutians south to California.

MARBLED MURRELET *Brachyramphus marmoratus* 9-10 (230-255)
A small, chubby, neckless sea bird. In summer, dark brown above, heavily mottled with brown and white below. In winter, upper parts

dark gray with white collar, white stripe on back above wing, and white under parts. Often dives when approached. CALLS. A loud, clear, whistled *meer, meer, meer,* etc., or *whee-er, whee-er.* HABITAT. Nests on limbs high in coniferous trees and in protected areas on the forest floor, on wooded hills and mountain slopes near, but some little distance from salt water; at other seasons, common on salt water, especially near shore. RANGE. Resident and breeder in suitable habitat from the Gulf of Alaska to California.

KITTLITZ'S MURRELET *Brachyramphus brevirostris* 7½-9 (191-230)
In winter, similar to the Marbled Murrelet, but the eye is surrounded by the white of the face and there is a complete, or nearly complete, black collar across the white breast. The bill is much shorter than in the Marbled Murrelet. CALLS. Not described. HABITAT. Salt water. RANGE. Summer resident and uncommon breeder along the Alaskan coast from Point Barrow south to Glacier Bay. Winters in southern part of the breeding range and rarely to coastal B.C. and Washington.

XANTUS'S MURRELET *Brachyramphus hypoleucus* 9½-10½ (242-268)
A small murre-like alcid, dark grayish black above and white below. No white wing patches as in the winter Marbled Murrelet, nor contrasting crown and back colors as in the Ancient Murrelet. May be characterized by bright white color on the under wings (flecked with a few dark feathers), the dark shoulder marks on the sides not extending downward to near the water in swimming birds, a relatively short and stout bill, and a broken and narrow eye-ring. CALLS. Harsh chattering notes. HABITAT. Salt water. RANGE. Rare to uncommon fall and winter and possible spring straggler north along the ocean coast to Queen Charlotte Sound, B.C. *Note.* The above plumage description is for the southern race, *Brachyramphus hypoleucus hypoleucus.* The northern race, *B. h. scrippsi,* differs in having dark sooty gray upper parts and a broad and broken eye-ring. Because it is sympatric in its breeding areas with the southern form, it probably represents a different species.

CRAVERI'S MURRELET *Brachyramphus craveri* 8½ (217)
Very similar to the Xantus's Murrelet but the underwing is grayish white to dark gray, never pure white; the bill is relatively long and thin, the upper parts are mostly brownish; and the eye-ring is broken and narrow. CALLS. Chattering noises are reported. HABITAT. Salt water and nearby areas for breeding. RANGE. Rare late summer straggler along the Oregon coast.

ANCIENT MURRELET *Synthliboramphus antiquus* 10 (255)
Upper parts solid dark gray in summer with white stripe going from eye back to nape and a black throat sharply set off from the white of the rest of the under parts. The white streaks on the nape and shoulders have given the name "ancient" in reference to the "hoary" tresses. Similar to the Marbled Murrelet in winter, but has the upper parts solid medium gray contrasting with the black cap. Often flies when approached. CALLS. A low shrill whistle. HABITAT. Winters and migrates on inshore waters of the open ocean and on the more open parts of straits and sounds. RANGE. Breeds from the Aleutians and the Alaska Peninsula south to Washington (very rarely), wintering and migrating from the Pribilof Islands southward along salt water to California. Rare fall straggler to northern Idaho and eastern Washington; very rare in spring.

CASSIN'S AUKLET *Ptychoramphus aleuticus* 8-9 (204-230)
This is the smallest alcid in the region. Upper parts blackish with small white spots over the eyes; throat and upper breast gray; rest of under parts white. Bill short, black, and with white spot on lower mandible. CALLS. A croaking rasping *kwee-kew*. HABITAT. Nests in colonies on rocky islets, either in crevices on cliffs or under boulders or in burrows in the ground. At other seasons, mostly in the offshore zone and seldom in inshore waters. RANGE. Breeds from the Alaska Peninsula south, irregularly and sometimes commonly along the ocean coast of the Northwest, wintering from Vancouver Island southward. Mostly seen off shore; a few in Puget Sound.

PARAKEET AUKLET *Cyclorrhynchus psittacula* 10 (255)
A small alcid with dark brown head and upper parts and white under parts. Bill small, upturned, and bright red; black in winter. Eye white. A wisp of fine white plume extending backward from the eye. In winter, similar but without plumes and with white of under parts extending onto the chin. CALLS. A low broken whistle, as *ch-u-u-eee, chu-u-u-eee*, rising in pitch. HABITAT. Mostly on the open ocean in off-shore zone during the non-breeding season. RANGE. Breeds on Bering Sea islands and the Aleutians, wintering from the Bering Sea south irregularly along the Northwest coast to Oregon and California, mostly off shore. Very rare in spring and summer in coastal salt water in Washington.

RHINOCEROS AUKLET *Cerorhincha monocerata* 14-15 (357-382)
A chunky alcid, larger than a murrelet and smaller than a murre. In winter, uniformly dark head, neck, and upper parts; remainder of under parts dirty white. In summer, similar to winter plumage, but with

67.　Horned Puffin (l.), Tufted Puffin (r.) (Fisher)

white mustaches and eye plumes and rhinoceros-like projection on yellowish-orange bill. CALLS. Growls, barks, and shrieking cries; usually silent on the water. HABITAT. Nests in burrows in colonies on islands along ocean coast; winters commonly on inshore salt waters and in straits and sounds, as well as open ocean. RANGE. Breeds along the coast from southeastern Alaska to California, wintering, often commonly, on salt water from Vancouver Island south to California. Apparently breeding more commonly in the more southern parts of the range than formerly.

HORNED PUFFIN *Fratercula corniculata* 14 (357) Figs. 65 and 67 This species is a stout chunky alcid with an enormous yellow and red bill. Upper parts blackish. White face and under parts separated from each other by black collar. Dark (red) horn-like growth projecting upward from upper eyelid. In winter, similar, but with cheeks gray and smaller blackish bill. CALLS. Mostly silent when feeding; whistling calls at nesting colonies. HABITAT. In winter and migration, mostly in the offshore zone; only dead birds washing in to shore. RANGE. Breeds on Bering Sea Islands and the coast of western Alaska south to the Aleutians, Glacier Bay, and Forester Island, just north of the Queen Charlotte Islands, and more recently farther south along the B.C. coast, perhaps to Washington; wintering generally in the breeding region, though occasionally southward on salt water to California. Several recent summer records for the ocean coasts of Washington and Oregon.

TUFTED PUFFIN *Lunda cirrhata* 15 (382) Figs. 66 and 67
A chunky dark-colored sea bird with a large triangular orange-red bill and long drooping pale-yellow ear-tufts. In winter, an all black bird with a small deep red bill. Cheeks dusky and ear tufts absent. CALLS. Mostly silent. HABITAT. Nests on islands along the ocean coast; usually in burrows; at other seasons, mostly over the open ocean and along outer coasts; seldom on island salt waters. RANGE. Breeds from northwestern Alaska and the Bering Sea islands south along the ocean coast to California. Winters well off shore along the Northwest coast from mostly north of Washington to the northern limit of open water.

PIGEONS

68. Mourning Dove (Fisher)

Pigeons are similar to the common domestic Rock Dove in mannerisms, flight, and bodily appearance. The bill and head are small, and the flight is swift with noisily flapping wings. The birds feed largely on the ground (noticeably bobbing the head) and in bushes, seeking grains, seeds, berries, and fruit.

Some 289 species of pigeons and doves occur variously around the World, but only four have been recorded in the Pacific Northwest. To

69. Band-tailed Pigeon (Pole)

a considerable extent, this is a tropical group. The author has seen large flocks foraging among the many species of fruit trees in the tropics of Central America and Africa where their distinctive calls are often their only clue to identity. Seeds and fruits make up the usual pigeon diet, though insects and other invertebrates are taken by a few species. Either arboreal or terrestrial, some species are highly gregarious, and many have a syncopated cooing "song". The very young birds are fed on "pigeon milk", a secretion produced in the crop of the parents.

The mournful cooing of the Mourning Dove is a standard feature of the arid interior of the Pacific Northwest. No farmstead is without this species and many persons' first experience with birds, as with the author's, is with the gentle "turtle dove" in the tall Lombardy poplars surrounding the farmhouse or country home.

PACIFIC NORTHWEST SPECIES
ROCK DOVE; DOMESTIC PIGEON *Columba livia* 14 (357)
The domestic pigeon of streets and pigeon lofts. Colors variable, usually with much blue, gray, and white. Rump white; black bands on wings; bill blackish. CALLS. The familiar rolling cooing of the

156

domestic bird. HABITAT. Mostly in urban and metropolitan areas and around farms where it nests, often in colonies, on buildings, to forage over streets, garbage cans, fields, and barnyards. In the arid interior, colonies may exist in rocky canyons in feral condition, as at Palouse Falls, Washington. RANGE. Resident in cities, farmsteads, and rocky canyon areas from Whitehorse, southern Yukon, southward.

BAND-TAILED PIGEON *Columba fasciata* 15-18 (382-459) Fig. 69
A large stout pigeon with dark-gray upper parts, ruddy under parts, white crescent across nape, and broad light band across tip of tail. May be identified at a distance by the fact that the Rock Dove rarely perches in trees. Yellow feet and black-tipped yellow bill. CALLS. An owl-like *hoop-ah-whoo*. HABITAT. Nests in bushes and small trees in gullies and small canyons in lower elevations, preferring wooded areas; moves to subalpine sections of mountains in late summer and early fall. RANGE. Summer resident and breeder from southwestern and northcentral B.C. south through the Northwest, being most numerous in western Washington and western Oregon. Winters from the Puget Sound south. Rare and local during spring and summer in Idaho, eastern Washington, and eastern Oregon.

MOURNING DOVE *Zenaida macroura* 11-13 (280-331) Fig. 68
A small, slender, brownish-gray pigeon with a pointed, tapering, white-edged tail; Robin size or larger; and with several large black spots on the wings. CALLS. A slow, solemn, mournful *coo-ah-oo, coo,cook, coo*. HABITAT. Prefers scattered groves of deciduous trees, as in windbreaks around farms, in hot arid parts of the interior; uncommon and irregular west of the Cascades, mostly in burns, logged-over country, and prairies. RANGE. Breeds from central Alaska, the southern Yukon, and central and southwestern B.C. south through the Northwest, wintering in the southern part of the region. Scattered winter records throughout the Northwest. More numerous east of the Cascades in the arid sections, but there are resident populations in the southern Puget Sound area. In Idaho, common summer resident throughout the state, but winters sparsely in Nez Perce and Latah Counties.

WHITE-WINGED DOVE *Zenaida asiatica* 11-12½ (280-319)
A brownish-grayish-colored pigeon with prominent white patches in the wings and white corners to the grayish tail. CALLS. A hoarse accented *cuck, cuck, cuck,oooo; coo-coo* or *coo-ee;* etc. HABITAT. Tall shrubs and low trees within a few miles of water. RANGE. Very rare straggler to Oregon, Washington, and B.C., mostly west of the Cascades.

CUCKOOS

70. Yellow-billed Cuckoo (Fisher)

PACIFIC NORTHWEST SPECIES

BLACK-BILLED CUCKOO *Coccyzus erythropthalmus* 11-12 (280-306)
Similar in appearance to the Yellow-billed Cuckoo, but lacks reddish in the outspread wings. The bill is entirely black. The undersurface of the tail is grayish brown with narrow, white, scalloped bars. A red eye-ring is present. CALLS. A soft rapidly-uttered series of *koo-koo-koo, koo-koo-koo, koo-koo-koo,* etc. HABITAT. Mostly deciduous woodlands. RANGE. Rare straggler on both sides of the Cascades north to southern B.C. and eastern Washington. Rare summer resident in southern Idaho.

YELLOW-BILLED CUCKOO *Coccyzus americanus* 12-13 (306-331)
Fig. 70
A slim long-tailed bird, a little larger than a Robin, with brownish-green upper parts and white under parts. Wings show reddish in flight. Upper bill dark; lower bill yellow. Tail white with large, scalloped, cross-wise black bars on under side. A shy seldom-seen bird of the

dense deciduous brush. CALLS. A long guttural series, *kuk-kuk-kuk-kuk, kuk, kuk, kuk, kyow, kyow, kyow;* also a series of soft, low cooing notes. HABITAT. Dense deciduous growth along larger streams and rivers, such as riparian willow woods with thick understory of shrubbery; mostly in the interior of the Northwest. RANGE. Rare local summer resident and breeder from B.C., western Washington, northern Idaho, and western Montana south through the Northwest. Much less numerous than formerly, especially west of the Cascades, though there is some indications that numbers may be picking up in a few localities, especially in Oregon and as a breeding bird in the Columbia Basin of eastern Washington.

OWLS

71.   Horned Owl (Fisher)

These are small to large, nocturnal or crepuscular, raptorial birds with characteristic facial disks and silent moth-like flight. The head is large and rounded with a relatively small hooked bill and large forward-directed eyes. The wings are large and the toes have hooked claws, the plumage is dense and fluffy, covering the base of the bill and often the toes. The voice is a hoot, deep or whistled.

Some 15 species of owls occur regularly or rarely in the Pacific

Northwest and are perhaps best characterized by their individual descriptions.

The owls, with their strange calls and silent relentlous hunting habits, have long fascinated and frightened humans and many are the legends of these ominous birds. Some 130 or so species of owls occur around the World and feed mostly on birds and mammals with other animal life in the minority. Most species are solitary and nocturnal. The food is usually swallowed whole and the bones and fur or feathers are regurgitated in the form of compressed pellets. Often a small pile of these pellets at the base of a tree indicates a roosting or feeding station of some owl. Foraging largely on small rodents, these are highly useful birds which should be strictly protected.

While the hoots of an owl floating mysteriously from some nearby woodlot may seem the epitomy of gloom and doom, we like to think, positively, of the lines from Shakespeare:

> To-whit, to-whoo, a merry note,
> While greasy Joan doth keel the pote.

PACIFIC NORTHWEST SPECIES

COMMON BARN OWL *Tyto alba* 14-19 (357-484) Fig. 72
A medium-sized, long-legged, earless owl with buffy and grayish upper parts and buffy-white under parts. Heart-shaped monkey-like face, dark eyes, and light coloration are distinctive. The breast has small dark spots. CALLS. Loud rasping hisses, loud screams, and rapid bill snappings. HABITAT. Nests in lofts of large barns (as well as in church steeples), usually in rural areas where a good supply of rodents, particularly rats, is available, as well as nearby trees for roosting. May also use hollow trees and cavities in cliffs and earthen banks. RANGE. Fairly common local resident from southern B.C., Washington, and northern Idaho southward through the remainder of the Northwest. Uncommon, though apparently increasing, resident in Idaho and eastern Washington. Fairly common in the Puget Sound country.

FLAMMULATED OWL *Otus flammeolus* 6-7 (153-178)
A tiny light gray owl with dark eyes and heavily mottled plumage. The ear tufts are very short. Smaller than the Screech Owl and much lighter than the Pygmy Owl, which has yellow eyes, this tiny fellow seldom hunts or calls before total darkness and is very poorly known, though apparently more numerous than commonly thought. CALLS. Single, soft, mellow hoots regularly repeated, as *hoo, hoo, hoo, hoo,* etc.; sometimes with a double *hoo-hoot, hoo-hoot,* thrown in. Though seemingly soft, these hoots carry to a considerable distance. HABITAT. Open or broken coniferous woods (especially of fir or yel-

160

low pine) and mixed second growth; scattered groves in desert mountain ranges are particularly favored. RANGE. Uncommon local summer resident and breeder as well as migrant from southern B.C. and Idaho south, mostly in wooded terrain (particularly yellow pine) east of the Cascades.

SCREECH OWL *Otus asio* 8-10 (204-255) Fig. 72
A small owl with conspicuous ear-tufts. Plumage intricately marked with spots and bars, but giving a general brownish or grayish appearance. Under parts lacking solid conspicuous stripes. Eyes are yellow. CALLS. A tremulous *oo, oo, oo-oo-oo-oo-oo-oo-oo-oo*, gaining in tempo toward the end; at a distance, only the final tremolo may be heard. Also a harsh squeaky *eek-it, eek-it*, etc. HABITAT. Open woodland, as well as second growth coniferous timber, near water; often in lowlands along river bottoms; frequents tree growth about houses in towns and orchards in the country. RANGE. Resident and breeder from the panhandle of Alaska south throughout the remainder of the Northwest, though tending to be rather local in occurrence and most numerous along the coast.

GREAT HORNED OWL *Bubo virginianus* 18-25 (459-637) Fig. 71
A large dark-brown owl, heavily marked below with cross-wise barrings and with a white collar across the throat. Conspicuous large ear-tufts or "horns" arise from the sides of the top of the head, whence the name. Some races are paler than the above description. One of the commonest of the owls and perhaps the one most frequently heard in the Northwest. CALLS. A solemn deep-toned series of four to eight hoots given in a definite rhythmical cadence according to sex. Male, *hoo-hoo, hoo, hoo* or *whoo-whoo-hoo, hoo, hoo;* female, *whoo-hoo-hoo, hoo-hoo, hoo.* The hoot of the female is higher pitched and more rapidly uttered. HABITAT. Woods and forests (both deciduous and coniferous), isolated groves or extensive tracts; requires only a protective roosting place, elevated nesting site, and nearby supply of mice. Common and widespread. RANGE. Resident and breeder in suitable habitat throughout the Northwest from the northern limit of trees southward.

SNOWY OWL *Nyctea scandiaca* 20-26 (510-663)
A large white owl, more or less marked with narrow brownish cross-bars. The head is round without "horns". CALLS. A hoarse raven-like hoot and a shrill tremulous whistle, though usually silent in the southern part of its range. HABITAT. Winter visitor in open places, ranging from ocean beaches to desert plains and from marshes and open sports fields to sand dune areas. RANGE. Breeds in the open

SAW-WHET OWL

BARN OWL

SHORT-EARED OWL

SCREECH OWL

72.   Some typical medium-sized Pacific Northwest owls (Schultz)

tundra areas from the Arctic Ocean south to central Alaska. Winters irregularly southward through the remainder of the Northwest, being most numerous about every four years, but showing an increasing tendency for more frequent southern invasions of the northern states and now some individuals recorded every year, even as early as September.

HAWK OWL *Surnia ulula* 15-17 (382-434)
A medium-sized, long-tailed, diurnal owl. Posture, when perched, is more inclined and not so erect as in the other owls. Occasionally it bobs its tail. Upper parts blackish, spotted with white; under parts whitish, barred with brown and with dark band across the breast. Blackish "sideburns" or grayish-white face. CALLS. A melodious trill. HABITAT. Breeds in the northern taiga; winters in open or broken woodlands (coniferous or mixed), second growth, snag areas in burns, etc. RANGE. Resident and breeder from northern Alaska and northern Yukon south to northern B.C., straggling southward in fall and winter to Washington, Oregon, and through Idaho. The paler Eurasian race has been recorded in northeastern Washington in winter.

NORTHERN PYGMY OWL *Glaucidium gnoma* 7 (178)
A small owl, the size of a large sparrow. Above, rusty brown, below, white, narrowly streaked with dark brown. Relatively long tail marked with white cross-bars. No ear tufts. Black patch on each side of hindneck. Similar to the Saw-whet Owl but smaller and darker. CALLS. A rapid series of mellow whistles ending with three detached deliberate notes, as *too-too-too....too-too-too, took, took, took;* often gives the whistled hoots singly, several seconds apart. HABITAT. Open or broken woods (coniferous or mixed), snag areas in burns, or logged over places; nests in woodpecker holes in stubs. RANGE. Common resident and breeder from southeastern Alaska and northern B.C. south through the forested parts of the Northwest. In Idaho, common resident in northern part of the state, irregularly invading lowland canyons and other areas in winter.

BURROWING OWL *Speotyto cunicularia* 9-10 (230-255)
A small, long-legged, round-headed, "earless" owl with brownish-tan upper parts heavily dotted with white, and white under parts spotted and barred with brown. White line over eye; short stubby tail. Characteristically bobs when disturbed. Usually seen during the day in open places, often standing on mound of dirt near nest hole. CALLS. A mournful dove-like hoot, as *cook-co-roo* or *cuck-coooo*. HABITAT. Dry, open, prairie country in the arid interior where it nests in ground

squirrel burrows that have been enlarged by badgers. RANGE. Uncommon local summer resident and breeder from southern B.C. southward, occurring mostly in the open arid interior. Winters in the southern part of the Northwest range from eastern Washington southward. Most of the scattered colonies west of the Cascades are now probably extirpated, but the species is reported wintering from western Oregon, southeastern B.C., and rarely western Washington. Much less common than formerly in the interior with agricultural development of the plains and prairies. Uncommon, though locally sometimes common, in southern Idaho and the Columbia Basin of eastern Washington.

SPOTTED OWL *Strix occidentalis* 18-20 (459-510)
This species is a large brown owl covered with numerous white spots. Flanks are heavily barred with white. Eyes dark, instead of yellow. Head round, without ear-tufts ("horns"). An extremely shy and secretive owl. CALLS. A high-pitched barking hoot, as *who, who-who, whoooo* or *hoo-oo, hoo-oo, hoo.* Also a shrill, rising, whistled *whee-eet.* HABITAT. Dense climax coniferous forests; frequents tree growth with dense canopies and low-spreading branches in shaded ravines with sparse undergrowth near water. RANGE. Uncommon, though locally fairly common, resident in suitable habitat from southwestern B.C. through western Washington and western and eastern Oregon, including both slopes of the Cascades. Very rare elsewhere in the Northwest. Noted in the mountains of northern Washington.

BARRED OWL *Strix varia* 18-24 (459-612)
This is a large brown owl with a heavy neck and fluffed out plumage. The eyes are dark brown and the pattern of barring on the under parts, cross-wise on the neck and breast and lengthwise on the belly is distinctive. Similar in size to the Great Horned Owl, but with thicker-appearing neck and without ear-tufts. CALLS. An emphatic heavily-accented series such as *hoo-hoo, hoo-hoo-hoo, hoo-hoo-a-aw* given in words rather nicely as *who-cooks-for-you, who-cooks-for-you-a-all.* Often begins hooting in the late afternoon and is easily imitated or squeaked up. HABITAT. Dense or mixed and broken wooded areas, often near water. RANGE. Resident in northern B.C. Increasing fall and winter visitor and now permanent resident and known to nest in Washington, Oregon, Idaho, and southern B.C. Most sightings are for northeastern Washington and northern Idaho. Strongly on the increase, especially as a winter visitor, even in the open arid areas.

GREAT GRAY OWL *Strix nebulosa* 24-33 (612-841)
A large, ear-less, yellow-eyed owl with a heavily striped and mottled

gray plumage. Large facial disks with dark concentric rings around the eyes. CALLS. A single, deep, booming hoot, as *whooooooo.* HABITAT. Dense coniferous or mixed coniferous-deciduous forests; in winter in broken woods, even visiting groves of trees in urban areas; at all elevations, though mostly in the mountains during the summer. RANGE. Local resident and breeder from central Alaska and northern Yukon (very rare) south throughout the forested regions of the Northwest where rare. Some southward movement of northern individuals in winter, but generally rare in the southern parts of its range. Fairly common breeder in eastern Idaho. Probably more numerous than commonly believed, as the author has found a number of them in various parts of the Northwest and the Fishers and he once shared the Ethel Wilson Campground in central B.C. with a pair.

LONG-EARED OWL *Asio otus* 13-16 (331-408)
A medium-sized owl with long ear-tufts or "horns" arising near the center of the head. Buffy to grayish, marked with length-wise streak- ings. The face is reddish. CALLS. A soft pigeon-like hoot, as *hoo, hoo, hoo* or *whoo-hoo, woo-hoo;* a variety of shrieks or screams near the nest; mostly silent, except during the breeding season. HABITAT. Most commonly found in aspen-willow or cottonwood growths along streams in the arid interior; also occurs in isolated groves or coniferous or mixed trees; somewhat variable in occurrence in winter and fre- quently enters residential areas in towns. The author once looked up from his desk to see a Long-eared Owl in the blue spruce just outside the study window silently observing him. RANGE. Local resident and breeder from central B.C. and southeastern Alaska south through the Northwest, east of the Cascades. Northern individuals move southward in winter. In Idaho, fairly common local summer resident and breeder and uncommon winter resident and visitor.

SHORT-EARED OWL *Asio flammeus* 13-17 (331-434) Fig. 72
A medium-sized owl; buffy in color, heavily streaked with dusky. Resembles a hawk, but flies more slowly and appears quite big- headed. Often seen in daytime, particularly over grain fields, meadows, and marshes. CALLS. A *whip-whip* or *weck-weck;* a *kiyow* like the bark of a small dog. Mostly silent except in the breeding season. HABITAT. Marshes, grassy tideflats, open grasslands, grain fields, airports, and even entering towns during snow winters. RANGE. Breeds in suitable open country from the Arctic coast throughout the Northwest. Winters from southern B.C. southward, often congregating in large flocks during stormy snowy weather. Un- common and local as breeder west of the Cascades, where mainly a

migrant and winter visitor; common east of the Cascades. Apparently somewhat reduced in numbers in recent years.

BOREAL OWL; TENGMALM'S OWL *Aegolius funereus* 9-12 (230-306)

An owl of mixed and coniferous forest that is larger than the Saw-whet Owl. Large head, earless, and with yellowish bill, the species has facial disks framed with black and the top of the head is heavily dotted with white. Under parts are streaked lengthwise. The upper parts are brownish, heavily dotted with white. CALLS. Reported to be like the winnowing of a Common Snipe, but rising in pitch. RANGE. Resident and breeder in coniferous forests from northern Alaska and northern Yukon south to northern B.C., and also to eastern Washington and the Salmon River Mountains of north central Idaho. Winters irregularly and rarely to eastern and western Washington, northern Idaho, and northern Montana. Very rare elsewhere in the Northwest.

SAW-WHET OWL *Aegolius acadicus* 7-8 (178-204) Fig. 72

A small owl without ear-tufts. Upper parts brown, spotted with white; under parts white, marked with wide brown length-wise stripes; tail is short. Has fluffy appearance, lacking the trim lines of the Pygmy Owl. Similar to the Boreal Owl but is smaller, browner, and with a streaked, rather than spotted, forehead and crown. CALLS. A rasping *say-ee* (whence the name); also a soft bell-like hoot uttered every few seconds (given by adults and the more commonly heard note). HABITAT. Open or broken coniferous woods, especially in the mountains; commonly comes to campfires of campers in the subalpine country; spends the winter in the lowlands. RANGE. Resident and breeder (occasionally fairly commonly in western Washington) in forested areas from southeastern Alaska and northern B.C. south through much of the Northwest; many individuals moving southward in winter.

GOATSUCKERS

73. Poor-will (Fisher)

The goatsuckers, or nightjars, are small- to medium-sized crepuscular and nocturnal birds with soft brownish plumages and insectivorous habits. The bill is small, somewhat hooked, and delicate, but the mouth is wide and very large and margined with long bristle-like feathers. The wings are long but the legs and feet are small and not adapted for grasping. The plumage is soft and loosely packed, echoing the relationship of this group to the owls. No nests are built. The animals feed on insects scooped up by the mouth in flight. The goatsuckers also resemble the owls in their nocturnal or semi-nocturnal habits.

Comprised of slightly less than 100 species, the goatsuckers are represented in our region by only two forms, as this order is primarily a tropical one. Many bizarre species are included in the Caprimulgiformes, ranging from the echo-locating oilbirds and the frogmouths to the potoos and nightjars.

In our Pacific Northwest, one of the most nostalgic of all bird sounds is the short whistled *per-jill-ip* that comes floating into the dusty ranch house from the nearby rocky hillside over in the sagebrush and yellow pine country. The birds begin to call just before complete darkness and their voices seem almost as detached as the fabulous calls of the Common Potoo of the tropics. Unlike the Nighthawk, these birds are seldom seen, though if one walks along a dirt road in Poorwill country in semi-darkness, he may see a bird start up from the road in front of him, fly some 75 or 100 feet at human eye level and settle back down to the dusty track. This behavior may be kept up for some little distance. Only uncommonly can one see them feeding on insects attracted to the light of a porch as the artist has portrayed one foraging by the porch of the author's summer cabin.

74.   Nest and eggs of the Common Nighthawk (Boggs)

COMMON NIGHTHAWK *Chordeiles minor* 8-10 (204-255) Figs. 74 and 77

The slender, long-winged, black-mottled, grayish bird seen hawking with erratic wing-beats for insects high in the twilight air. Close observation reveals white patches near the tips of the wings and on the throat. The call or booming dive often directs attention to the flying bird. CALLS. A nasal *beeship* in flight. The boom of the dive is caused by the rush of air through the feathers as the bird levels off at the end of the swoop. Often the dive is in the direction of the nest and may be aimed at the brooding female. HABITAT. Prefers open coniferous forests with exposed rocky or gravelly ground for nesting sites, mostly in yellow pine or lodgepole pine, as well as logged and burnt areas;

also the graveled roofs of flat-topped buildings. Forages in the air in the vicinity of the nest. RANGE. Summer resident and breeder from southern Alaska (rare) and the southern Yukon south through the remainder of the Northwest. Migrates throughout the range. Often common but seemingly becoming more irregular as a summer resident, especially in urban areas. Very rare winter straggler in the Northwest region.

75. Nest and eggs of Poor-will (Larrison)

POOR-WILL *Phalaenoptilus nuttallii* 7-8 (178-204) Figs. 73 and 75
A seldom-seen, but often heard, goatsucker similar to the Common Nighthawk in mottled-plumage and insectivorous diet, but differing from that species in smaller size, mottled grayish-brown color, rounded wings with white patches, completely nocturnal habits, and the custom of seldom flying more than a few feet above the ground. The Poor-will has white on the throat and corners of the tail. CALLS.

169

A single three-part call sounding like *per-jill-ip* or *pol-duc-ik;* a soft clucking note in flight. HABITAT. Dry rocky places in open terrain or sparsely timbered areas where daytime roosting is done on bare surfaces in the shade of brush, trees, or rocks; forages low (below 20 feet) over openings, roads, or trails. RANGE. Local summer resident and breeder from southeastern B.C. southward in the Northwest east of the Cascades. Rare elsewhere in the region covered by this manual. Found in hibernation in northeastern Washington in October by the author. Recorded breeding locally in southwestern Oregon. In Idaho, fairly common local summer resident and breeder, mostly in the southern part of the state.

76. White-throated Swift (Fisher)

SWIFTS

The swifts are dark swallow-like birds usually seen knifing through the air at considerable heights, alternating a few swift wing-beats with a glide on bowed wings. The mouth is large and the bill small, flat, and triangular. The tail is short, not reaching the tips of the wings when the latter are folded. The wings are blade-like with the wing feathers clinging together. The legs and feet are small and weak. These birds feed on flying insects which they scoop up in flight.

Of the some 80 species of swifts that inhabit various parts of the World, only three have been recorded in the Pacific Northwest. Of these, probably the Vaux's Swift is the commonest, being widely distributed throughout the coniferous forests of the region.

Much of the knowledge of Northwest swifts was recorded by Samuel F. Rathbun, a pioneer Seattle ornithologist, who spent many years and much diligent work in studying the habits and distribution of this fascinating group. Many of his observations are recorded in the Bent life history volume dealing with the swifts and related groups and make very interesting reading for a rainy day when the birder finds it difficult to be outside.

The valley of the south fork of the Stillaguamish River in Washington is an excellent place to watch Black Swifts, either on Mount Pilchuck or farther up the valley at Big Four. At the latter place in 1973, Jim Yaich and the author spent a pleasant summer afternoon watching some two dozen birds of this species flying low — and very fast — over the moraine of the glacier.

PACIFIC NORTHWEST SPECIES

BLACK SWIFT *Nephoecetes niger* 7 (178)
A large black-colored swift with a lightly forked tail. Somewhat like a Martin, but has long, narrow, sickle-shaped wings and flies and glides at great speed. CALLS. A loud high-pitched twitter, as a sharp *plik-plik-plik,* etc., given mostly near the nesting sites. HABITAT. Breeds on high mountain cliffs, canyon walls, and bluffs, frequently placing the nest on a ledge behind a waterfall; forages high in the air over forests, foothills, surrounding valleys, and saltwater sounds and the open sea, often at considerable distance from the nest. In fair weather, flies so high as to be out of sight, but on dull cloudy days may be seen low over the earth or water. RANGE. Local summer resident and breeder from southeastern Alaska through the mountains of B.C., Washington, Oregon, northern Idaho, and northwestern Montana. Nesting sites still unknown from Idaho, but individuals seen in the Selway-Bitterroot area in summer.

CLIFF SWALLOW

VIOLET-GREEN
SWALLOW

VAUX'S
SWIFT

COMMON
NIGHTHAWK

m.

77. Four aerial insect feeders (Schultz)

VAUX'S SWIFT *Chaetura vauxi* 4-5 (102-128) Fig. 77
A small brownish-gray swallow-like bird with long, stiff, slightly curved wings. In outline, like a Black Swift, but considerably smaller and without much of a tail. Twinkling bat-like flight is distinctive. The light throat is visible at close range. CALLS. A twittering *chip-chip-chip* or *twit-twit-twit-tweet-tweet;* silent during migration. HABITAT. Nests in hollow often burnt-out snags and trunks in coniferous forests; much less commonly in chimneys. Most foraging done in the airways following stream courses, clearings, burns, and immediately above the forest canopy. RANGE. Spring and fall migrant and summer resident from southeastern Alaska and northern B.C. south in coniferous forests through the remainder of the Northwest. In Idaho, fairly common, though local, summer resident and breeder in the conifer forest of the northern and central parts of the state. In several localities in the Northwest, huge flocks of 1,000 or more swifts frequent large chimneys (a la Chimney Swift style) apparently during migration.

WHITE-THROATED SWIFT *Aeronautes saxatilis* 6-7 (153-178) Fig. 76
A medium-sized swift, brownish-black in color, except for white throat, line down center of belly, and sides of rump. Fast, wheeling, swift-like flight and body outline are distinctive. CALLS. A shrill, twittering, descending *jee-jee-jee-jee,* etc., rapidly uttered. HABITAT. Nests in crevices and crannies on massive cliffs and canyon walls in the dry country, foraging widely over the surrounding valleys, foothills, and mountains. RANGE. Irregular scattered migrant and summer resident in southern B.C., eastern Washington, eastern Oregon (rarely to western Oregon), and southern Idaho. Recorded in early fall migration in northern Idaho. Late summer and fall migrant in southwestern B.C.

173

HUMMINGBIRDS

78. Calliope Hummingbird (Fisher)

Members of this group are tiny iridescent birds with long needle-like bills and rapidly beating wings. The flight is extremely rapid on vibrating humming wings, though the birds can hover motionless and even fly backwards. Feeding is done on the wing as the hummer inserts its bill into the corolla of some tubular flower and rapidly sucks up the nectar. The throat feathers of males have a metallic iridescence and glitter when struck by the light of the sun.

Some 319 species of hummingbirds grace certain fortunate parts of the New World, mostly its tropics. Nine species of hummers have been recorded in the Pacific Northwest, many of them rarely however.

These little fellows are often difficult to identify, as they seldom stay put long enough for a good view through binocs. This may account for the fact that only recently have we found certain of the species in the following accounts. They are best observed at the nest which is a tiny architectural jewel in itself. A second excellent spot is the hummingbird feeder where they are more or less immobile while sucking up the liquid food placed for them. The great number of species indicates an almost explosive adaptive evolutionary radiation into a variety of feeding types mirroring a parallel variety of flower types. Within their range, at least, no other bird group competes with them, and as is often the case in such situations, a great number of species is the result.

PACIFIC NORTHWEST SPECIES

MAGNIFICENT HUMMINGBIRD; RIVOLI'S HUMMINGBIRD *Eugenes fulgens* 5 (128)
A dark (sooty brown above and black below in male) long-billed hummingbird with a white spot behind the eye and a light yellowish-green chin in the male. As hummers go, this is a large species and the dark colors in both sexes are distinctive. CALLS. A sharp *chip*. HABITAT. Pine woods slopes and riparian deciduous growth along streams are preferred. RANGE. Very rare late summer and winter visitor to Oregon where there are two records: Steens Mountain and North Bend.

RUBY-THROATED HUMMINGBIRD *Archilochus colubris* 3½ (90)
Very similar in the males to the much more numerous Rufous Hummingbird but this species is separable by its grayish brown sides mixed with glossy green compared to the reddish sides of the Rufous. As is the case with the females of most species of the genus *Archilochus*, identification is not practicable and therefore descriptions of that sex are seldom given in this guide. CALLS. Various high-pitched squeals and squeaks. RANGE. Very rare straggler in southwestern B.C. (record not fully verified). Occurs in the northeastern and northcentral parts of the province.

BLACK-CHINNED HUMMINGBIRD *Archilochus alexandri* 3½-3¾ (90-96)
A "hummer" with a black chin contrasting with lighter under parts. Male, upper parts bronzy green, chin black with iridescent violet band above the white collar of the upper breast, and belly white with greenish wash. Female, like those of other hummingbirds, but lacks the ruddy color on the flanks and tail of the Rufous. Throat white, not black, as in male. CALLS. A characteristic loud buzzing or whirring sound in courtship flight of male; various hummingbird twitterings and a soft melodious warble. HABITAT. Nests and forages in deciduous riparian brush and small tree growth near water, in irrigated orchards, and suburban gardens. Usually found near standing or flowing water, mostly in the lowlands. RANGE. Local summer resident and migrant from southern B.C., northern Idaho, and northwestern Montana

79. Hummingbirds on their nests (Calliope above, Rufous below) (Boggs)

176

southward, mostly east of the Cascades in Washington and Oregon. Rare in winter in the southwestern part of the Northwest and southern Idaho. Uncommon summer resident in southern Idaho.

ANNA'S HUMMINGBIRD *Archilochus anna* 3½-4 (89-102)
The male is slightly larger than the Rufous Hummingbird, but may be distinguished from males of that species by the red throat and crown and the deep green on the back and sides. The female is similar to those of other Northwest species, but is slightly larger, darker green above, and has a somewhat heavier spotting of red on the throat. CALLS. A sharp *tchick;* a sqeaky "song"; a sharp *pop* made by the male at the bottom of its courtship dive. HABITAT. So far in the Northwest, mainly as a winter visitor, frequently feeders in urban and suburban gardens and in open lowland woodlands. RANGE. Uncommon, but rapidly increasing as permanent resident west of the Cascades; less numerous east of that range. Recorded breeding in southern B.C. (Vancouver Island) and in Washington and Oregon. Recorded as far north as Cordova, Alaska. Becoming fairly common as winter visitor in eastern Washington and B.C. in the last few years. Seemingly able to withstand sub-zero temperatures in the interior in winter but often succumbs to a protein deficiency. Recorded in winter from Idaho at Lewiston and Boise in recent years.

COSTA'S HUMMINGBIRD *Archilochus costae* 3¼ (83)
A small green-backed hummer in which the male has a deep purple crown and throat, the gorget extending as lobes far down the sides of the neck. CALLS. A soft *chick;* male's song is a hissing whistled *tss-see.* HABITAT. Typically desert environments, especially hillslopes, but also riparian growth and bordering woodlands. RANGE. Rare spring and summer visitor and very rare winter vagrant in western Oregon.

CALLIOPE HUMMINGBIRD *Stellula calliope* 3 (76) Figs. 78 and 79
A tiny hummingbird, much smaller than the Rufous. Male, throat white, streaked with lance-shaped lavender feathers; flanks dusky green; tail short and square (Rufous, longer and pointed). Also has white-tipped outer tail feathers. Female, similar to female Rufous Hummingbird, but smaller and with less reddish brown on tail. CALLS. A very low squeak or *tsip.* HABITAT. Nests and forages in and around deciduous brush patches in woodland openings, burns, meadows, and open hillsides from lowlands to subalpine regions. RANGE. Local, though occasionally common, summer resident and breeder from central B.C. southward through the Northwest, mostly east of the Cascade crest. Common breeder in northern Idaho.

BROAD-TAILED HUMMINGBIRD *Selasphorus platycercus* 4-4½ (102-115)

Male, green above with a bright rose-red throat. Trills in flight; other hummers produce a steady buzz but not an additional intense trilling pulsation as does the male of this species. Female, larger than the female of the Black-chinned Hummingbird; sides tinged with buffy on white; rufous wash on sides of spread tail. Trilling sound is probably the best field character. CALLS. A high thin *chip;* the loud rattling trill made by the male's wings is more obvious than other calls. HABITAT. Montane pine forests, particularly deciduous brush in clearings and meadows and along streams. RANGE. Uncommon to rare migrational straggler and rare summer resident in northern and southern Idaho, eastern and western Oregon, and southwestern Washington. Either increasing in numbers or being more efficiently identified.

RUFOUS HUMMINGBIRD *Selasphorus rufus* 3-4 (76-102) Fig. 79

Male, upper parts, sides, flanks, and tail reddish brown; throat iridescent fire-red; breast white. Female, upper parts and central tail feathers iridescent bronze or green; sides and outer tail feathers reddish brown, the latter with white tips, and the throat with or without an iridescent red spotting. The common hummingbird in the Northwest. CALLS. A light *tschick;* a low *tut-tut-tut-turr* accompanying the courtship performance of the male. HABITAT. Occurs in wide variety of open brushy or semi-open woods where flowers are abundant and nesting sites in low trees and high brush available. Seems to follow the blooming of the red-flowering currant, particularly on the west coast. RANGE. Common summer resident and breeder from southeastern Alaska and the southern Yukon southward through the Northwest to California, southern Oregon, and western Montana. Occasionally winters scatteringly through the breeding range. In Idaho occurs mostly in the northern and central parts of the state, being mainly a fall migrant in the southern portion.

ALLEN'S HUMMINGBIRD *Selasphorus sasin* 3-3½ (76-89)

A small hummingbird with a coppery or scarlet-colored throat, green back, and reddish brown rump, sides, and tail in the male. CALLS. A soft *chick* while feeding; a sharp *bzee* given by the male. HABITAT. Typically prefers gardens, shrubbery, and forest margins in the more humid areas. RANGE. Rare spring and/or summer visitor to southwestern Oregon and western Washington.

KINGFISHERS

80. Belted Kingfisher (female, l.; male, r.) (Fisher)

BELTED KINGFISHER *Ceryle alcyon* 11-14 (280-357) Fig. 80
A Robin-sized bird with blue-gray upper parts and white under parts,
a band of blue (blue and reddish in female) across the breast, a loose
crest, long heavy bill, and short tail. CALLS. A loud, rapid, rattling
kleck-kleck-kleck-kleck-kleck, etc. HABITAT. Almost always found
in the immediate vicinity of water — streams, rivers, lake shores, and
saltwater beaches, where small-sized fish are available and soft earth
or sandy banks for placing the nest tunnel. RANGE. Common and
widespread summer resident and breeder from central Alaska and the
Yukon south through the Northwest, wintering from southeastern
Alaska and southern B.C. southward where open water is to be found.

WOODPECKERS

81.   Pileated Woodpecker (Fisher)

These are stout chunky birds with chisel-like bills usually seen
hitching up the sides of trees or chipping off the bark with sharp bill
strokes. The undulating flight of several quick wing-beats and a
folded-wing dip is distinctive. The bill is strong and straight or nearly
so. The relatively short tail is usually stiff and used as a prop to hold
the lower part of the body away from the tree trunk. The legs are short
but provided with strong sharply-clawed toes. The nest is usually
placed in a hole drilled into a tree. Food consists mostly of grubs or
ants, often extracted by the bill or the long extensible tongue from
holes punched in the bark. Sapsuckers feed on sap draining from holes
they have drilled through the bark of certain trees.

The order Piciformes to which the woodpeckers belong is an immense and extremely varied one, containing such groups as the
jacamars, puffbirds, barbets, honey-guides, toucans, and
woodpeckers. All of these forms have one thing in common and that is
the fact that their bills are highly modified for their particular modes
of feeding, whatever they may be. Of the true woodpeckers, there are
about 179 species, of which 15 occur commonly or rarely in the Pacific

Northwest. All of them are specialized in digging prey out of wood or from in or under the bark of trees. A few, as the Pileated Woodpecker, dig massive holes in snags and stumps, others flake the bark for insects closer to the surface, while the sapsuckers include as a part of their diet the sap of trees.

PACIFIC NORTHWEST SPECIES

LEWIS'S WOODPECKER *Melanerpes lewis* 11 (208) Fig. 82
This is a dark-colored Robin-sized woodpecker with a black head and back, grayish collar and breast, and a red face and belly. The flight is crow-like and less undulating than in other woodpeckers. CALLS. Mostly silent, except for a harsh *churr* and a high-pitched *chee-up* given in the breeding season. HABITAT. Frequents open or broken coniferous or deciduous forests and woodlands where the trees or clusters of trees tend to be scattered. Often in recent burns. Commonly flycatches from isolated trees or snags. To be seen particularly in the river canyons in dry semi-forested mountainous or foothill country. RANGE. Irregular, though sometimes locally common, summer resident and breeder from central B.C. southward, mostly east of the Cascades, wintering in northern Oregon and occasionally in the coastal belt and eastern Washington north to southern B.C. Common breeder in central Idaho (Salmon River). May no longer breed in western Washington.

RED-HEADED WOODPECKER *Melanerpes erythrocephalus* 10 (255)
A medium-sized woodpecker with a deep red head, bluish-black upper parts with large white wing-patches and rump, and white under parts CALLS. A variety of harsh and soft scolding notes, particularly a *queer, queer, queer* or *chur-chur*. HABITAT. Open semi-wooded areas, such as woodlots in agricultural regions. RANGE. Rare summer, fall, and winter straggler to southern B.C. and southern Idaho (where possible breeder).

ACORN WOODPECKER *Melanerpes formicivorus* 9 (230)
A strikingly colored woodpecker with a black and white face, red crown, black ear-patches and nape, black back and wings (with white wing-patches and rump), black and yellow breast, and white under parts narrowly streaked with black. CALLS. A strident *yacob, yacob, yacob* and a variety of raucous calls and scolds. A very noisy bird. HABITAT. Prefers oak or mixed oak-pine woodlands. RANGE. Local resident in Oregon, but increasing in the Willamette Valley. Has been found near Vancouver and Washougal, Washington and in the oak woods country north of the Columbia both east and west of

82. Red-shafted Flicker (l.); Lewis's Woodpecker (c.); Yellow-naped and Red-breasted Sapsuckers (r.) (Schultz)

Goldendale in the same state. A recent record (1979) from Fort Simcoe in western Yakima County, Washington.

YELLOW-BELLIED SAPSUCKER; RED-NAPED SAPSUCKER
Sphyrapicus varius 8-9 (204-230) Fig. 82
A small woodpecker with a varied striped black, white, and red appearance (male), red crown bordered with black, red throat, and black and white wings, back, and tail. The belly is light yellow, streaked with black on the sides. The female is somewhat duller with less red on the throat. In the field, the birds seldom appear as bright as the bird guide artists make them. CALLS. A sharp descending *kee-yer, kee-yer,* or *tzew;* some single harsh notes; makes use of drumming on resonant objects, usually producing an erratic series of knocks often ending with a detached beat or two. HABITAT. Prefers semi-open pine and fir as well as alder, cottonwood, aspen, or birch woods, often near water; forages on dead trees for insects as well as harvesting the sap and inner bark of birches and alders. RANGE. Irregular local summer resident and breeder from the central and southern Yukon (apparently increasing) and northeastern B.C. south through the forests of the interior of the Northwest. Rare on the western slope of the Cascades and in the Puget Sound region in migration. In Idaho, fairly common summer resident and breeder throughout the state. Winters sparsely, but regularly, in the lowland portions of the breeding range. (Includes the varieties *varius* and *nuchalis.)*

RED-BREASTED SAPSUCKER Sphyrapicus ruber 9 (230) Fig. 82
A smallish woodpecker with a bright red head, neck, and breast. The wings, back, and tail are black, spotted and striped with white. The rump is white. There is a strikingly white wing-stripe. CALLS. A nasal squealing *chee-arr.* A slow patterned drumming, often on a resonating surface or object. HABITAT. Prefers mixed and coniferous timber, where it will drill alders, maples, willows, cedars, and hemlocks. RANGE. Summer resident and breeder from southeastern Alaska eastward to northeastern B.C. and southward and westward in the Cascades to western B.C., western Washington, and western Oregon. Winters in the southern part of the Northwest range as far north as southwestern B.C. and in the entire Olympic Peninsula. (This taxon includes *"S. v. daggetti".)*

WILLIAMSON'S SAPSUCKER *Sphyrapicus thyroideus* 9-10 (230-253)
Male, upper parts black, except for white stripes above and through the cheeks, red throat, and white patches on the wings and rump. Chest black; sides mottled; belly yellow. Female, black and white

zebra-like stripes on back, barred sides, brown head, white rump, and yellow belly. CALLS. A nasal *chee-r-r-r*. Drumming sounds like those of the Yellow-bellied Sapsucker. HABITAT. Open to semi-open coniferous forests, especially of yellow or lodgepole pine or subalpine firs, mostly in the upper montane and subalpine forests. RANGE. Uncommon local summer resident and breeder, mostly in semi-open forests in the mountains, from southeastern B.C. and western Montana southward, east of the Cascade crest. Rare west of the Cascades.

NUTTALL'S WOODPECKER *Dendrocopos nuttallii* 7 (178)
A small black and white woodpecker with a conspicuously ladder-striped back. Face with black and white stripes; speckled forehead; reddish crown; black-spotted white outer tail feathers. CALLS. A double-noted *tick-et, tick-et, tick-et*, etc. and a thin rattle. HABITAT. Foothill and montane forests of pine, oak, and other deciduous species, as well as orchards and nut groves. RANGE. Very rare straggler to southern Oregon.

DOWNY WOODPECKER *Dendrocopos pubescens* 6-7 (153-178) Fig. 135
A small woodpecker with white or smoke-gray under parts, black and white stripes on head, and upper parts mostly black with white patch in middle back and white spots on wings; tail black with white outer feathers containing a few black bars. Bill about one-half to two-thirds of an inch long. Female lacks the males red bar on the nape. CALLS. A loose whinny-like series of notes descending in pitch toward the end; also a flat *tchink* or *pink*. HABITAT. Prefers the deciduous or mixed coniferous-deciduous woods, often along streams, mostly in the lowlands. Also in orchards and urban areas. Frequently joins titmouse flocks in fall and winter. RANGE. Resident and breeder from central Alaska and the southern Yukon south throughout the remainder of the Northwest, but somewhat more local in distribution and more closely tied to preferred habitat than is the Hairy Woodpecker. Uncommon in southern Idaho.

HAIRY WOODPECKER *Dendrocopos villosus* 8-10 (204-255)
Very similar to the Downy Woodpecker in color but much larger — size of a Robin instead of large sparrow. White outer tail feathers and without black bars; bill is about one inch long. CALLS. A kingfisher-like rattle; also a loud *kee-ip* or *kip*. HABITAT. Prefers the broken semi-open parts of the denser, more mature, coniferous forests, but also in logged-over or burned areas. Common in the yellow pine and montane forests. Wanders to a greater variety of habitats in winter, frequently joining in with flocks of chickadees and nuthatches (the

"titmouse" flocks). RANGE. Resident and breeder throughout forested areas of the Northwest.

83. White-headed Woodpecker at nest (Boggs)

WHITE-HEADED WOODPECKER *Dendrocopos albolarvatus* 9 (230) Fig. 53
A medium-sized woodpecker, wholly black except for immaculately white head and white wing-patches. Male has red patch on nape.

CALLS. A sharp harsh *witt* or *witt-witt;* often a series of *witts* run together in a kingfisher-like rattle. HABITAT. Mostly in yellow pine forests in the drier parts of the Pacific Northwest where it prefers hard-shelled, but internally decayed, trees for nest holes and foraging which it does creeper-like. RANGE. Irregular local resident from northern Washington and northern Idaho southward, east of the Cascade crest. Rare to southern B.C. Sometimes almost rare or absent in certain areas that would appear favorable.

NORTHERN THREE-TOED WOODPECKER *Picoides tridactylus* 9 (230)

A medium-sized woodpecker with black upper parts spotted with white; top of head of male golden yellow; white markings down center of back; under parts dirty white, heavily barred on the sides with black. Barred sides distinguish this species from the Hairy Woodpecker. Differs from the Black-backed Three-toed Woodpecker by the presence of white bars on the back. CALLS. A short sharp *kuck*. HABITAT. Frequents open subalpine forests and burns in the high mountains, but also in dense stands of coniferous timber. Often seen on the lower parts of tree trunks. RANGE. Resident and breeder from northern Alaska and northern Yukon (more numerous than the Black-backed Three-toed Woodpecker) south, mostly in semi-open forests of the mountains, to the southern part of the Northwest. Tends to be uncommon and local in distribution; most numerous in snag forests of burns, especially at the higher elevations, as well as mature montane forests. More widely distributed and ecologically varied than the Black-backed Three-toed Woodpecker.

BLACK-BACKED THREE-TOED WOODPECKER *Picoides arcticus* 9-10 (230-255)

Similar to the Northern Three-toed Woodpecker but lacks any white on the back. Male has lemon-yellow crown patch. Sides are barred. CALLS. A sharp *tchik* or *tchuk;* a kingfisher-like rattle; a loud shrill cry. HABITAT. Prefers lodgepole and yellow pines, subalpine groves of mountain hemlock and subalpine firs, and particularly standing snags in recent burns or insect-ravaged areas (often called "silver forests" in the Northwest); mostly in the mountains. RANGE. Resident and breeder from central Alaska (where rare) and the southern Yukon (uncommon) south in the mountain forests through the Northwest, mostly east of the Cascade crest. Moves to lower forested elevations in winter. Seemingly more numerous than the Northern Three-toed Woodpecker east of the Cascades because of its preference for burns. Commonly frequents lodgepole pines, both live and dead.

YELLOW-SHAFTED FLICKER *Colaptes auratus* 13 (332)
Similar to the much more common Red-shafted Flicker but with the
under surfaces of the wings and tail yellow and red band across the
nape. No red stripe on sides of head. CALLS. A loud *wick-up, wick-
up, wick-up,* etc.; a sharp *pee-up.* HABITAT. Similar to that of the
Red-shafted Flicker. RANGE. Uncommon, though irregular,
migrational straggler and winter visitor. Summer resident in the
northern half of B.C. and the central and southern Yukon. *Note.* The
so-called "Gilded Flicker" which has adapted to the desert niche and
is characterized by yellow wings and tail and a red mustache is
reported as a very rare migrant in southwestern Idaho.

RED-SHAFTED FLICKER *Colaptes cafer* 12-14 (306-357) Fig. 82
and 84
A large woodpecker with brown back and wings barred by black;
gray-white under parts spotted with black; black collar; grayish head;
red under surface of wings and tail; and white rump patch. Male has
black mustache marks. A red nape patch common to both sexes.
CALLS. A *wick-wick-wick-wick-wick,* etc. (mating call, mostly commonly given); *wick-up, wick-up, wick-up,* etc. (in short series); *pee-up*
(given singly). HABITAT. Occurs widely from sea level to tree line in
broken or semi-open woodlands and forests and in urban and sub-

84. Red-shafted Flicker and nest hole with young (Boggs)

urban areas where dead and decaying trees are present and hard-surfaced utility poles, trees, and metal objects for drumming. Also forages on the ground, as for ants. RANGE. Resident and breeder is forested to more or less open country throughout the Northwest from central B.C. southward. Moves out of the more northerly latitudes and highest elevations in winter. *Note.* The author does not feel that the facts of reality are expressed by a promiscuous lumping of species because of certain amount of hybridization in some over-lapping parts of ranges. Accordingly, certain species currently considered conspecific, as with the flickers, are maintained as separate entities in this manual. The flicker problem has been analyzed and reported upon by Kenn Kaufman in *Continental Birdlife,* Vol. 1, No. 1, February, 1979. Divergence, hybridization, and introgression in the genus *Colaptes* are carefully considered with comments on field identification. Since classic binomial, or even trinomial, systematics cannot adequately handle the problem, it seems best to recognize the modes of evolutionary divergence by traditional species designation.

PILEATED WOODPECKER *Dryocopus pileatus* 17-18 (434-459) Fig. 81
A large, black, crow-sized woodpecker with a red crest, white stripes down sides of neck, and large white wing-patches. Male has red mustache. CALLS. Like the mating call of the flickers but louder, higher-pitched, and rising in pitch at the beginning; various other notes. The loud singly-spaced bill strokes are distinctive. HABITAT. Prefers dense coniferous forests, particularly of Douglas fir and yellow pine, where standing dead trees and snags are available for foraging and the placing of nest holes. Often in canyons or valleys near streams. RANGE. Regular, and sometimes fairly common, resident from northern B.C. southward through the Northwest, preferring dense coniferous forests and shunning the open arid regions. Uncommon resident in central Idaho but not found below the Snake River Plain.

KINGBIRDS

85. Western Kingbird (Fisher)

Kingbirds are intermediate in size between sparrows and robins with grayish or blackish upper parts and yellowish or whitish under parts. They are like flycatchers in habits and mannerisms but rather more outgoing in "personality". The tail is shorter than the wing and may be edged or tipped with white. The adults have a bright-colored patch (yellow, orange, or red) concealed on the crown and visible only when the bird is excited.

This is the first of the groups treated here in the family Tyrannidae, the so-called "tyrant flycatchers". There are about 360 species in the family around the World, most of them tropical in distribution; 32 are found in North America. Six kinds of kingbirds have been recorded in the Pacific Northwest, some fairly common, others rare. Two species occur regularly in our region. The Eastern Kingbird has a somewhat wider distribution in open brushy country while the Western Kingbird prefers the more arid agricultural and canyon areas. Most of the populations of both species are to be found east of the Cascades; a few occur scatteringly west of that range in the western lowlands, mostly in open country.

86.   Eastern Kingbird (Schultz)

PACIFIC NORTHWEST SPECIES

EASTERN KINGBIRD *Tyrannus tyrannus* 8-9 (204-230) Fig. 86
A large black and white flycatcher with a noticeably "extroverted"
personality. Head and back sooty gray; wings brown; tail with black
and white band at tip; throat and under parts grayish white. A concealed patch of red on crown, revealed when excited. CALLS. Commonest call is a *tzi-tzee*. A shrill crying *kip-per, kip-per,* etc.; also a
tsee, tsee, tsee. HABITAT. Prefers open sparsely wooded areas, as
orchards and tree groves near water (stream or lake margins). Seems
to shun the drier rockier habitats. Often in windbreaks and shade trees
about ranches. RANGE. Summer resident and breeder from the
southern Yukon and northeastern B.C. south to (uncommonly) western
Washington and western Oregon, and (commonly) to that part of the
lowland Northwest east of the Cascades. Very rare in other parts of
the Northwest, including southeastern Alaska. Tends to be rather
local but common as summer resident in southern Idaho.

TROPICAL KINGBIRD *Tyrannus melancholicus* 8-9 (204-230)
A gray-headed kingbird with a grayish chin, greenish back, and yellow under parts. The tail is all brown and slightly forked. CALLS. A rapid, rising, high-pitched chatter. HABITAT. Open semi-wooded habitats and agricultural areas, as well as the wooded or brushy borders of lakes and streams. RANGE. Rare, but regular, summer and late fall straggler northward to B.C. and Washington, mostly along the coast, but records for the interior.

GRAY KINGBIRD *Tyrannus dominicensis* 9 (230)
A large pale-gray kingbird with whitish under parts and sooty ear-patch, wings, and tail. CALLS. A loud *pe-cheer-y* note, constantly given. HABITAT. In normal distribution, prefers coastal areas, both natural tree growth and urban plantings. However, stragglers to our region may be found in almost any wooded or semi-wooded habitat. Like gold, they are "where you find them", one of the reasons why most of us are birders. RANGE. Very rare straggler to the Pacific Northwest. Status uncertain.

WESTERN KINGBIRD *Tyrannus verticalis* 8-9 (204-230) Fig. 85
Similar in tyrannical personality to the Eastern Kingbird. Head and back pale gray; wings brown; tail black, bordered on sides with white; throat white, breast grayish; and rest of under parts yellow. Orange patch on crown usually concealed (as with the Eastern Kingbird). Tail pattern and colors of under parts distinctive in the two common Northwest kingbirds. CALLS. A loud *whit* or *ker-whit;* various twittering notes. An early morning song of *kit, kit, fee-dee-dee-dee.* HABITAT. Found in dry open areas in the arid country of the Northwest where it prefers canyon walls, scattered trees, power poles, ranch buildings, windmills, etc. Not so dependent on the vicinity of water as is the Eastern Kingbird. RANGE. Summer resident and breeder from southern B.C. southward in suitable habitat through the interior of the Northwest, mostly in the arid interior east of the Cascades. A few breeding records for western Washington and Oregon. More ecologically restricted than the Eastern Kingbird.

CASSIN'S KINGBIRD *Tyrannus vociferans* 9 (230)
Very similar to the Western Kingbird, but with a darker gray head, darker green back, white chin contrasting with a gray breast, and no obvious white outer tail feathers. CALLS. A harsh *churr* and a *kee-deer;* a high-pitched series, *kee-dee-dee-dee,* etc. HABITAT. Open, semi-wooded areas. RANGE. Rare summer visitor to Oregion.

THICK-BILLED KINGBIRD *Tyrannus crassirostris* 9 (230)
A large kingbird with a very thick bill, brownish upper parts, whitish

throat and breast, and pale yellow belly. The tail is grayish brown without any white markings. Bird appears "big-headed". CALLS. A loud *kit-er-reer* or *kit-er-ree* or *ker-ee.* HABITAT. In our region as a straggler, probably in open sparsely wooded country. RANGE. Very rare fall straggler to the Northwest. One specimen record for southwestern B.C.

PHOEBES

87. Black Phoebe (Pole)

These are medium-sized flycatchers that seem to prefer open areas with scattered trees and buildings. Farmsteads and abandoned buildings are much to their liking, as are bridges and riparian growth, particularly in the case of the Black Phoebe. Our species all share the habit of jerking their tails downward. They also prefer to nest under overhanging structures or rocky projections. They usually perch in the open where their calls direct attention easily to them.

PACIFIC NORTHWEST SPECIES

EASTERN PHOEBE *Sayornis phoebe* 7 (178)
A large flycatcher with a dark head and back, black bill, no eye-ring or wing-bars, dirty white chin and breast, grayish flanks, and habit of wagging its tail side-ways as well as up and down. CALLS. An emphatic *feebee, feebee,* etc, hence the name; also a sharp *chip.* HABITAT. A variety of habitats but usually near water where streambanks and bridges afford nesting sites. Also utilizes sheds, buildings, and man-made structures of various kinds where there is overhead cover to the nest. RANGE. Summer resident and breeder in northeastern B.C. Very rare migrational straggler elsewhere in the Northwest south to Oregon.

BLACK PHOEBE *Sayornis nigricans* 6-7 (153-178) Fig. 87
An entirely black flycatcher with a white belly. Tips the tail downward and upward, as in the other phoebes. CALLS. A sharp *tsip* or soft *tseeeee;* also a repeated *pi-tsee, pi-tseer.* HABITAT. Tree branches, bridges, buildings, or other structures near water in wild as well as residential areas in towns. The nest site must be overhung. RANGE. Resident in southwestern Oregon. Rare fall and/or winter visitor elsewhere in southwestern Idaho, western Oregon, eastern Washington, and B.C. Recorded in early spring along the ocean coast in Washington and at Vancouver, B.C.

SAY'S PHOEBE *Sayornis saya* 7-8 (178-204)
A large flycatcher with a dark-brown head, grayish breast, and reddish-brown belly. Bill and feet are black, back brown, tail black, throat brownish gray. This pattern and lack of white in the tail separates this species from the kingbirds. CALLS. A *phee-ur* or *pit-pee-ur.* HABITAT. Open dry regions mostly in the arid interior where scattered bushes or trees provide lookout perches and interconnecting flyways for low-level foraging, and also where there are suitable canyon walls, old buildings (such as abandoned ranchsteads), isolated gas stations, etc., where protected nest sites are to be found. Often found at abandoned shacks or sheds in the open country. RANGE. Summer resident and migrant from northcentral Alaska and the central Yukon

south through the Northwest, mostly east of the Cascades, but rarely west of that range. Occurs uncommonly to rarely as winter visitor in such protected places as Lewiston, Idaho and the Okanagan Valley of B.C., as well as in eastern Oregon. One of the very earliest of the spring migrants. Rare in winter and early spring in western Washington and western Oregon.

FLYCATCHERS

Flycatchers are small sparrow-sized birds usually seen perched upright (occasionally jerking the tail) on snags or tips of limbs from which they dart forth to seize large passing insects. Most of them are best identified by their vocal notes and habitat preferences.

Insectivorous birds feed in a number of ways. It is interesting to note that these different techniques of foraging prevent the various groups of insect-eating birds from competing with each other and make sure that the insects in their different habitats are all equally worked upon. Besides vacuums, nature may be said to also abhor competition and over-lapping of ways of life! Certain groups of birds glean the insects, their larvae and eggs, from surfaces of tree trunks, leaves, flowers, and the ground. Others scoop up the aero-plankton at

88.   Ash-throated Flycatcher (Fisher)

various levels and at different times of the day and night. This particular group, the flycatchers, seize single large insects that they have sallied forth from perches to obtain.

Some 15 species of flycatchers and pewees have been recorded in the Pacific Northwest — some commonly and some rarely. This is a fascinating group, the author's favorite, though many are rather difficult for the tyro to identify. This is particularly true of the genus *Empidonax,* the little green flycatchers. Experience, careful attention to details, and checking such clues as vocal notes, subtleties in behavior, and habitat will help. But, if you think life with flycatchers in the Northwest is complicated, try the tropics!

PACIFIC NORTHWEST SPECIES

SCISSOR-TAILED FLYCATCHER *Muscivora furficata* 12-15 (306-382)
With a Kingbird-sized body, this pale gray flycatcher has a tail much longer than any other Northwest flycatcher. Head and body are pale ash-gray, paler, below; concealed scarlet crown patch; delicate salmon-pink sides, abdomen, and wing linings; upper surface of the wings gray-brown. Tail extremely long (7-10 inches), scissored, and deeply forked with the outer feathers white with black tips. The adult female is smaller and has a shorter tail. CALLS. A hard *keck, kew;* a rapidly repeated *ka-leep, ka-leep, ka-leep,* etc., and a variety of interrupted bickering notes. HABITAT. Mostly dry, open, brush or sparsely treed country. RANGE. Rare migrational and post-breeding straggler to eastern Oregon, Idaho, and southeastern and southwestern B.C.

WIED'S CRESTED FLYCATCHER *Myiarchus tyrannulus* 9-10 (230-255)
A kingbird-sized flycatcher with a grayish-brown back, brown head, and dark bill. The throat is grayish and the belly is yellow. Similar to the Ash-throated Flycatcher, but darker, with darker gray throat and breast and deeper yellow on the belly. CALLS. A loud clear whistle; a short double-noted call accented on the second syllable, as *prr-rreep;* a sharp single *weep.* HABITAT. Scattered groves of deciduous woodland and riparian growth in the desert country (typical habitat). RANGE. Very rare fall migrational straggler to southwestern B.C. One record, near Vancouver.

ASH-THROATED FLYCATCHER *Myiarchus cinerascens* 8-9 (204-230) Fig. 88
Like a kingbird in size and mannerisms, but has no white in the tail. Head brown; remainder of upper parts grayish brown with two white

89. Olive-sided Flycatcher (l.); Willow Flycatcher (r.) (Schultz)

wing-bars. The tail is bright reddish brown; the throat and breast gray, belly pale yellow; bill and feet black. CALLS. A variety of sounds, such as *peewheeur, pee-whit, pr-r-rip,* or *chee-chip, chee-chip,* etc. HABITAT. Prefers scattered small trees or areas of large bushes with interconnecting flyways for low-level foraging flying. Junipers and large sagebrush are particularly favored. A dry country bird. RANGE. Local irregular summer resident and breeder from central Washington and southern Idaho south through the Northwest, mostly east of the Cascades (a few west-side records). Has been recorded in B.C. Uncommon fall visitor in western Oregon and rare winter visitor in that state. Regular but uncommon in summer at the Columbia National Wildlife Refuge in Washington.

OLIVE-SIDED FLYCATCHER *Nuttallornis borealis* 7-8 (178-230) Fig. 89

A large dark-colored flycatcher usually seen perching at or near the top of a dead tree at a considerable height above the ground. Dark gray upper parts and brownish-gray under parts with a narrow white stripe or "zipper" down the middle of the front from the throat to the belly, separating the dark chest patches. Bill large; lower mandible slightly lighter than the upper. White patches on the sides of the rump. CALLS. A loud hard *pip-pip, pip-pip-pip,* etc. SONG. A loud ringing *pip-pee-up, pew* or *whi-whee-whew.* Described by Florence Merriam Bailey as "Quick, three beers!" Often carrying to a considerable distance, this loud ringing cry is one of the nostalgic sounds of the wilderness. HABITAT. Frequents ridge and hill tops where it perches on the highest snags or tree crowns in the vicinity and forages forth horizontally from such places. Never abundant, but scattered over the high points from lowlands to subalpine areas. RANGE. Migrant and summer resident from central Alaska and the central Yukon south in suitable habitat through the remainder of the Northwest.

EASTERN WOOD PEWEE *Contopus virens* 6½ (166)

Very similar to the Western Wood Pewee, but very slightly lighter in color. Best separated by voice. CALLS. A lazy whistled *pee-a-wee,* rising in pitch on the third note. HABITAT. Same as that of the Western Wood Pewee. RANGE. Rare visitor to eastern Oregon. *Note.* This species is very difficult to separate from the following and non-specimen records from the Northwest may be doubtful.

WESTERN WOOD PEWEE *Contopus richardsoni* 6-7 (153-178) Fig. 90

A sparrow-sized flycatcher, slightly larger than the *Empidonax* group. Dark grayish brown above; dirty-white throat and belly; grayish breast; two white wing-bars; no white eye-ring. Bill relatively large; lower mandible dark. CALLS. A mild descending *pee-eer.* Also a slurred *hee-za-wip, purr-deer* which rises in the first phrase and falls in the second and is given in the evening. *Note.* Many flycatchers have two or three different songs which are given in the early morning (dawn song), during most of the day, or in the evening. HABITAT. Prefers deciduous, mixed deciduous-coniferous, or open coniferous (as yellow pine) woodlands provided with airways between trees where it forages at intermediate to rather high (canopy level) strata. Bare horizontal branches sought for nesting sites. Common in urban parks and well-treed residential areas. RANGE. Migrant and summer resident from central Alaska and the central Yukon south through the remainder of the Northwest.

90.   Western Wood Pewee on nest (Boggs)

YELLOW-BELLIED FLYCATCHER *Empidonax flaviventris* 5-6 (128-153)
Upper parts (including head) greenish; wings blackish (two buffy-white wing-bars); tail grayish brown; eye-ring buffy; under parts (including throat) pale yellow, tinged with greenish on breast. CALLS. A liquid *cha-leek;* a plaintive *pee-whee.* HABITAT. A moist woodland or riparian growth *Empidonax*. Forages in the lower airways beneath the tree branches, but chooses the top of tree leaders for singing. RANGE. Summer resident and breeder in northeastern B.C.

ACADIAN FLYCATCHER *Empidonax virescens* 5¾ (147)
Very similar to the Alder Flycatcher, but with more greenish upper parts; though impossible in the field to tell by sight from that species or probably the Least Flycatcher. The voice is the best character. CALLS. A short *peet* or *peep*. Song is an accented (second syllable) *ka-zeep*. A muttered twittering given in flight. HABITAT. Prefers deep deciduous woodland where it forages along and around the lowest branches. RANGE. Very rare in northeastern B.C. Very rare fall straggler elsewhere in the Northwest, mostly along the Washington-Idaho border migration route.

WILLOW FLYCATCHER *Empidonax traillii* 5-6 (128-153) Figs. 89 and 91
A small flycatcher with greenish-brown back, gray breast, dirty-white

198

throat and belly, light eye-ring, and two white wing-bars. Bill large and broad with the lower mandible entirely straw-colored. CALLS. A sharp *whit*. SONG. A bright snappy *areek, ree-pee-oo* or a hurried *reets-pee-oo* or even shortened to a very emphatic *dee-deer*. HABITAT. Brushy places and low alders, birches, and willows near swamps, lake shores, or streams, from the lowlands up into the montane forest zone. Dense brush is preferred and the foraging is done in the short air-ways between brush patches and contained trees. Scotch broom plantings, if thick and extensive enough, are favorite haunts. Unfortunately, the species seems to be diminishing in numbers lately in the Northwest. Whether this is due to habitat removal, insecticide and pesticide pollution, or other factors is unknown. RANGE. Summer resident and breeder from southern B.C. southward through the Northwest in preferred habitat. Tends to be irregular in distribution and apparently on the decrease.

ALDER FLYCATCHER *Empidonax alnorum* 5-6 (128-153)
Very similar to the Willow Flycatcher but with slightly more greenish upper parts, paler wing-bars, and slightly shorter bill. Best separated by voice. CALLS. A low *wit*. SONG. A raspy *fee-bee-oo* or *fee-beer*. HABITAT. More inclined to forage higher in trees than the Willow Flycatcher. RANGE. Summer resident and breeder in northern, northeastern, and southcentral B.C. and the southern Yukon. Some

91. Willow Flycatcher on nest (Boggs)

individuals may migrate southward through the Washington-Idaho border corridor.

LEAST FLYCATCHER *Empidonax minimus* 5-5½ (128-140)
A small flycatcher with grayish-green upper parts, throat, and breast, and a white belly. Similar to the Alder-Willow complex, but throat is greenish and the back more grayish; wings brownish black; two dull white wing-bars. Best told by voice and occurrence in open tree groves. CALLS. A dry brittle *che-beck* often repeated rapidly in a long series. HABITAT. Open deciduous or mixed deciduous-coniferous woodland, edges of forest clearings, woodlots, orchards, and suburban shade trees. RANGE. Summer resident and breeder from the southcentral and southeastern Yukon south to southern B.C. and Montana, and sparsely farther south in eastern Washington and northern and southern Idaho. Apparently increasing along the east slopes of the Cascades in Washington. Rare west of the Cascades. Recorded as fall migrant in the Washington-Idaho migrational corridor and in a similar corridor in eastern Idaho.

HAMMOND'S FLYCATCHER *Empidonax hammondii* 5-6 (128-153)
A small flycatcher with an olive-gray back; dark gray head, throat, and breast (breast darkest); yellowish or dirty white belly; light eye-ring; and two white wing-bars. Bill relatively small and narrow and entirely blackish brown. Appears in the field to be dusky-backed, sooty-breasted, and short-tailed. Tail is wagged up. CALLS. A soft *pit, pee-zeet,* or *tsur-r-p*. SONG. A soft colorless *se-put, tsur-r-p, see-leep* or *see-dick, brizick, see-dick*. Given with great vigor early in the morning. HABITAT. Prefers the dense, more or less pure, coniferous forests of the mountains and foothills, having retreated from the western lowlands with the elimination of much of the Douglas fir forest and tending to shun the rain forests. Probably most numerous in the mixed-species and coniferous and yellow pine forests of the interior where there is relatively little undergrowth. Forages from 20 to 100 feet above the ground and seeks shaded airways. RANGE. Common summer resident and breeder from southeastern Alaska and southern Yukon south in preferred habitat through the Northwest, tending to occur more in the foothills and mountains.

DUSKY FLYCATCHER *Empidonax oberholseri* 5-6 (128-153)
A small flycatcher with medium gray head, shoulders, and breast, and a creamy wash in the white of the breast and on the belly. The breast is not darker than the throat or belly. Back is greenish. Bill relatively small; lower mandible dull straw color. In color, this species is very similar to the Hammond's, but has a lighter throat and breast (buffy

gray, instead of clear dark gray). Appears in the field to be gray-backed, light-breasted, long-tailed, and larger than the Hammond's. The tail is wagged up. CALLS. A sharp high-pitched *pew-whit* or *pee-wick*. SONG. A jerky *tsip, pr-r-rit, tsip, tsee-eet*, similar to the song of the Hammond's Flycatcher, but given in four parts and with the second part double-noted and higher in pitch. The four-part song is rendered continuously in the early morning before dawn. During the day, the 4th phrase is usually omitted. In the late afternoon, especially on cloudy days, the song is a plaintive *deer, deer, deer-whit, deer, deer-whit*, etc. HABITAT. Prefers the more open mixed coniferous-deciduous and deciduous woods and tall brush areas (willows, aspens, alders, buckbrush, serviceberry, and ninebark) where shrubs are available for nesting, open flyways for foraging (forages from 10 to 50 feet), and medium-sized trees for perching. Basically a tall shrub bird with interpolated taller deciduous or coniferous trees needed for guard mounting. Prefers drier habitats than those of the Hammond's Flycatcher. RANGE. Common summer resident and breeder from southern Yukon and northwestern B.C. south through the Northwest in suitable habitat. Less numerous west of the Cascades (rare to very uncommon).

GRAY FLYCATCHER *Empidonax wrightii* 5-6 (128-153) Figs. 92 and 93
A flycatcher of the sagebrush, juniper, and yellow pine country with brownish-gray upper parts and light gray under parts. Belly white. Bill black above, lower mandible noticeably flesh-colored (particularly toward the base). White eye-ring and wing-bars (two) present. Tail is wagged down. CALLS. A faint *chi-wip, cheep*, or *hesick*. SONG. A slow *chebec, cheep* with several seconds delay between the two elements of the song. HABITAT. Prefers semi-open sagebrush and/or juniper areas where there are bare patches of ground, sagebrush gullies, open yellow pine groves where perching and nesting are done in low trees. In its northward advance along the east slopes of the Cascades in Washington, to be found mostly in the lower yellow pine belt. Forages from the ground to 25 feet. RANGE. Summer resident and breeder from central Washington and southern Idaho southward, east of the Cascades. Very rare elsewhere in the Northwest, mostly as migrational straggler. Has been extending its range into eastern Washington, including the Blue Mountains, in recent years, mostly in yellow pine. Found breeding as far north as Twisp, Washington in summer of 1980.

WESTERN FLYCATCHER *Empidonax difficilis* 5-6 (128-153)
A small flycatcher with a greenish or grayish head, greenish-brown

92.　Gray Flycatcher on nest (Boggs)

93.　Habitat of the Gray Flycatcher (Boggs)

back, yellowish under parts, yellowish eye-ring, and two white wing-bars. Bill relatively wide, upper mandible brownish black, lower mandible wholly straw colored. The tail is wagged up. CALLS. A sharp metallic *chip, ting,* or *pseet.* SONG. A rising series of three detached notes, as *tsee-dick, tseep, tsee-eet,* the last note being slurred upward; often repeated several times and modified, as *tsee-eet, tsee-tick, tseep, tsee-eet, tsik, tsee-eet,* etc. HABITAT. To be found in dense-shaded coniferous and mixed coniferous-deciduous forests in the lowlands, mostly west of the Cascades. Most numerous in the dense dark rain forests. Forages up to 40-50 feet and nests in crevices in the bark of tree trunks or between tree roots. In the interior, occurs scatteringly in the densest parts of the coniferous woods, usually along streams. RANGE. Migrant and summer resident from southeastern Alaska, central B.C., and western Montana southward. East of the Cascades tends to be very local and irregular in distribution, but often common in preferred habitat west of that range. Rare winter visitor in western Oregon. In Idaho, uncommon irregular summer resident in the northern and western northcentral part of the state. Recently reported in winter in eastern Washington (December 1978). Apparently increasing in summer on the east slopes of the Cascades.

LARKS

94. Skylark (Fisher)

PACIFIC NORTHWEST SPECIES

SKYLARK *Alauda arvensis* 7-7½ (178-191) Fig. 94
A trim sparrow-like bird with a thin narrow bill, streaked brown appearance, small crest, and white outer tail feathers. Has the interesting habit of singing on the wing for several minutes at a time, hovering in position and then slowly fluttering to the ground. The claw of the hind toe is much elongated. Walks on bent legs on the ground, as if continously crouching. CALLS. A melodious *tree-kee*. SONG. A high-pitched twittering warble given as long as 2-3 minutes while the bird is awing. HABITAT. Open areas such as airports, golf courses, and large meadows. RANGE. Resident in the Victoria, B.C. area at the southern tip of Vancouver Island and well established permanent resident on San Juan Island, Washington. Regular migrant and summer resident in the western Aleutian Islands, Alaska.

HORNED LARK *Eremophila alpestris* 7-8 (178-204) Fig. 95
A plump, large-sparrow-sized, brownish bird with a black collar below a yellow or white throat; head conspicuously marked with yellow or

white and a strong black mustache streak; grayish-white to yellowish under parts contrasting with the black tail; usually seen walking (not hopping) in fields, shores, or other barren areas. Often erects black feather tufts ("horns") over eyes. CALLS. A sharp rolling *slik-seesik, slik-slee-sik.* SONG. A high-pitched twitter, as *tsip, tsip, tsip, tee-dee-dee.* HABITAT. Prefers the open plains and croplands of the interior where often abundant, as well as the high bare plateaus of the mountains in summer, descending to lower, but open elevations in winter, as west of the Cascades. Common along the sides of roads in the dry country. RANGE. Summer resident and breeder from northern Alaska and the northern Yukon south in appropriate open habitat through the remainder of the Northwest; wintering from southern B.C. southward in open areas of the northwestern states.

95. Horned Lark on nest with young (Boggs)

SWALLOWS

96. Purple Martin (Fisher)

Swallows are sparrow-sized birds usually seen flying through the air with very graceful flight. May be confused with the swifts, but lack the fast sailing flight, bowed wings, and stiff wing-beat of that group. The bill is short and flat, the wings long and pointed, and the legs and feet short and weak. The body of swallows is strongly streamlined for fast flight and the plumage is compact and often iridescent. Individuals commonly perch on wires but seldom in leafy trees.

Some 78 species of swallows occur around the World, of which we have seven in the Pacific Northwest. They are a neat compact group, well characterized, which feed on aerial insects which they scoop up with their wide-gaped bills and expert flight.

TREE SWALLOW *Tachycineta bicolor* 5-6 (128-153) Fig. 97
A swallow of the country-side; appearing in urban areas usually as the earliest migrating swallow. Head (except throat) and back, bluish black; wings and tail, greenish brown; throat, breast, and belly are white. Similar to the Violet-green Swallow but lacks white rump patches and sides of face. CALLS. A soft *silip* or *seery;* a series of short rattling notes, as *tsip, prup, tsip, prrup-prup, tsip, pr-rup,* etc.

HABITAT. Frequents the more open rural areas, especially over or near water. Commonly nests in holes in snags, standing in or near water, as drowned cottonwood trees in beaver ponds. Not common in urban areas, though may briefly visit them in spring migration. RANGE. Summer resident and breeder from northcentral Alaska and southwestern Yukon southward through the remainder of the Northwest. Rare erratic winter straggler west of the Cascades in the southern part of the Northwest. One of the earliest of the spring migrants, often appearing in early February.

97. Tree Swallow at nest hole (Boggs)

98. Purple Martin nest boxes on pilings (Boggs)

99. Purple Martin in nest box (Boggs)

VIOLET-GREEN SWALLOW *Tachycineta thalassina* 5 (128) Fig. 77
Crown and back dark green; nape and rump violet; wings and tail
violet green; face (to above the eye), breast, belly, and sides of rump
white. In flight, appears to have a white rump. CALLS. A twittering
tsee-tseet, tseet-tselt-tseet, etc.; *chee, chee, chee;* a sharp *chee-cheet;* a
yip or *yeep* like a lost baby chick. HABITAT. Occurs widely in the
lowlands where it frequents settlements and prairies west of the
Cascades and in urban areas and open Transition Zone timber to the
east of that range. The commonest swallow in cities and towns, where
it forages to elevations of several hundred feet. RANGE. Summer resident and migrant, as well as breeder, from central Alaska and the
central Yukon southward through the Northwest. A few linger till late
in the fall and rarely over-winter in the southern part of the region.
May appear as early migrant in the spring in February, though most
come in March.

PURPLE MARTIN *Progne subis* 7-8 (178-204) Figs. 96, 98, and 99
Our largest swallow. Male, entirely blue-black. Female, similar, but
more grayish brown above and dingy white below. CALLS. A loud
sheep-shear and *keerp;* a harsh buzzing *bizz-z-z,* given in anger or fear.
HABITAT. Formerly entirely restricted to downtown building areas,
but now spreading to pilings along salt water and to colonial nesting
houses. Spotty in distribution and nowhere common, except in post-
nesting roosts, such as the famous one at Lower Green Lake in Seattle
during the 1940s where as many as 4,000 birds would congregate
nightly. RANGE. Irregular local summer resident and breeder from
southwestern B.C. south, mostly west of the Cascades (rare east of the
range). Also in northeastern B.C. Very rare in northern and southern
Idaho.

ROUGH-WINGED SWALLOW *Stelgidopteryx ruficollis* 5 (128)
A dark-colored swallow of the water courses. Upper parts dark
brown; breast and throat light ashy brown; rest of lower parts white.
CALLS. A sharp *prit, preet,* or *pree-eep.* HABITAT. Prefers immediate vicinity of water, particularly slow-moving streams and rivers
where suitable nesting sites in the form of banks are available. Often
along irrigation ditches and canals in the lowlands. Forages low over
the water. RANGE. Summer resident, migrant, and breeder from
northern B.C., the southern Yukon, and southeastern Alaska
southward in the Northwest in suitable habitat. Rare winter visitor in
the Northwest states.

BANK SWALLOW *Riparia riparia* 5 (128)
A grayish-brown swallow with a conspicuous dark-brown collar on

the breast separating the white throat from the white belly. Usually seen in the vicinity of steep banks or road cuts where its manner of nesting is distinctive. CALLS. A weak burry *br-rit,* often rapidly repeated as a harsh twitter. HABITAT. Restricted to areas where proper sand or earth banks are present for placing of the burrows for nesting which are clustered in colonies. Foraging is done over water or land in the vicinity of the colony. River bluffs, sides of dry or wet gulches, road and railroad cuts, etc., are frequented. RANGE. Summer resident and breeder from northcentral Alaska and the central Yukon south in preferred habitat through the remainder of the Northwest, mostly east of the Cascades, though a few records west of that range (probably migrants).

BARN SWALLOW *Hirundo rustica* 6-7 (153-178)
A large swallow with a deeply forked tail. Upper parts bluish black; throat and breast brick red; belly orange. CALLS. A short sharp *kvit, kvik-kvik,* etc., with a dry rattling of the bill; alarm note is an emphatic *kleet-ik.* SONG. A harsh rolling succession of notes often long continued. HABITAT. Frequents vicinity of water for foraging and nesting sites. Must have overhanging facilities (natural or man-made) for the latter. Water for drinking a necessity. Adapting well to the edifices of man, such as bridges, barns, and covered walkways and eaves. RANGE. Summer resident, breeder, and migrant from northcentral Alaska and the southern Yukon south through the Northwest. Rare winter visitor. Prefers areas near water.

CLIFF SWALLOW *Petrochelidon pyrrhonota* 5-6 (128-153) Fig. 77
This species is distinguished from other swallows by its tan rump patch, square tail, buffy-white forehead, dark reddish throat, white belly, and burnished blackish wings and back. CALLS. A short low *chur;* the dry twittering, sounding like the squeaking of a rusty door, is distinctive. HABITAT. Usually in the vicinity of water for drinking, muddy shores for nest building materials, and insect-laden airways for foraging. In addition, rough rock surfaces for attaching nests (canyon walls, cliffs, and weathered walls of buildings). RANGE. Summer resident and migrant, as well as breeder, from central Alaska and central Yukon south in suitable habitat through the Northwest. Very rare in early winter as migratory straggler. Not as abundant recently as in former years.

WAGTAILS

100. Water Pipit (Fisher)

The wagtails and pipits comprise the family Motacillidae of some 48 World species, three of which have been recorded in the Pacific Northwest. They are medium- to small-sized birds with thin slender bills, long legs for walking — not hopping — and long toes and nails. The hind toe claw is often considerably elongated. They have a habit of wagging the tail up and down, hence the name.

The Water Pipit is the commonest of the three wagtails in the Northwest. It is one of the few birds that breeds in the Arctic-alpine Zone in the high mountains. Here, in the summer amid the fields of rocks, snowbanks, and low-growing forbs, one finds these slender long-tailed birds with their bobbing tail-wagging walk moving about over the barren surfaces or flying close to the ground with a soft "pipit" call note. They are birds of the open places and great numbers of them nest in the far north where they seemed to the author, on his several trips to the Arctic, to be the most abundant bird of the tundra. With us in the Pacific Northwest, however, they spend the summers in the region above timberline, till colder weather in September forces them down to the open places in the lowlands, such as the tideflats, fallow fields, meadows, shores, and other similar open areas.

211

101. Water Pipit nest and young (Boggs)

PACIFIC NORTHWEST SPECIES

WHITE WAGTAIL *Motacilla alba* 7 (178)

The strikingly contrastive color pattern of this pipit-like bird is distinctive. The crown, collar, and/or throat and breast, and tail (white outer feathers) are black. The sides of the head and forehead, as well as the throat, are whitish as are the breast and belly. The male has a black throat and breast in spring. The wings are black, extensively marked with white. CALLS. A two-parted *tsa-weep.* SONG. A seldom-heard twittering. HABITAT. Open areas, such as farmlands, meadows, and rocky places, often near water. RANGE. Breeder and summer resident in western Alaska; rare migrant in the Aleutian Islands. Rare migrational straggler, February to June, west of the Cascades in the Northwest and south to eastern Oregon.

RED-THROATED PIPIT *Anthus cervinus* 6 (153)

Similar to the Water Pipit, but this species has an unspotted brick-red throat, less of an eye-stripe, and more of a striped crown and back. In winter, the throat is whitish while the breast and sides are spotted and striped with sooty-brown. CALLS. A sharp *choop,* a hoarse *tsee-ah,* and a *tsweerp.* SONG. A series of thin *tswees.* HABITAT. In migration, open areas (mudflats, wet meadows, and agricultural fields). RANGE. Rare summer visitor and breeder in the Bering Strait region.

Very rare, irregular, migratory visitor southward in the Northwest, mostly in flocks of Water Pipits, and west of the Cascades and along salt water and ocean coast, though there are more than 60 records for California and the species must pass through our region, there seems to be only one record (San Juan Island, Washington, late summer) for the Pacific Northwest.

WATER PIPIT *Anthus spinoletta* 6-7 (153-178) Figs. 100 and 101
A sparrow-sized ground bird of the open places that walks (not hops) and constantly bobs its tail. Upper parts grayish brown; tail dark with white outer feathers; light line over eyes; under parts buffy, streaked on breast and sides with dusky. Bill slender. CALLS. A short sharp *tsee-teep* or *pi-pit*. SONG. A staccato series of *chuweets;* also a *tsr-ee, tsr-ee*. HABITAT. Prefers the open tundra of the high mountains in summer, moving down in September to the open areas in the lowlands, such as tideflats, beaches, and fields. RANGE. Summer resident and breeder in open tundra areas throughout Alaska and the Yukon south in alpine tundra to northern California and central Idaho. Winters and migrates through the Northwest states and southern B.C., wandering widely. Mostly a migrant in eastern Washington and northern Idaho.

SHRIKES

102. Northern Shrike (Fisher)

PACIFIC NORTHWEST SPECIES

LOGGERHEAD SHRIKE *Lanius ludovicianus* 9 (230) Fig. 103
Very similar to the Northern Shrike, but is slightly smaller and
without the markings on the breast. The bill is sharply hooked at the
tip. CALLS. A harsh scolding *bzee, bzee.* SONG. A halting, varied,
Mockingbird-like collection of notes and phrases, often in pairs, as
queedle, queedle, queedle. HABITAT. Occurs in open country with frequent perching posts for prey-spotting and brushy thickets or low trees
for nesting. Sagebrush and juniper commonly utilized. RANGE. Summer resident and breeder from southern B.C. south through the
remainder of the Northwest, mostly east of the Cascades (no definite
breeding records for west side). Uncommon as winter straggler, both
east and west of the Cascades in Washington. In Idaho, common summer resident and breeder in the southern part, but more as a spring
migrant in the northern portion of the state.

NORTHERN SHRIKE *Lanius excubitor* 9-10 (230-255) Fig. 102
A grayish Robin-sized bird with a black facial mask, wings, and tail

(with white outer feathers). Breast is faintly barred. CALLS. Various harsh calls, such as a *chuk-chek,* or mewing *jaaeg,* though usually silent in winter. SONG. A variable warbled song reminiscent of the songs of the mimic thrushes. HABITAT. Breeds in broken or semi-open country in the northeastern part of our region, moving southward in winter through open terrain and preferring areas where there are adequate lookout posts for spotting prey. RANGE. Summer resident and breeder from northern Alaska and central Yukon south to southern Alaska and northern B.C., wintering from central Alaska and the southern Yukon southward, mostly east of the Cascades, but regularly in the Puget Sound area.

103. Loggerhead Shrike (Schultz)

104. Phainopepla (Pole)

PHAINOPEPLA *Phainopepla nitens* 7½ (191) Fig. 104
A large-sparrow-sized blackish bird with a prominent crest and large white wing patches. The female is brownish gray with grayish wing-patches. The flight is erratic and fluttering on slow wing-beats. CALLS. A liquid thrush-like *quirt*. SONG. A varied succession of mellow, but weak, two- and three-parted notes. HABITAT. Scattered woodlands and riparian brush and trees in the desert country. RANGE. Very rare migratory straggler in eastern and western Oregon.

WAXWINGS

105. Bohemian Waxwing (Fisher)

PACIFIC NORTHWEST SPECIES

BOHEMIAN WAXWING *Bombycilla garrulus* 7-8 (178-204) Fig. 105
Similar to the more common Cedar Waxwing, but grayer and with
white and yellow spots on the wings and a reddish-brown patch under
the tail. Appears to have twice the bulk of the Cedar Waxwing.
CALLS. A low trilled whistle, as *zir-r-r* or *zree-ee*. HABITAT. Breeds
in open conifers woodlands, muskegs, etc., in the northern part of the
Pacific Northwest, migrating southward to winter in the berry- or
fruit-producing lowlands, particularly suburban areas, parks, ar-
boretums, etc. RANGE. Local summer resident and breeder from
central Alaska and the Yukon south to northern Washington,
northern Idaho, and very sparsely southward. Winters from the
southern Yukon south to Washington, Oregon, and Idaho, mostly
east of the Cascades, often in large flocks.

CEDAR WAXWING *Bombycilla cedrorum* 6-7 (153-178) Fig. 106
A sleek brown bird with a long crest and a broad yellow band at the tip
of the tail; without white and yellow spots on wings and reddish-

brown under tail area found in the Bohemian Waxwing. In winter, feeds like a thrush, but in summer, like a flycatcher or swallow. The yellow belly is distinctive. CALLS. A high, thin, lisped *zee*. HABITAT. Prefers willows, alders, maples, and other deciduous trees (also some mixed coniferous), visiting fruit producing trees and flycatching in interspersed airways. Common in orchards. Wandering more in winter to the more varied southern habitats. RANGE. Summer resident and breeder from southeastern Alaska and northcentral B.C. south through the Northwest, wintering from southern B.C. south. In Idaho, uncommon local summer resident in the southern part, but more numerous as summer resident and winter visitor in the northern portion of the state.

106. Cedar Waxwing (juvenile, 1; adult, r.) (Schultz)

DIPPERS

107. Dipper (Fisher)

AMERICAN DIPPER *Cinclus mexicanus* 7-8 (178-204) Fig. 107
A dark slate-colored bird, the size of a large thrush and shaped like a
large chunky wren; conspicuous white eyelid and short stubby tail.
Usually seen in or near water where its continuous bobbing action and
blinking white eyelids are characteristic. CALLS. A loud insistent
jigic, jigic, jigic, etc. SONG. Loud, clear, and wren-like. HABITAT.
Occurs along cold, clear, fast-flowing mountain streams where shaded
waters provide adequate invertebrate food and wet canyon walls or
waterfalls for nesting sites. Occasionally found along the margins of
alpine lakes. Mostly in the mountains, but will occur along proper
habitat to sea level, dropping to the lowlands in winter. RANGE.
Resident and breeder from central Alaska and the central Yukon, as
well as the Aleutian Islands, south in the mountains and foothills
through the remainder of the Northwest. Moves to lower elevations
and lowlands in winter.

WRENS

108. Rock Wren (Fisher)

These are small, nervous, brownish birds with long slender bills and tails that are often rakishly carried almost perpendicular over the back. They are solitary and aggressive in nature. The wings are short, curved, and rounded, while the plumage contains much brown. The wings and tail are usually conspicuously barred. The wrens feed mostly on insects and have loud bubbling songs which are often rapidly repeated.

There are about 63 species of wrens, six of which are to be found, commonly or rarely, in the Pacific Northwest.

One of the interesting items the bird student learns in his hobby is that the different species and genera vary not only in color and size, but in personality and in seeming intelligence. Contrast the stately heron with the vivacious wren, the crafty jay with the stodgy coot. People have noted these differences for ages and comparisons to human types have often been made in the literature. Rimsky-Korsakoff, recognizing this anthropomorphism, makes the goddess of spring, in her fantastically beautiful opening aria in the opera, *The Snow Maiden,* sing of the migrating birds who resemble the merchants, farmers, soldiers, etc. What esthetically attractive things are our birds!

ROCK WREN *Salpinctes obsoletus* 5-6 (128-153) Figs. 108 and 111
A grayish-colored wren with grayish-brown white-spotted back, white
stripe over eye, buffy-white corners at end of tail, grayish breast finely
streaked with brownish, and a pale grayish belly. CALLS. An
emphatic *tick-eer.* SONG. An accented *tee-oo, tee-oo, tee-oo;* or
sounding like *flee-flee-flee-flee.* HABITAT. Prefers the more sunlit
cliffs and rock walls of canyons and basaltic outcroppings, as well as
talus slopes. Wanders to the rocky subalpine areas of the mountains
after the breeding season. RANGE. Summer resident, breeder, and
sparse winter visitor from southern B.C. south through the Northwest,
mostly, but not entirely, east of the Cascade crest. Occasionally found
in rocky places in high alpine areas. Occurs in the San Juan Islands.
Most individuals winter south of the region covered by this manual,
though a few winter through the Northwest in protected lowland
areas.

109. Bewick's Wren (upper l.); Winter Wren (upper r.); Long-billed Marsh Wren
(lower l.); House Wren (lower, r.) (Schultz)

110. Canyon Wren at nest (Boggs)

CANYON WREN *Salpinctes mexicanus* 5½-6 (140-153) Fig. 110
A wren of the dry rocky canyons. Upper parts brownish, finely
speckled with black and white; tail bright reddish brown, crossed by
several narrow black bars. Lower cheeks, throat, and upper breast
white. Rest of under parts reddish brown. Contrasting white throat
and dark brown body are distinctive. CALLS. A sharp wren-like *chee-*

chee. SONG. A unique brilliant "waterfall" of melody starting high and cascading downward on descending slurred double notes as *tee, tee, tee, tsee-ee, tsee-ee, tsee-a, tsee-ah, tsoo-ee, tsoo-ee.* HABITAT. Prefers partly-shaded walls of canyons and outcroppings, as well as rock slides where the proper crannies for nesting occur. Does much foraging in the shadows. Favors cliffs bordering rivers in the arid interior. RANGE. Local resident and breeder from southcentral B.C. and northern Idaho southward through the Northwest, mostly in open arid country of the interior. Very rare in winter in southern Idaho. Tends to be very irregular in distribution.

LONG-BILLED MARSH WREN *Cistothorus palustris* 4-5 (102-128) Fig. 109
A marsh-inhabiting wren with a white line over the eye and conspicuous black and white striping on the back. Remainder of upper parts brown; under parts mostly light. CALLS. A harsh *churr, churr, churr.* SONG. A preliminary emphatic *tuk, tuk, tuk,* followed by an explosion of clicking, buzzing, and sputtering sounds. HABITAT. Restricted to patches of cattails and bulrushes standing in shallow fresh water, where it often nests in colonies. RANGE. Summer resident and breeder from central B.C. southward in suitable habitat through the Northwest. Winters in Washington and Oregon, mainly in the milder western portions.

BEWICK'S WREN *Thryomanes bewickii* 5 (128) Fig. 109
Separated from other wrens by the grayish-white under parts, white line over eye, solid brown upper parts, and small white spots along sides of the tail. CALLS. A sharp *whit-whit* or *bsht.* SONG. A bright *sister, sweet, sweet, sweet;* "spring song" consists of a few weak introductory notes followed by a descending trill. HABITAT. Occurs in gardens and parks in urban areas, logged tracts, slash areas, and old burns; also common in drift logs along saltwater beaches. RANGE. Resident and breeder from western and southcentral Washington southward along the east slope of the Cascades and westward. Rare straggler to central Washington; to extreme southeastern Washington as a winter resident in lowland riparian habitat. Very rare in southern Idaho.

WINTER WREN *Troglodytes troglodytes* 4 (102) Fig. 109
A small, dark, solid-brown wren with a short stubby tail. To be seen in the deep dark woods, sneaking through the underbrush and over fallen logs. CALLS. A sharp *chick* or *chick-chick.* SONG. A prolonged, high-pitched, quavering warble, very rapidly uttered and sounding much like escaping steam from a leaking valve. HABITAT. A wren of

the deep, dark, coniferous woods, where it occurs along the moss- and fern-covered downed logs and tangled bushes, foraging on or close to the ground. Prefers the deepest densest parts of the forests. It is interesting to note that this is the common wren or "Jenny Wren" of English and European parks and gardens. The different habitats that the same species will occupy in separated parts of its range are often interesting, if not downright baffling. We wonder, however, whether the elimination of the once thick forests of Britain forced the wren to adapt to a changed environment. Are we seeing this phenomenon taking place in our own country? RANGE. Summer resident and breeder from the Aleutian and Pribilof Islands and southern Alaska and southern Yukon south in coniferous forests through the Northwest. Winters through much of the breeding area and tends to wander at that season to more open areas. As a breeder, shuns the open plains areas, restricting itself to the coniferous forests.

HOUSE WREN *Troglodytes aedon* 4-5 (102-128) Fig. 109
A small, energetic, brownish bird without distinctive markings. Similar to the Marsh Wren, but lacking white spots on the back; differs from the Canyon and Winter Wrens in having light-gray under parts, and from the Rock Wren in its unmarked throat and absence of reddish buff tail edging as well as its shorter bill. CALLS. Harsh rasp-

111. Rock Wren at nest (Boggs)

ing notes as a scolding *chur, chur,* or *chee, chee,* etc. SONG. A hurried descending *tsee-tsee, wheedle-wheedle-wheedle, widdle-widdle-widdle,* sometimes ending with an upward slurred *chur-whee.* HABITAT. Prefers the vicinity of human habitats, old orchards, farm junk piles, and old buildings, as well as burnt stumps of old conifers in open burns and pastures. Commonly nests in woodpecker holes in farm buildings, cabins, and stumps. Forages at or near the ground. RANGE. Summer resident and breeder from southern B.C. south, through the remainder of the Northwest, mostly east of the Cascades; uncommon west of that range. Very rare winter visitor in the Northwest states.

MIMIC THRUSHES

112. Mockingbird (Fisher)

The species of this group (family Mimidae) are grayish or brownish Robin-sized or larger birds with loud songs and shrubby habitats. The bill is long and slender and often down-curved and the tail is relatively long. The young have speckled breasts. The mimids are often called mimic thrushes because of their loud thrush-like songs and the tendency in this group to imitate the songs of other birds, the Mockingbird being the prime example of this trait.

225

GRAY CATBIRD *Dumetella carolinensis* 8-9 (204-230) Fig. 113
A slender blackish-gray bird, the size of a towhee, with a black cap and reddish-brown patch at the base of the tail underneath. CALLS. A mellow *phut, phut;* a cat-like *mayee.* SONG. Variable and often mimicking other songsters. HABITAT. Prefers dense deciduous thickets near water, as well as the shrubby edges of woodlands and brushy gardens. RANGE. Summer resident and breeder from southern B.C. south through the lowlands of the Northwest, mostly east of the Cascades. Rare erratic winter straggler. Less numerous as summer resident in southern Idaho.

113. Catbird (Schultz)

NORTHERN MOCKINGBIRD *Mimus polyglottos* 9-11 (230-255) Fig. 112
This "many-tongued" bird, with its long gray tail and snowy white patches, is about the size of a skinny Robin. Upper parts are ash gray, wings black (with white patches); mid-tail feathers dark; outer-tail feathers white for entire length. The under parts are grayish white; the iris yellow. This species has no black on the head as do the shrikes and can be distinguished from the Townsend's Solitaire by its lighter under parts, large white wing patches, yellow eye, and absence of an eye-ring (a noticeable white eye-ring in the solitaire). CALLS. A melodic *tee-er, tee-er,* and a noisy *tchair.* SONG. Mimicking the songs of a number of species, often repeating the song several times before picking up another "borrowed" tune. Other mimic thrushes may repeat other

bird songs once or twice, but Mockingbirds often repeat such songs several times. HABITAT. Occurs mostly in brush patches, thickets, and open woods in the Northwest. RANGE. Uncommon to rare irregular visitor throughout the year to the lowlands of the Northwest northward to southern B.C., though found more often in fall and winter. Several summer records in western Washington in 1980.

SAGE THRASHER *Oreoscoptes montana* 8-9 (204-230) Fig. 114
Size and shape of a Robin. Upper parts grayish brown with white line over eye and narrow dark streaks on buffy face. Throat white; under parts buffy white, usually heavily streaked with small brownish spots. Often seen perched on top of a sagebrush bush from which it sings lustily. CALLS. A low *chuck, chuck;* a whistled *whee-er.* SONG. A musical succession of deep-throated warbled phrases often repeated at some length. HABITAT. The open sagebrush plains of the arid interior. Sometimes found in riparian growth along streams. Forages below the tops of the bushes. Numbers strongly reduced with the continued "reclamation" of sagebrush land. RANGE. Summer resident and breeder in suitable habitat (sagebrush) from southcentral B.C. and central Idaho southward through the Northwest, mostly east of the Cascades. Occurs very locally in western Washington, as in the San Juan Islands, western Oregon, and southwestern B.C. in the nonbreeding season. Very rare in winter in eastern Oregon.

114. Sage Thrasher (Schultz)

BROWN THRASHER *Toxostoma rufum* 10-12 (255-306)
A bright, slim, Robin-sized, reddish-brown bird with long bill and tail.
Upper parts light reddish brown; two wing-bars; under parts white or
buffy white, heavily streaked and spotted on breast and sides with
dark brown; iris yellow. Could be confused with thrushes but has a
much longer tail. CALLS. A loud hiss, a three-noted whistle, a sharp
clicking *smack*. SONG. Mockingbird-like with double-noted phrases
and occasional mimicking of other birds. HABITAT. Brush and
woodland borders in arid open country. Feeds on the ground, as do
most of the thrashers. RANGE. Rare summer and migrational visitor
to Oregon, southern Idaho, eastern Washington, and western B.C.

CURVE-BILLED THRASHER *Toxostoma curvirostre* 11 (280)
A dull gray thrasher with a long curved bill. Tail is dull brownish gray,
throat white, and breast and belly dirty white to buffy white, heavily
spotted with large grayish and buffy-gray spots. Eye is red. Sides of
head light gray. Two inconspicuous white wing-bars. CALLS. A two-
or three-noted whistle, as *whit-whee;* various trills and chattering calls.
SONG. A long irregular, but melodious, carol of various short phrases
with almost no repetition. HABITAT. Dry desert country with scattered shrubs and cactus. RANGE. Very rare late summer visitor to
southern Oregon.

LeCONTE'S THRASHER *Toxostoma lecontei* 12 (306)
A large very pale gray thrasher with a long strongly down-curved bill.
Brown eye. Plumage mostly without markings, except for darker ear
patches and thin dark mustache marks at sides of whitish throat.
CALLS. A soft three-noted *ti-ti-rup*. SONG. Varied and similar to
other thrashers but loud and melodious. HABITAT. Prefers open,
arid, barren desert areas, especially those covered with shadscale
(Atriplex). RANGE. Very rare in southwestern Oregon (one record).

CALIFORNIA THRASHER *Toxostoma redivivum* 12 (306)
A large evenly-brown-colored thrasher with a long strongly-curved
bill. A black-marked face (ear patches and mustache marks) and a
white throat. Tail is long and rounded. Under tail coverts and belly are
reddish. Eye is dark brown. CALLS. A harsh *tchak* or *cheep;* a purring
churr; and a liquid *glip* or *prip*. SONG. Similar to that of the
Mockingbird but harsher. HABITAT. Densely brushed desert and
semi-desert foothills, riparian growth, parks, and residential areas.
Forages the ground beneath heavy cover. Prefers more densely
vegetated habitats than most thrashers. RANGE. Very rare early spring visitor to southern Oregon.

BLUEBIRDS

115. Mountain Bluebird (l. female; r. male) (Fisher)

PACIFIC NORTHWEST SPECIES

WESTERN BLUEBIRD *Sialia mexicana* 6-7 (153-178) Fig. 116
A sparrow-sized bluish-appearing bird. Male, head, throat, wings, and
tail blue; breast, sides, and back reddish. Belly white. Female, similar,
but paler; blue on head and back replaced by sooty gray. CALLS. A
mild whistled *pew, pew, pew;* a hard snapping note, as *chuck.* SONG.
A short mild *chee, cheer-lee, churr* carol. HABITAT. Prefers open or
broken woodland with plenty of scattered low lookout perches, open
ground for hovering foraging, and woodpecker or knot hole nesting
sites in dead trees or short snags. Burns, clearings, or open pine groves
are particularly sought after. Also open farming country. RANGE.
Local summer resident and breeder from southern B.C. south through
the Northwest, wintering rarely from the lowlands of western
Washington southward; rare to uncommon in the region in late fall
and winter. In Idaho, uncommon local summer resident and breeder
in the northern part of the state.

MOUNTAIN BLUEBIRD *Sialia currucoides* 6-7 (153-178) Figs. 115 and 123

A mostly blue sparrow-sized bird. Male, upper parts sky blue, throat and breast grayish buff. Female, blue of the male replaced by greenish gray; rump bluish gray. CALLS. A soft low *pew* or *churr*. SONG. A short, clear, caroling warble given mostly in the early morning. HABITAT. Prefers open areas or large clearings with scattered snags or fence posts with hole nesting sites. Perching sites on rocks, small trees, or broken snags necessary. Blue coloration may offer concealment from low-flying insect prey. Prefers more open country than does the Western Bluebird. RANGE. Summer resident and breeder from central Alaska and central Yukon south through the Northwest, mostly east of the Cascades, though locally in high alpine plateaus in that range and occasionally as low as 2-3,000 feet on the west slopes. Winters in Oregon and southward (rarely northward). Rare in winter in Idaho.

116. Western Bluebird (male, r.) (Schultz)

SOLITAIRES AND WHEATEARS

117. Townsend's Solitaire (Fisher)

PACIFIC NORTHWEST SPECIES

TOWNSEND'S SOLITAIRE *Myadestes townsendi* 8-9 (204-230) Fig. 117

A slender grayish bird, almost Robin size. Dark gray in color, white eye-ring; tail black with white outer feathers; buffy patch in middle of black wings. Resembles a flycatcher in aerial foraging habits. CALLS. A short, metallic, whistled *pink,* easily imitated and sure to bring the bird to the whistler. SONG. A sustained, loud, finch-like warble, most closely resembling the song of the Purple Finch. HABITAT. Prefers mountainous terrain where it often nests in cut banks along roads in dense dark woods just under the overhanging rim. Seeks the first places to be free of snow in spring. Also nests between roots at the bases of trees or in crannies in upturned roots of fallen trees. Flycatches from relatively high perches. Moves to lowlands in winter. Often migrates in large flocks through subalpine areas in early fall. RANGE. Summer resident and breeder from eastcentral Alaska and southern Yukon south through the Northwest, mostly in mountainous terrain. Winters from extreme southern B.C. southward. Rather local in occurrence, both as breeder and winter visitor. Abundant in winter in the Juniper Forest reserve of eastern Washington.

231

WHEATEAR *Oenanthe oenanthe* 6 (153)

A contrastively colored sparrow-sized bird of the open tundra, rocky slopes, hillsides, and sand dunes of the far north. In male, crown and back grayish blue, black patch through eye bordered above and below with white lines. Wings and tip and central part of tail black. Rump and upper outer tail feathers white. Female is similar, but black replaced with brown and white with buff, except on the tail. Moves by hopping, constantly bobbing and waving its tail up and down. CALLS. A high-pitched, banjo-like *chack-chack*. SONG. A thin, chattery, melodious warble. HABITAT. Prefers stony and shrubby tundra and barren mountain sides above timberline. RANGE. Breeds in northern Alaska and the central and northern Yukon. Very rare straggler to the Pacific Northwest (southwestern B.C. and eastern Oregon).

THRUSHES

118.   Veery (Fisher)

The typical thrushes are shy, modestly-colored, woodland or forest birds with pleasant flute-like songs and Robin-like bills. Foraging is done mostly on the ground where earthworms and insects are procured and in bushes and small trees where berries and fruits are gathered. The spotted-breasted species are very similar in appearance and must be identified with care when studied visually. The songs are very distinctive, and, since thrushes are more often heard than seen, the beginner in bird study will find it useful to become acquainted with these notes.

The family Turdidae, the thrushes in the broad sense, are a large group numbering somewhat over 300 species. Bluebirds, solitaires, wheatears, robins, and spotted-breasted thrushes make up the representation in the Northwest. Many have pleasing voices and, in fact, the Gray Solitaire of the New World tropics is considered by many birders to be the finest of singers.

PACIFIC NORTHWEST SPECIES

VARIED THRUSH *Zoothera naevius* 9-10 (230-253) Fig. 121
This is a bird of the dense forests, very similar to the Robin, but with orange eye-stripe and wing-bars and a black band across a salmon-red breast. The remainder of the head, back, and tail is bluish slate. CALLS. A low *cherk*. SONG. A slow series of detached drawn-out notes, each of a different pitch, resembling single notes blown on a harmonica. HABITAT. Occurs in dense, heavy, coniferous timber in the foothills and mountains where it forages mostly over the moss-covered floor and occasionally to the lower branches of trees. Descends to the lowlands in winter (commonly urban yards and gardens) but re-enters the forests in March and April to follow the retreating snowline. RANGE. Summer resident and breeder from central Alaska and central Yukon southward, west of the Cascades to California and, east of that range, to northeastern Oregon, northern Idaho, and northwestern Montana. Winters at lower elevations from southern B.C. southward.

VEERY *Catharus fuscescens* 7½ (191) Fig. 118
This is a shy thrush of the dense woodlands and thickets along streams. Upper parts uniform brown. Throat and upper breast buffy, lightly spotted with brownish. Rest of under parts whitish. The most indistinctly spotted of our typical thrushes. CALLS. A low *phee-oo*. SONG. A descending series of double notes, as *whee-a, whee-a, vee-er, vee-er* of deep flute-like quality given usually in the late afternoon and evening. HABITAT. Occurs mostly in thick willow and alder (or other deciduous) riparian growth along streams where it forages and sings in the densest places. RANGE. Summer resident and breeder from northcentral B.C. southward in preferred habitat through the Northwest east of the Cascades. Less common and irregularly distributed in the open southern part of the region. More numerous east of the Cascades than west of the range where records are few.

GRAY-CHEEKED THRUSH *Catharus minimus* 7¾ (198)
Very similar to the Swainson's Thrush, but grayish cheeks and throat and is slightly larger; somewhat less buffy below and lacks an eye-ring. Best identified by voice. CALLS. A downward slurred *wheeoo,* somewhat like the call of a Nighthawk. SONG. Very similar to that of the Veery but rises in pitch at the end, not falling as in the other species. HABITAT. The northern spruce forests, near tree line in the mountains, and in the stunted growth near the northern latitudinal tree line. The most northerly occurring of the spotted-breasted thrushes in North America. RANGE. Summer resident and breeder from the northern limit of trees in Alaska and the northern Yukon south to southwestern Alaska and northern B.C. Of accidental occurrence in fall in Idaho.

SWAINSON'S THRUSH *Catharus ustulatus* 7 (178) Fig. 120
A shy brown-backed bird with a slender bill, spotted breast (small greenish-brown spots arranged in streaks), and a tail of the same color as the back. Throat, breast, and eye-ring buffy. CALLS. A querulous *quirt* or whistled *whit-whee;* a harsh whinnying *ker-hee-ee-ee.* SONG. A melodious series of flute-like notes as *wher-wher, wheelia, wheelia, wheelia;* the two introductory notes are on the same pitch, but each of the following phrases climbs upward. At distance may sound like *real-you, real-you.* HABITAT. Prefers shaded alder, maple, or willow thickets along streams or bodies of water where it forages in low wet foliage and on the ground. Also in coniferous woods with dense understory of deciduous brush. Sings mostly in the evening till dark. RANGE. Summer resident and breeder from central Alaska and the central Yukon south through the Northwest in the lowlands and middle elevations in the mountains. Rare winter visitor west of the Cascades.

HERMIT THRUSH *Catharus guttatus* 7 (178)
A shy brownish-backed bird with a slender bill, spotted breast (the large sooty-brown spots arranged in streaks), and reddish tail and rump; throat and breast white or buffy. Somewhat larger than a sparrow. CALLS. A whistled *chee* or low *chuck.* SONG. A series of detached trilled phrases, each introduced by a prolonged clear note of marvelous flute-like quality; the song sections (introduction plus trill) often alternated in higher and lower pitches. HABITAT. Occurs in the subalpine and upper montane forest areas in summer where scattered trees for singing posts and nearby meadows for surface foraging are available, migrating in the lower areas in spring and early fall. A thrush of the subalpine groves where its beautiful song is a delight to the mountain hiker. RANGE. Summer resident and breeder from central

119. Swainson's Thrush on nest (Boggs)

120. Varied Thrush at nest with young (Boggs)

235

Alaska and the central Yukon south in the mountains of the Northwest, wintering from eastern and western Washington (uncommon), northern Idaho (rare), and Oregon southward (rarely northward). Uncommon migrant through the lowlands.

WOOD THRUSH *Hylocichla mustelina* 8 (204)
Characterized by clear brownish upper parts and whitish under parts which are entirely covered by large round black or dark brown spots. Throat and ear patches streaked with gray and white; a white eye-ring. CALLS. A short sharp *quirt;* a *pit, pit, pit;* or a low *tuck, tuck.* SONG. A short melodious series of usually three notes, the first high, the second low, and the third a high trill, as *cedar-lee.* HABITAT. Prefers deciduous woodlands, particularly near water, frequently the ground and lower branches of the over-hanging trees. RANGE. Rare migrational straggler in southern Idaho and eastern Oregon.

121. American Robin (Pole)

ROBINS

AMERICAN ROBIN *Turdus migratorius* 8-10 (204-253) Figs. 119 and 122
The familiar bird of our backyards and lawns. Head, wings, and tail blackish; white streaks on the throat; back grayish; bill yellow; under parts brick red. Characteristically flips its tail upon alighting on a branch or wire. CALLS. Various short sharp notes; a loud thin hiss (food call of young). SONG. The familiar series of rising and falling phrases, usually four in number and repeated many times. HABITAT. Requires soft earth for worms, mud for lining the nest, bushes and low trees for nest sites, and berries and fruit as provided by urban lawns and gardens, forest edges, and the shores of lakes and rivers. Strongly territorial during the nesting season but gathers in large flocks in late fall and winter. RANGE. Summer resident and breeder throughout the Northwest from the limit of trees in Alaska and the Yukon south. Winters from southern B.C. southward. Recently recorded in winter from the southern Yukon. In Idaho, common summer resident throughout, but a common winter resident mostly in the southern portion, especially in the junipers of the southeastern part; uncommon in the northern portion of the state in winter.

122. Young Robin on nest (Boggs)

123. Mountain Bluebird at nest with young (Boggs). Note the spotted plumage of the young, a characteristic of many thrushes. Compare with the preceding figure (122).

BABBLERS

124. Wrentit (Fisher)

WRENTIT *Chamaea fasciata* 6½ (166) Fig. 124
A small, long-tailed, loose-feathered, brownish-gray bird of the dense brush and chaparral with a wren-like behavior. Seldom seen but easily heard. Forages within the shrubbery and rarely leaves the fastnesses of such cover. CALLS. A series of double notes, as *weeka, weeka, weeka, weeka,* etc. a rasping purring, as *prr, prr, prr.* SONG. A long series of loud notes on one pitch and accelerating into a trill at the end, as *yip, yip, yip-yip-yip-yip-yiter-tr-tr-tr-tr-r-r-r-r.* HABITAT. Dense brush, especially of evergreen broad-leaved species, on hillsides and lower mountain slopes and along streams. RANGE. Uncommon resident and breeder in the lowlands of western Oregon, mostly in the southern half and primarily along the coast in the northern part of western Oregon. Rare in southwestern Washington. A few stragglers along the Columbia River as far east as near the mouth of the Snake River. One record for the Puget Sound area.

OLD WORLD WARBLERS, GNATCATCHERS, AND KINGLETS

125. Blue-gray Gnatcatcher (Fisher)

This is an immense family of some 325 species scattered pretty well around the planet. Three groups are represented in the Pacific Northwest avifauna: the gnatcatchers, a small group of 12 New World forms; the Old World warblers, a large group of extremely difficult birds to separate (a few penetrate North America); and the kinglets, New World representatives of the firecrest group.

PACIFIC NORTHWEST SPECIES

BLUE-GRAY GNATCATCHER *Polioptila caerulea* 4-5 (102-128)
Figs. 125 and 126
A tiny grayish bird resembling a miniature Mockingbird but with kinglet habits. Blue-gray above and white below. Tail long and black with white on the outer-most feathers, often cocked in a wren-like fashion. Head blue-gray with a black stripe extending across the forehead and along the sides of the crown forming a conspicuous U-shaped mark; white eye-ring present; bill short and thin. A restless active insect forager. CALLS. A quick *ting* or thin *zpee* or

126. Blue-gray Gnatcatcher at nest with young (Boggs)

chee. SONG. Thin, squeaky, and difficult to hear. HABITAT. Open deciduous woodlands, brushy thickets with interspersed mature trees, and riparian woods. RANGE. Uncommon summer resident and breeder in southern Idaho, southeastern Oregon, and in southern and southwestern Oregon north to Medford, Crater Lake, and Big Lake. Very rarely north to southwestern B.C. and western Washington as a migrational straggler and winter visitor.

ARCTIC WARBLER *Phylloscopus borealis* 5 (128) Fig. 127
Closely resembles a vireo; greenish above and buffy white below with a conspicuous light eye-line. Bill is slender and sharp-pointed. Very active in foraging and continuously flicks its wings. CALLS. A husky *tssp* or *tsick;* a rattling *drr-drr-drr.* SONG. A high-pitched *tsik, tsik, tsik, zi-zi-zi-zi.* HABITAT. Prefers the broken woods and brush patches of the far north, especially near streams. Deep dense birch thickets are particularly sought after. RANGE. Summer resident and breeder in western and central Alaska. Very rare fall migrational straggler to western Washington (Seattle, October 14, 1978). *Note.* This record is considered doubtful by some authorities, and is included mainly to emphasize the need for careful observation, note-taking, and preferably photographs in recording unusual species.

127. Arctic Warbler (Pole)

RUBY-CROWNED KINGLET *Regulus calendula* 3-4 (76-102)
A tiny denizen of the shrubbery and woodlands with an out-sized voice. Upper parts grayish green; under parts dirty white; eye-ring and wing-bars white; center of crown red in male, but rarely visible. CALLS. A sharp *chit-it* and a *chleyew* rapidly uttered. SONG. A rapid *see-see-see, tee-tee-tee-tew-tew, wher-her-hee, wher-her-hee, wher-her-hee;* also given by Harry Nehls as *chee-ti-tutu-tutu-cheeva-cheeva-cheeva-weetu-weetu-weetu-weet.* The elements of the song are somewhat variable and individuals have a habit of aborting certain parts. HABITAT. Prefers brushy, rather dense, coniferous growth with open edges, especially fir, lodgepole pine, and hemlock. Forages from intermediate levels downward and places the nest at medium

heights in trees. Wanders widely to a variety of habitats in winter. RANGE. Summer resident and breeder from central Alaska and the central Yukon south through the Northwest, wintering from southern B.C. southward, often commonly, in suitably protected places, mostly west of the Cascades. Common breeder in southern Idaho mountains.

GOLDEN-CROWNED KINGLET *Regulus satrapa* 3-4 (76-102) Fig. 128
A tiny bird of the tall conifers with greenish-gray upper parts, brownish white under parts, white and black stripes over the eye, and an orange-red crown bordered by yellow. The crown is solid yellow in the female. Usually seen in high branches of coniferous trees. CALLS. A thin *see, see, see.* SONG. A rising series of thin *sees,* dropping into a chatter at the end. HABITAT. Prefers dense, tall, coniferous forests (especially Douglas fir) where it forages high in the canopy and places its nest near the tips of branches. Wanders to more varied wooded habitats in winter. RANGE. Summer resident and breeder from southern Alaska and the southern Yukon south through the Northwest, wintering and migrating from central B.C. southward.

128. Golden-crowned Kinglet (male, l.; female, r.) (Fisher)

TITMICE

129. Chestnut-backed Chickadee (Fisher)

The titmice of the family Paridae contain some 14 species in North America of which we have six in the Pacific Northwest. These birds are placed in various families and genera by different workers and perhaps represent a point of view rather than actually related or unrelated groups. All of this is of little importance to the birder who enjoys birds for their own sake. And in this esthetic sense, few groups of birds are better appreciated and loved by the amateur ornithologist than the chickadees. Resident in their chosen ranges, these little gems of bird life are commonly found in coniferous timber or deciduous woods and brush where their sprightly actions and cheery songs and calls are to be seen and heard in all weather, even in the midst of swirling snowstorms and biting sub-zero cold. Tame and gentle, chickadees allow the closest approach of any bird and thus are special friends of the bird student. In winter, they travel in flocks and the bright tinkling of their calls often is the only bird song in the somber landscape.

A series of tinkling *bseets* out in the rose hedge announces the appearance of a little troop of bushtits in the garden. They go about their inspection of the insect situation in a business-like manner, slowly

244

moving through the hedge and continually uttering the little call note. In a few minutes, they are gone and the bugs in the roses have been materially reduced.

The birder has to go to southernmost parts of the Northwest to find the Plain Titmouse, a drab-looking member of the group with certain chickadee-like calls. Its discovery, however, is well worth the effort.

PACIFIC NORTHWEST SPECIES

BUSHTIT *Psaltriparus minimus* 4 (102)
This species is a tiny drab-gray bird, smaller than a chickadee, with a brownish cap, grayish body, very short small bill, and a long tail. It commonly travels in flocks through the bushes and small trees. CALLS. A light *bseet* and similar notes more or less continually uttered. A light rapid trill used by a flock in unison is the alarm note. HABITAT. Prefers tall shrubs and small tree thickets, especially near water, such as willows and small conifers. Ocean spray is a favorite. Common in residential areas where there is considerable growth of ornamental shrubbery. RANGE. Resident and breeder from southwestern B.C. (including southern Vancouver Island) south in the coastal belt to California and locally in southcentral Washington, eastern Oregon, and southern Idaho. Occasional straggler as far east as the Walla Walla area in Washington.

130. Mountain Chickadee at nest hole (Boggs)

BLACK-CAPPED CHICKADEE *Parus atricapillus* 4-5 (102-128) Fig. 135

A small chickadee with a black cap and bib, white cheeks, gray back, and dirty-white under parts. CALLS. A soft *tsick;* a clear *chick-a-dee-dee-dee;* a plaintive whistled *hee-hee, heer-heer* or *fee-bee-a, fee-bee-a* given in spring. HABITAT. Occurs mostly in deciduous or mixed deciduous-coniferous woods and thickets near water in low to intermediate elevations, seldom penetrating the denser forests. RANGE. Resident and breeder from central Alaska and westcentral Yukon southward in preferred habitat through the remainder of the Northwest (exclusive of Vancouver Island). Moves rather widely in winter.

MOUNTAIN CHICKADEE *Parus gambeli* 5 (128) Figs. 130 and 135

Similar to the Black-capped Chickadee, but has a white line through the cap over each eye. Back, sides, and wings are grayish brown. CALLS. "Chickadee" note similar to that of the Chestnut-backed Chickadee but slower and more nasal, as *zicka, dya, dya, dya.* SONG.

131. Boreal Chickadee and Plain Titmouse (Pole)

132. Plain Titmouse at nest hole (Boggs)

A loud whistled *hee-heeee, ho-hoooo,* sometimes sounding like the "Three Blind Mice" tune. HABITAT. Prefers the open to semi-open coniferous forests of the mountains generally and pine-covered areas of the interior in particular. In the Cascades-Coast Range complexes, primarily a species of the timberline areas. Open woods for foraging, snags for old woodpecker holes are necessities. Common in the yellow pine areas. RANGE. Resident and breeder from northwestern B.C. south through the mountains of the Northwest, mostly east of the Cascade crest, though occasionally wandering westward, particularly in fall and winter. Moves to the lowlands out of the coniferous forests in winter.

BOREAL CHICKADEE; HUDSONIAN CHICKADEE *Parus hudsonicus* 5½ (140) Fig. 131
Similar to the more widely distributed Black-capped Chickadee, but is dark in color with grayish-brown cap and back, dull reddish sides, brownish-black throat patch, and grayish sides of head, breast, and belly. CALLS. A slow hoarse *zick-a-day-day.* HABITAT. Prefers open to semi-open coniferous or mixed coniferous-deciduous woods, mostly in the more northern mountainous areas of our region. RANGE. Resident and breeder from the northern limit of trees south to the mountains of northcentral and northeastern Washington and northern

247

Idaho. Recorded in the lowland foothills of northeastern Washington and northern Idaho in late summer, fall, and winter.

CHESTNUT-BACKED CHICKADEE *Parus rufescens* 4-5 (102-128) Fig. 129
Similar to the Black-capped Chickadee but has a reddish back, brown cap, brownish-black throat, reddish sides, and whitish under parts. CALLS. A harsh *check-check;* "chickadee" note similar to that of the Black-capped, but more nasal in quality and uttered more rapidly. There is no whistled "spring song". HABITAT. Prefers dense coniferous forests where it forages in the higher parts of the trees. Western lowlands and mountains preferred where proper timbered habitat is available, often along streams. RANGE. Resident and breeder in southwestern Alaska, western B.C. (including Vancouver Island), western Washington, and western and southcentral Oregon, and locally in the mountains and heavy lowland forests of southeastern B.C., eastern Washington, eastern Oregon, northern Idaho, and western Montana.

PLAIN TITMOUSE *Parus inornatus* 5 (128) Figs. 131 and 132
The only small gray-backed bird with a pointed crest in the Northwest. It is uniformly gray to gray-brown with no distinctive markings. Although the crest may not always be noticeable, the plainness and chickadee-like behavior reveal its identity. CALLS. A hearty *tsick-a-dee-dee, tsee-tse-tse-sicka-dee, weety-weety-weety,* or *peter-peter-peter.* HABITAT. Prefers juniper-pinyon, juniper, or other open dry country coniferous woods and deciduous thickets. RANGE. Resident and breeder in southern Oregon and southern Idaho (south of the Snake River). Rare north of the Snake River in southern Idaho.

NUTHATCHES

These are chunky little birds smaller than sparrows that are often seen creeping down the bark of tree trunks or ranging along branches hunting for insects. The bill is slender and long as the head, while the tail is very short. The plumage is soft and fluffy and without bars, streaks, or spots. The nuthatches seem large-headed. They are most often seen working down a tree trunk, up-side down.

At present, there are considered to be about 24 species of nuthatches and relatives around the World, three of which occur in the Pacific Northwest and are widely distributed in the region. Widest ranging and most common is the Red-breasted Nuthatch with its red breast and white line over the eye. Somewhat irregular in distribution

133. White-breasted Nuthatch (female, 1.; male, r.) (Fisher)

is the White-breasted Nuthatch. One must look in the yellow pine forests of the interior for a sight of the tiny Pygmy Nuthatch.

PACIFIC NORTHWEST SPECIES

PYGMY NUTHATCH *Sitta pygmaea* 4 (102)
A small nuthatch with a brownish-gray head, bluish-gray back, black ear-patch, white spot on nape, and buffy under parts. CALLS. A moderate *kit, kit, kit,* etc., in flocking; a rapid *ti-di, ti-di, ti-di,* etc. HABITAT. Prefers yellow pine groves often on foothill ridge-tops, where it forages among the crowns and higher branches of the trees. Nests are placed at least 30 feet above the ground in dead snags or tree trunks. A tree-top nuthatch. RANGE. Resident and breeder from southern B.C. south through the interior of the Northwest. Rare vagrant west of the Cascades; most records for spring and summer. In Idaho, common in suitable habitat in the northern part, but irregular and local in southern Idaho (not present in southeastern portion).

RED-BREASTED NUTHATCH *Sitta canadensis* 4-5 (102-128) Fig. 135
A small nuthatch with a black head and white line over the eye; rest of upper parts bluish gray; under parts, including throat, reddish brown.

CALLS. A nasal *nyenk* or *nyat,* etc., repeated a number of times; also an endless *kit-kit-kit-kit,* etc., which seems to be an alarm note. HABITAT. Occurs in coniferous and mixed forests and woodlands where fir trees are a preferred species for foraging. Dead snags a necessity for nesting. Searches for food in the branches of trees. RANGE. Resident and breeder from southeastern Alaska and the southern Yukon south through the Northwest, wandering somewhat in fall and winter, sometimes invading the lowlands in great numbers.

WHITE-BREASTED NUTHATCH *Sitta carolinensis* 5-6 (128-153) Figs. 133 and 134

A large nuthatch with a black crown and nape, bluish-gray back, and white sides of head, shoulders, and under parts. CALLS. A nasal *tan, tan, tan;* a low mellow *too, too, too;* also a sharp nasal *keer, keer.* HABITAT. Occurs mostly in pine woods in the more arid interior; also at timberline in the mountains. Snags needed for nesting and it forages on the rough bark of tree trunks. Uncommon around the wooded edges of prairies, clearings, and burns west of the Cascade axis. RANGE. Scattered local resident and breeder from central B.C. southward, wandering somewhat to adjacent parts of the Northwest lowlands in winter. Common in the oak woods south of Puget Sound.

134. White-breasted Nuthatch at nest hole (Boggs)

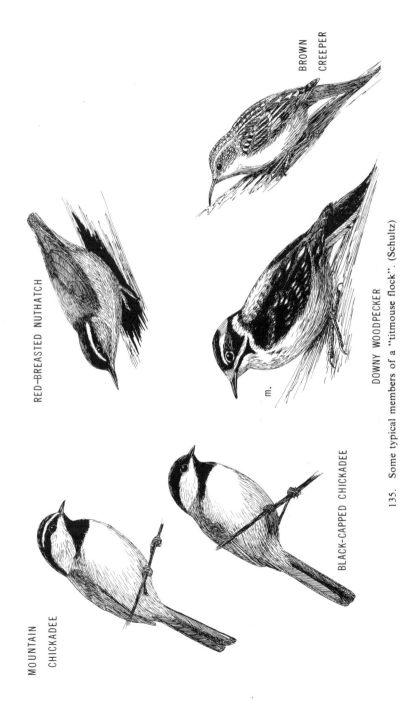

MOUNTAIN
CHICKADEE

RED–BREASTED NUTHATCH

BROWN
CREEPER

DOWNY WOODPECKER

BLACK-CAPPED CHICKADEE

135. Some typical members of a "titmouse flock". (Schultz)

251

CREEPERS

136. Brown Creeper (Fisher)

BROWN CREEPER *Certhia familiaris* 5-6 (128-153) Figs. 135 and 136

A small, black-streaked, brownish, warbler-sized bird with a long curved bill and a long tail; under parts grayish. Usually seen creeping up the bark of a tree trunk which it closely resembles in color. CALLS. A faint sustained kinglet-like *tsee* or *tsick,* usually given in pairs, which separates it from the Golden-crowned Kinglet's call. SONG. A weak lisping series on several pitches, such as *tsee-tsee-tsee-ti-ti-tsee,* not cascading downward like that of the Golden-crowned Kinglet, but closer and louder. Most notes of the creeper are probably mistaken for those of the kinglet. HABITAT. Forages on trunks and larger branches of coniferous trees, particularly fir and hemlocks, in dense mature forests. In foraging, begins at the base of a tree and climbs upward, circling the trunk, till the higher branches are reached, then flies down to the base of the next tree. Often heard, but seldom seen. RANGE. Resident and breeder from southcentral Alaska and the southern Yukon southward through the Northwest in coniferous forests, occasionally invading the lowlands in considerable numbers.

252

ARCTIC BUNTINGS

137. Chestnut-collared Longspur (male) (Pole)

In the treatment of the following groups, this manual makes a marked departure from the arrangement of most guides of the past in separating the sparrow-like and finch-like birds into two major groups, the buntings of the family Emberizidae and the true finches of the family Fringillidae. The two groups are only distantly related and resemble each other through convergent evolution of seed-eating characters rather than on the basis of close relationship. Our North American sparrows are really buntings. The family Emberizidae is a very large one, numbering some 554 species around the World of which we have 49 species in the Pacific Northwest.

The Arctic Buntings are of special interest to Pacific Northwest birders as they are mostly on the scarce side, to be found primarily in the winter-time in open wind-swept habitats, and are ambassadors from the far northern climes that most people never see. It has been the good fortune of the author to see several of these buntings on their boreal breeding grounds where they show off their interesting and often contrastive plumages on the barren tundra and rock. As men-

253

tioned earlier in this manual, if we would seek birds such as these in winter in our southern region, we must visit habitats as close to the summer ecotypes as possible. These are birds that are well worth searching for.

PACIFIC NORTHWEST SPECIES

RUSTIC BUNTING *Emberiza rustica* 5¾ (147)

Head of male with striking black and white pattern (black crown and broad stripe through eye; white line over eye and white throat). Rusty collar, sides, and back. White belly. Mustache marks indistinct. Duller in winter and like female. Female, paler with black replaced with rusty. Outer tail feathers mostly white in both sexes. Cinnamon streaks on white breast and sides are distinctive. CALLS. A sharp *tick*. SONG. Short, melodious, and rather tinkling. RANGE. Uncommon on Kiska, Adak, and Amchitka Islands in the Aleutians. Recorded in fall in the Queen Charlotte Islands, B.C. Like so many far northern species, a few individuals may straggle southward in fall migration, evidently trying the North American migration route, rather than the Asiatic one.

McCOWN'S LONGSPUR *(Calcarius mccownii* 6 (153)

A gray-headed brownish bird of the open grassy country with a black crown, mustache, and patch on breast. Throat white; rest of under parts gray, fading to white on abdomen. Central tail feathers and tip of tail black, remainder of tail white. Large chestnut patch at bend of wing. Female and fall immature, brown above and buffy below, lacking most of the black and gray of spring; a few black feathers scattered on the breast; faint chestnut tint at bend of wing. Best field mark is characteristic tail pattern. CALLS. A dry rattling sound. SONG. Clear warbles, given in flight. RANGE. Rare visitor to southern B.C. Possible rare summer resident in southeastern Idaho where it has been recorded in late winter. Very rare late summer and fall visitor east of the Cascades in the Northwest states.

LAPLAND LONGSPUR *Calcarius lapponicus* 6-7 (153-178)

A sparrow-like bird with upper parts streaked with black, a brownish nape, and whitish or buffy under parts streaked with small black spots along the sides and across the throat (to form a collar). Tail black, edged with white. CALLS. A rattling twittering series of *chirs* and a whistled *too-ee* in flight. HABITAT. Open areas in the lowlands in winter and migration; commonly on mudflats and ocean beaches and dunes, often in company with Horned Larks and other Arctic buntings, as well as Water Pipits. In the interior, prefers open windswept plains and stubble fields. RANGE. Summer resident and breeder in the Aleutians, Alaska, and the central Yukon, especially along the coasts of the Arctic Ocean, migrating and wintering regularly and often commonly from southern B.C. southward, mostly in the open areas along the ocean coast and in the arid interior. Rare winter visitor in southern Alaska and the Aleutians. Common in migration through the southern Yukon. Occasionally seen in early fall along the Washington coast; very rare in western Washington in summer (one record of a vagrant individual).

SMITH'S LONGSPUR *Calcarius pictus* 6½ (166)
A distinctively marked longspur with (in male) a black ear-patch (white dot in center) and crown. Line over eye and chin white. Under parts pinkish buff. Upper parts brown-streaked. White outer feathers (all the way to the tips). Female, similar, but duller, with striped breast and sides and without pinkish buff under parts. Male in winter, like the female. A black and white patch on the shoulder of the male in all plumages. CALLS. A rapid series of clicking notes. HABITAT. Prefers open areas in migration, such as fields, meadows, airports, etc. RANGE. Summer resident and breeder in northern Alaska (Brooks Range) and central Yukon and in scattered areas in central Alaska and northwestern B.C. Rare migrational straggler as far south as northwestern Oregon, especially in the fall. Some doubt has been expressed as to the validity of the Oregon records.

CHESTNUT-COLLARED LONGSPUR *Calcarius ornatus* 6¼ (159)
Fig. 137
Male in summer is most characteristic with its striped yellow, white, and black face and chestnut-colored nape and back contrasted with the black breast and belly. The female is a plain striped sparrow-like bird of no particularly identifiable pattern. The winter male is similar to the summer plumage, but the black under parts are more or less hidden by buffy feather tips. CALLS. A liquid *til-lip;* twittering notes of alarm. SONG. A weak high-pitched series of notes usually given in flight. HABITAT. Grassy plains and prairies. RANGE. Uncommon migratory and winter visitor in B.C. and elsewhere in the Northwest; occurs mostly along saltwater beaches, jetties, etc. Summer records in Washington are of vagrant coastal strays. Very rare in spring in southern Idaho.

SNOW BUNTING *Plectrophenax nivalis* 6-7 (153-178)
An uncommon winter visitor to open plains, occasionally mixing in with Horned Larks and other Arctic buntings. Mostly white with crown, nape, sides of breasts, and back brownish; wings and tail black

and white. CALLS. A clear whistled *teer* or *tee-oo,* uttered in flight; a musical rolling whistle; a conversational *tut-tut-tut-tew;* and a harsh *bzz.* HABITAT. Prefers in winter and migration the open beaches, tideflats, and sand dunes of the ocean coast and the broad grasslands and stubble fields of the interior. Often visits the sides of extensive road cuts and other exposed soil surfaces. RANGE. Summer resident and breeder from the Arctic coasts of Alaska and the Yukon south to the Aleutians and Kodiak area, wintering south from southern Alaska through the Northwest, mostly east of the Cascades but often common in open areas along the ocean coast, as at Leadbetter Point, Washington.

McKAY'S BUNTING *Plectrophenax hyperboreus* 7 (178)
Similar to the Snow Bunting, except that this species is much whiter. In summer almost entirely white; in winter, much lighter with very little color on the head and back. CALLS. A twittering song given by the male in flight. RANGE. Summer resident and breeder on Hall and St. Matthew Islands of the Bering Sea, wintering on the coast of western Alaska and the Alaskan Peninsula. Straggles very rarely to the Northwest coast (two records; Ocean Shores, Washington, winter of 1978-79; Portland, Oregon area, March 1980).

SPARROWS

138. Savannah Sparrow (Schultz)

The sparrows are small compact birds with short, conical, canary-like bills which are similar in size and body shape to the House Sparrow. For the most part, the sparrows are brownish in color and heavily streaked on the back. They feed largely on seeds which are expertly hulled by the cone-shaped bill. Sparrows are primarily ground feeding birds, less commonly foraging in brush and trees. Although some species are rather similar in appearance, the songs are distinctive and close attention to plumage color details and habitat will help for ready identification.

Twenty-four species of sparrows occur, commonly or rarely, in the Pacific Northwest. They range from such brush-inhabiting kinds as the Song, Lincoln's, and Fox Sparrows to those of the open meadows and prairies, as the Savannah, Grasshopper, and Vesper Sparrows. The best way to identify sparrows is to mentally list the possible species that might be present in the habitat you are currently studying. With such a group in mind, be alert for their particular field marks and vocal notes. If you have done your home work well, by memorizing the birds and their characteristics, you will know what to look for and may well be able to find it. Remember, Sherlock Holmes used to say that the reason he found obscure clues was that he was looking for them. Careful study of this book, other guides as those listed in the bibliography, particularly the excellently illustrated ones by Peterson and Robbins, as well as examination of museum displays and specimens will do much to improve your ornithological I. Q. with sparrows as well as with the other Northwest birds.

PACIFIC NORTHWEST SPECIES

FOX SPARROW *Passerella iliaca* 6-7 (153-178)
A large plump sparrow with clear dark brown or reddish brown (no streaks) upper parts, whitish under parts heavily streaked with dark brown triangular spots which aggregate into a large dark blotch in the center of the breast, and a reddish tail (not always apparent in the field). CALLS. A Song Sparrow-like *tseet* or soft *tsook;* a sharp *tchek,* harsher than that of the Song Sparrow. SONG. A loud, brilliant, but unhurried *sweet-sweet, cheer, chillup-chillup.* HABITAT. In summer, prefers dense brush in open woods or along water. In the arid country, commonly resorts to willow and aspen thickets or ceanothus patches in the woods or as scattered clumps on bare montane slopes where the snow drifts or cornices heavily in winter, leaving moist areas in summer. Forages by scratching on the ground in dense dark areas. Migrates and winters in dense brush patches often in city parks and urban areas. Mostly breeds at intermediate to alpine elevations. RANGE. Summer resident and breeder from limit of trees in Alaska and the Yukon south along the coast to northwestern Washington and in the interior in suitable habitat in the foothills and mountains through the region. Winters from southern B.C. southward, mostly west of the Cascades. In Idaho, summer resident and breeder in suitable habitat throughout the state; rare in winter.

SONG SPARROW *Passerella melodia* 5-6 (128-153) Fig. 139
The "small brown sparrow" of backyards, brushy areas, and semi-open woods. Rusty or grayish brown above, streaked on back with darker; under parts white, streaked with brown; dark spot in middle of breast. CALLS. A sharp hoarse *chwick,* also a soft *seet.* SONG. Begins with an introductory *chit-chit-cha-wee,* followed by various runs and trills. Percy Taverner used to render it as *"Pres-pres-presbyteri-eri-erian".* HABITAT. Requires low dense brush and moist ground in which to forage. Distributed widely in such places west of the Cascades but in the interior, more restricted, preferring brush along stream and lake margins. Occurs commonly in proper habitat in urban gardens, along brush-covered fields, and in the brush, marshes, and

139. Song Sparrow (Schultz)

driftwood on saltwater beaches. Common in the western lowlands, but sparser in the interior, except near water. RANGE. Common summer and permanent resident from the Aleutians, southern Alaska, and the southern Yukon south throughout the Northwest, wintering in much of the region except the colder interior of the far North. In Idaho and eastern Washington, less numerous in winter and restricted mostly to the lowlands at that season. Greatest area of abundance is in the humid coastal belt west of the Cascade range.

LINCOLN'S SPARROW *Passerella lincolnii* 5-6 (128-153)
Like a pale Song Sparrow, but with grayish throat bordered with black lines, buffy band (containing narrow black streaks) across the breast and along the sides, a small dark spot in the middle of the breast (not in a large blotch as in the Song Sparrow), and grayish-brown or olive-brown upper parts streaked with dark. Belly white. Much shyer than the Song Sparrow and more difficult to find and observe. CALLS. A junco-like *check* or *tsup*. SONG. A sweet gurgling roll, rising in pitch

at first and then dropping toward the end. HABITAT. Prefers brush at the edges of wet mountain meadows or along small streams or intermittent water courses, mostly in the upper montane and lower subalpine areas. Migrates and winters in brush along water. RANGE. Local summer resident and breeder in suitable habitat from northcentral Alaska and central Yukon south in the mountains of the Northwest, wintering from southwestern B.C. southward through the region including eastern Washington (the Yakima Valley). Much more common in the lowlands in late summer and fall migration than in spring migration.

SWAMP SPARROW *Passerella georgiana* 5½ (140)

A dark-colored Song Sparrow-like bird with a bright red crown, back and wings; the back two-striped with darker colors. In fall, the crown is streaked with black and with a buffy stripe down the mid-line. Under parts, face, and line over the eye are grayish; with whitish belly. Fall adults are buffy on the under parts, heavily streaked on the breast and sides. Very similar in habits and appearance to the Lincoln's Sparrow, but the breast in spring is clear gray, not streaked. CALLS. A metallic *chink*. SONG. A trilled series of single or double notes, which is long, loud, and melodious, somewhat reminiscent of the song of a Chipping Sparrow, but slower and more musical. HABITAT. Freshwater marshes and aquatic margins. A ground-foraging bird. Also visits somewhat drier habitats in migration. RANGE. Summer resident and breeder in northeastern and eastcentral B.C. Rare, but regular, spring, fall, and winter visitor west of the Cascades in Washington and Oregon.

HARRIS'S SPARROW *Zonotrichia querula* 7-8 (178-204)

A large sparrow with black lores, chin, and throat; dusky grayish crown; whitish face (back of eyes); brownish back (streaked with dark); and whitish under parts, heavily streaked on sides. Two white wingbars. Young of the year have white chin and buffy sides of head. Winter adults are similar to spring birds but have a grayish crown and the blacks in the color pattern are weaker. CALLS. A loud metallic *spink*. SONG. A slow mournful *tee, tee, tee, tee, whee-whee-whee-whee-whee*. HABITAT. In migration, frequents shrubbery, scattered small trees, thickets, and suburban gardens. RANGE. Uncommon to rare, but regular, winter visitor and migrational straggler from southeastern Alaska south through the Northwest on both sides of the Cascades. Sharply increasing in numbers in recent years, or at least being more commonly identified. In Idaho, rare visitor in late winter and early spring.

260

140. White-crowned Sparrow (juvenile, l.; adult, r.) (Schultz)

WHITE-CROWNED SPARROW *Zonotrichia leucophrys* 5-6 (128-153) Fig. 140

A medium-sized sparrow with clear gray breast and under parts; crown conspicuously striped with black and white and brown back streaked with dark. CALLS. A sharp metallic *pink*. SONG. A slow, plaintive, nasal series of notes sounding much like *oh-gee, kitty-did-scare-me; oh-jay-gee-jay-gee;* or *air-tsay-tsee-tsay;* depending on subspecies. HABITAT. Prefers brush, thickets, and forest edges in open situations providing singing perches, suitable damp ground beneath for foraging, and dense cover for protection. Common in brush along salt water, but in the interior east of the Cascades prefers the subalpine country. Migrates through the lowlands in spring and along the alpine ridge tops in late summer and fall. RANGE. Common summer resident and breeder from the limit of trees in Alaska and the Yukon south through the Northwest in the lowlands west of the Cascades and in the subalpine of the mountains east of that range. Winters from the southern Yukon southward, mostly in protected habitats. In the interior, tends to breed locally and irregularly mostly in the subalpine areas of the mountains, though it is a common spring migrant at lower levels.

WHITE-THROATED SPARROW *Zonotrichia albicollis* 6-7 (153-178)

Resembles the White-crowned Sparrow, but has a conspicuous white throat and a yellow spot between the eye and the bill. CALLS. A harsh *chink* and a slurred *tseet.* SONG. A plaintive series of whistled notes sounding much like *oh, Sam, Peabody-Peabody-Peabody.* Vies with the Hermit Thrush as a famous nostalgic singer of the wilderness. HABITAT. As winter visitor and migrant for most of the Northwest, prefers open brush and small-tree thickets. Nests in similar habitat in northern part of the region. RANGE. Summer resident and breeder from the southern Yukon (rarely) south to northeastern B.C. Uncommon, but regular, local and migrational straggler in the remainder of the Northwest, on both sides of the Cascades and as far north even as central Alaska. As a wintering bird, increasing in numbers in the Northwest states, particularly west of the Cascades. Occasional in spring and early summer in northern Idaho and northeastern Washington and in the Washington-Idaho border zone.

GOLDEN-CROWNED SPARROW *Zonotrichia atricapilla* 6-7 (153-178)

A large sparrow with clear grayish-brown under parts, broad black line over eye, dull yellow crown, and brownish upper parts which are streaked on the back with black, except for the neck and lower head which are the same gray as the under parts. CALLS. Very junco-like, but louder, as *tchip.* SONG. A minor, descending slurred *dee-er, dee-er, mee,* like "three blind mice" whistled very slowly. HABITAT. Prefers brush, broken woodland, and urban areas for migration in the Northwest of a character denser and darker than that frequented by the White-crowned Sparrow. Breeds in brushy open-tree areas at moderate to higher elevations in the mountains of the northern part of our region. Migrates through the low country in the spring but mostly along the subalpine rides in fall. RANGE. Summer resident and breeder from northwestern Alaska south along the coast to southeastern Alaska and from the southern Yukon south to southern B.C. and the northcentral Cascades of Washington, mostly in the mountains. Winters and migrates through the Northwest from southern B.C. southward. May occasionally occur as a migrational wave in the lowlands west of the Cascades. More scattered in the interior (Idaho and northeastern Washington) where it seems to be more of a fall migrant. Fairly common spring migrant along the eastern foothills of the Cascades; much less common fall migrant with a few individuals spending the winter around feeding stations.

SAVANNAH SPARROW *Ammodramus sandwichensis* 5-6 (128-153)
Fig. 138

A small, light-colored, heavily-streaked sparrow with a yellow line over the eye, a white line through the center of the crown, and a short notched tail. A poorly developed dark spot in the center of the breast. Similar to the Song Sparrow but yellow line above eye and white stripe on crown distinguish it. This sparrow usually walks when on the ground. CALLS. A soft *tsup.* SONG. A faint insect-like *tset-tset-tsa, wzzzzt, subut* or *tsee-tsee-tsa-tseeee-tsay.* HABITAT. Breeds in large moist to semi-moist meadows and alfalfa fields, particularly in the arid interior, but also in meadows and grassy places in the coastal lowlands and along salt water. Those remaining in winter frequent beaches and salt grass and salicornia flats near saltwater beaches on the sounds and ocean coast. RANGE. Summer resident and breeder along the Arctic slope in Alaska and south through the coastal and interior country to the southern border of the Northwest and beyond. Winters irregularly and locally from southern Yukon southward.

SHARP-TAILED SPARROW *Ammodramus caudacuta* 5½ (140)

Very similar to the Grasshopper Sparrow but with a dark gray midline through the crown, more strongly striped back, and rich buffy face and sides (the latter striped with darker brown). CALLS. A sharp *chuck.* SONG. A wheezy insect-like trill, as *tee-tee, sheeeeee.* HABITAT. Wet grassy meadows and marshes in the interior and salt marshes on the ocean coast. RANGE. Summer resident and breeder in northeastern B.C.

LeCONTE'S SPARROW *Ammodramus leconteii* 5 (128)

A small sparrow of wet meadows and marshes with a blackish back marked with four buffy stripes. Under parts buffy; sides streaked with black; white center stripe on crown; yellowish line above eye and black line back of eye. Cheeks gray; nape pinkish-brown; tail pointed. Distinguished from the similar Savannah Sparrow by absence of streaking on the breast. CALLS. A short insect-like buzz. SONG. Insect-like, ending with a chip, as *tse-bzzzzzz-tsip.* HABITAT. Wet meadows and marshes; matted tall grass meadows near water. RANGE. Summer resident and breeder in northeastern B.C. Rare spring and fall migrational straggler in the Washington-Idaho border migration corridor and elsewhere in eastern Washington.

BAIRD'S SPARROW *Ammodramus bairdii* 5½ (140)

An open prairie sparrow, similar to a Savannah Sparrow but with a strong buffy suffusion on the striped head, nape, and band across breast. The spots in the breast streaks are stronger than in the Savan-

141. Open yellow pine habitat of the Chipping Sparrow (Boggs)

142. Chipping Sparrow at nest (Boggs)

nah. The outer tail feathers appear whitish. A clear, dark buffy, unstriped crown stripe. CALLS. A soft *tzip*. SONG. Begins with several *tzips* followed by a musical trill on a somewhat lower pitch. HABITAT. Grain fields, weedy patches, and dry grassy prairies with occasional shrubs. RANGE. Very rare fall migrant in southwest Idaho (Owyhee Country).

GRASSHOPPER SPARROW *Ammodramus savannarum* 5 (128)
A small, black-streaked, grayish sparrow of the grassy rocky places with buffy unstreaked under parts. Easily separated from the Savannah Sparrow by the much shorter tail and unstreaked under parts. Flight is weak and fluttery. CALLS. A slurred *til-ik*. SONG. An insignificant insect-like *tset-tset, tsur* or *tset-tset-tseeee*. HABITAT. Occurs mostly in the interior where it frequents the bunchgrass of the lower Transition Zone where occasional rocks project above the turf to provide singing posts. In drier rockier grassland than the Savannah Sparrow and seems to shun areas that are very heavily grazed. RANGE. Local irregular summer resident and/or migrant from southern B.C. south, mostly through the arid interior of the Northwest. Rare west of the Cascades (as a migrational straggler) in southwestern B.C. and Oregon (one breeding record in Willamette Valley). In Idaho, uncommon irregular summer resident and migrant in the northern portion, showing strong attachment to the preferred habitat. Local breeder in southeastern Idaho.

TREE SPARROW *Spizella arborea* 6 (153)
Very similar to the Chipping Sparrow, but may be separated from that species by the larger size, single round black spot in the center of the breast, two conspicuous white wing-bars, and black (upper) and yellow (lower) mandibles. Lacks the white line over the eye found in the Chipping Sparrow. CALLS. A sharp *tseet;* a musical *teeler* or *teel-it.* SONG. A metallic canary-like series beginning with two or three high notes and ending with a rapid warble. HABITAT. To be found scatteringly in weedy fields and brush patches in the open country of the arid interior. Breeds in brushy willow and alder thickets. RANGE. Summer resident and breeder from the Arctic coast of Alaska and the Yukon south to northern B.C., wintering through the Northwest, mostly east of the Cascades, but scatteringly west of the range, from the southern Yukon (rarely) southward.

CHIPPING SPARROW *Spizella passerina* 5 (128) Figs. 141 and 142
A small sparrow with clear gray under parts, a bright red cap, white line over eye, and black line through the eye; back brown, streaked with black. CALLS. A faint *tsip*. SONG. A dry, rapidly uttered,

monotonous series of *chips,* all on one pitch. HABITAT. An "edge bird", preferring the margins of coniferous or deciduous groves, roads, clearings, and burns in the forest, open subalpine country, and open arid areas if there is timber nearby. Foraging is done in the open places but the trees are needed for cover and nesting sites. RANGE. Summer resident, migrant, and breeder from northern B.C. and central Yukon south throughout the Northwest. Very common in the Northwest states in suitable forest edge habitat. Uncommon to rare late fall and winter visitor, mostly in the southern part of the Northwest region.

FIELD SPARROW *Spizella pusilla* 5-6 (128-153)
Very similar to the Tree Sparrow, but lacks the blackish mid-breast spot. No streaking on under parts in adults. A slight buffy wash on the breast and sides. CALLS. A soft *tsip.* SONG. A pleasing series of two long clear whistles followed by an accelerating trill. HABITAT. Brushy fields, abandoned farm lands, and woodland borders. RANGE. Very rare spring and late summer visitor to the Northwest. Records for Oregon.

BLACK-CHINNED SPARROW *Spizella atrogularis* 5¼ (134)
A small sparrow with grayish head (black chin and patch before the eye), breast, and sides; striped brownish wings and back, and notched tail. Belly is grayish white. Female, similar, but lighter and without black chin and eye-spot. CALLS. A soft *tsip.* SONG. A series beginning with several long notes accelerating into a weak trill but with a marvelous carrying power. HABITAT. Open brush-covered slopes, especially on mountains and foothills, in the desert country. RANGE. Very rare spring and early summer migrational straggler in Oregon.

CLAY-COLORED SPARROW *Spizella pallida* 5-5½ (128-140)
A small bird very similar to the Brewer's Sparrow but with more buffy on the back and sides and not so dull and gray as is the Brewer's. Streaks on face are more strongly marked. Hind neck is dark gray. CALLS. A weak *chip.* SONG. Two to four weak insect-like buzzes. HABITAT. Patches and thickets of small trees and brush near standing or running water, often aspen groves or brushy openings in woodlands. RANGE. Summer resident and breeder in northeastern B.C. and rarely in the Okanagan area of that province. Rare in migration (spring, summer and late fall) in eastern and western Washington, northern Idaho, and Oregon (where very rare in winter in northwestern part of state). May breed in the Spokane area.

BREWER'S SPARROW *Spizella breweri* 5 (128)
A small sparrow of the higher, drier, open country of the Northwest, with streaked grayish-brown upper parts and grayish unstreaked under parts. Crown is gray, finely streaked with sooty brown. CALLS. A soft *tsip.* SONG. A long rambling canary-like series of trills, buzzes, and chops, usually delivered in the evening. A most delightful sound in the open sage country. HABITAT. Prefers the open sagebrush or plains country of the interior where hedgerows or scattered brush provide singing posts and nesting sites. Forages on the ground and in bushes. Often found in association with the Vesper Sparrow. RANGE. Summer resident and breeder from the southern Yukon south in suitable habitat through the Northwest entirely east of the Cascades. Very local and less common than formerly in northern Idaho. Has been sharply reduced with the progressive destruction of the sagebrush biome and elimination of brushy hedgerows in the grain country.

VESPER SPARROW *Pooecetes gramineus* 5-6 (128-153)
A bird of the meadows and open farmlands, resembling a pale Song Sparrow or Savannah Sparrow but with white eye-ring, brown shoulder patches, and conspicuous white outer tail feathers showing in flight. CALLS. A short *tsook.* SONG. Somewhat similar to that of the Song Sparrow, but opening notes are not hurried (of these, first two are soft and low, second two notes are higher in pitch) as *see-chee, sweet-sweet, ti-ti-ti-ti, chu-chu-chu-chu.* HABITAT. To be found in sagebrush plains, grasslands with occasional bushes, the open glacial outwash prairies at the southern end of Puget Sound, and occasionally along salt water. Tends to work into the open parts of the yellow pine zone. Though foraging is done on the ground, brush tops are necessary for singing posts. RANGE. Summer resident and breeder from central B.C. south through the Northwest, mostly in suitable habitat east of the Cascades. Less common in large open places west of that range, as in the prairies south of Puget Sound. Very rare winter visitor, both east and west of the Cascades. Tends to be rather local in occurrence and most likely to be found in open semi-arid to arid plains regions.

LARK SPARROW *Chondestes grammacus* 6 (153)
A large field sparrow with striped red, white, and black head; brownish-gray upper parts streaked with darker brown; white under parts with black spot in middle of breast; and dark-brown tail with prominent white corners and edges. Tail pattern is distinctive in flight. CALLS. A weak *tsip.* SONG. An irregular series of clear notes and musical trills, interspersed with harsh *buzzes* and *churrs.* HABITAT.

Prefers open sagebrush and bunchgrass with scattered brush and trees in which it sings and nests. Juniper areas are ideal and it seems to favor areas with large shrubs. RANGE. Summer resident and breeder from extreme southern B.C. south in the arid lowlands of the Northwest east of the Cascades and in western Oregon. Rare fall and spring visitor west of the Cascades in the Northwest states. Rather local in distribution, preferring sagebrush, shrubby, and juniper-clad areas. Noted uncommonly in winter in protected places east of the Cascades.

BLACK-THROATED SPARROW *Amphispiza bilineata* 5 (128)
A gray desert sparrow with black forehead and throat and two white face stripes; cheeks are gray. Under parts plain whitish; wings brownish-gray; tail blackish (white edging difficult to see unless tail is spread widely in flight). CALLS. A tinkling *wee-eet*. SONG. Two clear *cheets* and a trilling *cheeeeeeeeee*. HABITAT. A bird of the hot dry sagebrush and hopsage plains. RANGE. Rare, though locally common, resident and breeder in southeastern Oregon and southern Idaho in suitable habitat. Rare migrational straggler to western Oregon, western Washington, eastern Washington, northern Idaho, and B.C. Reported as common summer resident and breeder in the southern Idaho Birds of Prey Study Area and adjacent Owyhee County.

SAGE SPARROW *Amphispiza belli* 5-6 (128-153)
A sparrow with a black dot in the middle of the breast and a gray head conspicuously marked with black and white bars above the eyes and through the cheeks. Rest of upper parts grayish brown, streaked with blackish. Under parts whitish. CALLS. A sharp *tick*. SONG. A high thin *tsit, tsit, tsee-you, tee-a-tee*. HABITAT. In our area, mostly confined to sagebrush flats and slopes, where it forages on the ground and in the lower parts of the shrubbery. Usually stays hidden below the tops of the bushes. RANGE. Summer resident, migrant, and breeder in suitable habitat in eastern Washington, eastern Oregon, and southern Idaho. Tends to be rather local in occurrence. Rare west of the Cascades; most being seen in late winter and early spring. Rarely recorded in southern B.C. east of the Cascades.

RUFOUS-CROWNED SPARROW *Aimophila ruficeps* 5½ (140)
A dark, drably-colored, brownish sparrow with a black streak on each side of the throat and a reddish brown crown-patch. Spends much time on the ground and frequently refuses to flush into the air when startled, preferring to run through the ground cover. CALLS. A sharp *chirp* or a mewing *dear, dear*. SONG. A wren-like warble with trills interspersed. HABITAT. Rocky brushy areas near streams. RANGE. Very rare straggler to southern and eastern Oregon.

JUNCOS

143. Slate-colored Junco (Pole)

Juncos are sparrow-like ground birds with conspicuous white outer tail feathers, black or gray heads sharply cut off from the white under parts, and white bills. Nesting and feeding are done mostly on the ground where the birds are usually seen by the bird student. Juncos commonly visit urban areas and backyards in the winter, often appearing about the time of the coming of the first snows, whence the old name of "snow bird" that was sometimes given them. In the interior of the Pacific Northwest, they are common in winter, often constituting a considerable portion of the wintering bird population at that season.

The systematics of this genus have been chaotic in the literature for years and the present lumping is no solution. It seems best to consider this group an unusual one and to recognize the traditional species so that the variant (sibling?) taxa may not be lost sight of.

PACIFIC NORTHWEST SPECIES

WHITE-WINGED JUNCO *Junco aikeni* 6½ (166)
Very similar to the Slate-colored Junco, but with two white wing-bars.

In addition, the wing feathers are more or less margined and tipped with white. CALLS and SONG. Similar to those of the Slate-colored Junco. HABITAT. Yellow pine forests, especially brushy clearings and burns. In migration, usually joins other species of juncos. RANGE. Very rare migrational straggler and summer visitor to southern Idaho.

SLATE-COLORED JUNCO *Junco hyemalis* 6 (153) Fig. 143
A junco with uniform blackish-gray head, breast, sides, wings, and back. Belly white. CALLS and SONG. Very similar to those of the Oregon Junco but slightly higher pitched. HABITAT. In our area, usually mixed in with migrating or wintering flocks of the Oregon Junco in such habitats as open brush, parks, residential areas, and the edges of groves of trees. Breeds in more open coniferous and mixed woods in the northern part of the Northwest region. RANGE. Summer resident and breeder from the limit of trees in northern Alaska and the Yukon south to northern B.C., wintering uncommonly south through the Northwest, mostly east of the Cascades, but some regularly west of that range. In Idaho, uncommon winter visitor in the northern portion; less so in the southern part.

144. Oregon Junco at nest with young (Boggs)

145.   Oregon Junco feeding young (Boggs)

OREGON JUNCO *Junco oreganus* 5-6 (128-153) Figs. 144 and 145
A junco with rusty-red upper back, pinkish-brown sides, and a gray or black head. Both sexes have a pink bill and white outer tail feathers; head grayer in the female. Young are brownish gray above, buffy white below, heavily streaked, but with white outer tail feathers. The intensity of the dark heads and red backs varies according to sex, age, and geographic race. CALLS. A sharp *chek* or *tsip* and a *tew-tew-tew*. SONG. A simple trill, similar to that of the Chipping Sparrow, but more musical and varied. HABITAT. For breeding, open or broken forest or woodland areas with scattered brush and some grassy spots required. Nests commonly on the ground in grassy brushy areas in the yellow pine zone. In winter, wanders widely, mostly to the lowlands where it is to be seen at the edges of timber near protecting brush and in urban parks and gardens. RANGE. Summer resident and breeder from southeastern Alaska and central B.C. south in suitable habitat through the Northwest, wintering from B.C. southward. Rare in the southern Yukon.

GRAY-HEADED JUNCO *Junco caniceps* 5½-6 (140-153)
A junco with a bright reddish-brown back, pale gray head, ashy-gray sides and wings, and a white belly. CALLS. A sharp *chek*. SONG. A loose single-pitched trill. HABITAT. Dry forests in desert mountains.

RANGE. Summer resident and breeder in the mountains of southern Idaho south of the Snake River. Rare migrational straggler and possible winter visitor in eastern Oregon and southwestern B.C. Recorded in winter in southern Idaho.

TOWHEES

146.   Green-tailed Towhee (Fisher)

PACIFIC NORTHWEST SPECIES

GREEN-TAILED TOWHEE *Pipilo chlorurus* 6½ (166) Fig. 146
A brownish and greenish towhee with reddish crown, dark gray forehead, white streaks on face, and rest of upper parts grayish brown. Bright yellow on edge of wing; tail yellow green. Under parts with white throat (bordered by sooty mustache marks), grayish breast and sides, and dirty white belly. CALLS. A towhee-like *pee-you-ee.* SONG. A loud bright *chip-cheer-chur-chee-chee-chee,* reminiscent of the typical towhee "drink your tea" pattern. HABITAT. Occurs scatteringly in brush, mostly on hillsides and in gulches and arroyos where it forages near the ground. RANGE. Local summer resident, breeder, and migrational straggler in central and southern Oregon, southern Idaho, and the Blue Mountains of southeastern Washington.

147. Rufous-sided Towhee (adult, l,; juvenile, r.) (Schultz)

RUFOUS-SIDED TOWHEE *Pipilo erythrophthalmus* 7-8 (178-204)
Fig. 147
A Robin-like bird of the shrubbery. Male, head and upper parts black
with numerous white spots on wings; sides reddish, belly white.
Female, similar, but head dark slaty or brown. Conspicuous red eye.
Young are dark grayish above, buffy brown below, and heavily
streaked. Tail has white corners as in adults. CALLS. A complaining
mee-ay-ee, a *ma-reeee,* or a drawled *hreeeeeee.* SONG. A rather
colorless *chiddle-chiddle-chiddle-chiddle.* HABITAT. Prefers dense
brushy areas in the open or in broken woodland. Forages on the
ground, but frequently flies to the top of a bush or the lowest limb of a
small tree for singing. RANGE. Summer resident and breeder from
southern B.C. south through the Northwest. Winters mostly west of
the Cascades; less commonly east of that range. In Idaho, common
summer resident in the northern and southern sections, though occasionally seen in winter, mostly in the southern parts.

BROWN TOWHEE *Pipilo fuscus* 8-9 (204-230)
A large brown-colored towhee with a dark buffy throat (dark-streaked
on the sides), dark-brown crown and tail, and a reddish patch under
the tail. CALLS. A light *tsip* and a stronger *chip.* SONG. A rapid
series of *chips.* HABITAT. Oak and riparian woodlands, brushy canyons, and urban gardens and estates. RANGE. Resident and breeder
in southwestern Oregon. Rare visitor to eastern Oregon.

CARDINAL GROSBEAKS AND BUNTINGS

148. Black-headed Grosbeak (female, l.; male, r.) (Pole)

Another of the groups of the immense bunting family is that of the cardinal grosbeaks and buntings. For the most part, these are highly-colorful birds with the type of contrastive pattern that we tend to link with tropical species. Though tropical birds are often very attractive, some of the best-looking birds are in our region, as witness the buntings and Black-headed and Rose-breasted Grosbeaks. In fact, some birders feel that the Painted Bunting, which has rarely visited us in the Northwest, is the most beautiful of North American birds.

Certain of the seed eaters around the World have very large conical bills. At one time this character was thought to be indicative of a close evolutionary relationship. Now we know that anatomical features such as this are often the result of parallel adaptation and have been arrived at independently. Thus, we have "grosbeaks" among the buntings, as well as among the true finches (as witness the Pine Grosbeak). Another example of the process of convergent evolution, as it is called, is to be found among those birds that make a living in the fashion of our North American meadowlarks. The Dickcissel, soon to be mentioned, appears somewhat like these species. The author studied a bird in East Africa a few years ago that was a dead ringer for the meadowlark, as regards color pattern and habits. What is there about the meadowlark "profession" that requires a particular uniform? For that matter, why do raccoons and raccoon dogs (an Old World species of canid) need eye masks? Nature is a fascinating realm to study and speculate about!

PACIFIC NORTHWEST SPECIES

DICKCISSEL *Spiza americana* 6¼ (159)
Reminds one of a miniature meadowlark, but is half the bulk of those species. The male with its partial black collar, yellow breast, and prominent yellow line over the eye is distinctive. The female has no black collar but a yellow breast streaked with dark brown, along with a buffy line over the eye. SONG. A bright staccato *dick, dick, dickcissel,* the number of song elements varying in number. HABITAT. Grassy meadows or hay or brushy fields. RANGE. Very rare migrational straggler to western and eastern Oregon and southwestern B.C.

ROSE-BREASTED GROSBEAK *Pheucticus ludovicianus* 8 (204)
Male, easily recognized by its black head and upper parts (wings and shoulders marked with white), large light-colored bill, rosy breast, and distinctive white under parts. Female, heavily streaked on white or buffy-white under parts with a large bill. CALLS. A high-pitched *tick.* SONG. Somewhat Robin-like but more rapid and varied. Resembles closely the song of the more numerous (in our region) Black-headed Grosbeak. HABITAT. Deciduous and mixed woods, especially near water. RANGE. Summer resident and breeder in northeastern B.C. Rare migrational straggler, possible breeder, and winter visitor elsewhere in the Northwest; more records for Oregon than for other Northwest states. Apparently increasing in numbers and occurrence in the region, especially in Washington.

BLACK-HEADED GROSBEAK *Pheucticus melanocephalus* 7-8 (178-204) Figs. 148 and 149
A shy large-billed bird of the lowland woods. Male, head black; back black, streaked with buff; tail black with white corners; wings black with white bars and white patch in the primaries. Collar, rump, breast, and sides rusty; belly yellow. Female, brownish, streaked with white; under parts rusty, paling on belly; bills grayish; best recognized by color of breast and bill and by song. CALLS. A sharp *eek.* SONG.

149. Black-headed Grosbeak on nest (Boggs)

Very similar to the carol of the Robin, but faster in tempo and more varied; the *purdeet-chee-wee-oo* phrases are more characteristic. HABITAT. Frequents deciduous woods, particularly the edges of clearings and groves of mixed timber where it forages and sings from large deciduous trees such as cottonwoods, alders, and maples. Often to be found at the base of a branch near the trunk of the tree. RANGE. Summer resident, breeder, and migrant from central and southern B.C. south through the Northwest being possibly slightly more numerous east of the Cascades, but uncommon in the drier areas.

BLUE GROSBEAK *Passerina caerulea* 6½-7½ (166-191)
A large all-blue (except for brownish wing-bars) bunting with a large dark bill. Female is light buffy brown and streaked. CALLS. A sharp *spink*. SONG. A finch-like warble. HABITAT. Brush and low trees near water and woodland edges. RANGE. Migrational straggler in western Oregon and eastern Washington. Very uncommon local summer resident and breeder in southern Idaho (Elmore County).

INDIGO BUNTING *Passerina cyanea* 5½ (140)
Male, an indigo blue bunting with more or less blackish wings. Female, an obscurely marked bunting with solid greenish-brown upper parts, clay-colored breast, and grayish-brown belly. CALLS. A

sharp *tsick*. SONG. Has been described as *zwee, zwee, zwee, zerry, zerry, tsu, tsu*, trailing off at the end. HABITAT. Mixed brush and trees, edges of woods, and abandoned farmsteads. RANGE. Uncommon to rare migrational straggler to various parts of the Northwest, but apparently more regularly in the southern portion of the region. Also occasionally found in the Washington-Idaho border migration zone. June and July records may indicate breeding.

LAZULI BUNTING *Passerina amoena* 5 (128) Fig. 151
A common bird of the brushy gullies and slopes in arid areas. Male, head, neck, and back bright blue; wings and tail dusky blue; breast reddish; belly white; wing crossed with white wing-bars. Female, brownish above, lighter below; wing-bars whitish. CALLS. A sharp *tsip*. SONG. A rapid, high-pitched, rambling warble made up of several phrases, each on a different level of pitch. Somewhat resembles the song of the American Goldfinch. HABITAT. With us, prefers brushy hillsides, burns, riparian shrubbery, and town gardens where adequate brush is available. Forages in the bushes, but sings from the tips of branches or from low trees. RANGE. Summer resident, breeder, and migrant from western and southern B.C. south through the Northwest, mostly east of the Cascades. Less common, though regular, west of that range. Somewhat closely restricted to preferred habitat.

PAINTED BUNTING *Passerina ciris* 5¼ (134)
A beautiful bunting, which in the male has a blue head, greenish yellow back, red rump, brownish red wings and tail, and red under parts. Female, light greenish yellow, darker on the upper parts. CALLS. A sharp two- or three-noted chirp; a soft, sharp, metallic *tsick*. SONG. A soft high-pitched warble. HABITAT. Brushy woodland and swampy thickets. RANGE. Rare late spring visitor to eastern Oregon (Malheur).

LARK BUNTING *Calamospiza melanocorys* 6-7½ (153-191) Fig. 150
Spring male: black with large white wing patches. Fall male, female, and immature: brown, streaked on breast; black patch on belly, white patch on wings (wings of male blackish); large bluish bill. CALLS. An unmusical *chug, chug, chug*, or a sweet *whoo-ee* uttered in flight; each repeated several times. SONG. A chorus of soft clear notes and trills. HABITAT. Open plains and prairies with mixture of both grass and sagebrush. RANGE. Uncommon local summer resident and breeder in southern Idaho. Has been recorded in B.C. Very rare fall and winter visitor in scattered parts of the Northwest.

150. Lark Bunting (male, l.; female, r.) (Pole)

151. Lazuli Bunting (female, l.; male, r.) (Schultz)

278

TANAGERS

152. Western Tanager (Fisher)

The tanagers constitute the third of the three groups of the Emberizidae, the first two being the buntings and American Sparrows and the cardinal grosbeaks. The tanagers are a large group of some 239 species, mostly tropical. Only three — two very rare — have been recorded in the Pacific Northwest, though the third, the Western Tanager, is widely distributed in the proper habitat. Many of the tanagers are very brightly colored, adding another interesting feature to the areas they inhabit, though in the tropics, one finds that bright colors are often not very visible in the dense rainforest vegetation. The author's favorite in Central America is the beautiful Blue-gray Tanager. Our Western Tanager, however, rates highly with many western birders. Tanagers feed on insects and fruit and are forest and woodland birds.

PACIFIC NORTHWEST SPECIES

SUMMER TANAGER *Piranga rubra* 7½ (191)
A dull rosy-red tanager in the male. Female, light greenish above, orange-yellow below, with dark green wings and tail and yellowish bill. No wing-bars in either sex. CALLS. A rapid *chick-tucky-tuck.*

SONG. Resembles the song of a Robin but is softer and more melodious. HABITAT. Open woodlands and suburban areas. RANGE. Very rare late fall migrational straggler west of the Cascades; noted also in extreme eastern Washington and in eastern Oregon.

SCARLET TANAGER *Piranga olivacea* 7¼ (185)

Male, in summer, a beautiful scarlet red tanager with black wings and tail and light-colored bill. Female, greenish yellow (brighter on under parts) with dusky wings and tail. Winter male is similar to the female, but has blackish wings and tail. CALLS. A buzzy *chip-churr.* SONG. Robin-like but hoarser. HABITAT. Mature deciduous or mixed woodlands and suburban areas with many shade trees. RANGE. Very rare straggler to B.C. and eastern Oregon.

WESTERN TANAGER *Piranga ludoviciana* 6-7 (153-178) Fig. 152

A brilliantly-colored summer resident of our coniferous forests. Male, head red; wings, middle of back, and tail black; rest of body and wing-bars yellow. Female, upper parts greenish yellow; wings dusky with yellowish-white wing-bars; under parts dull yellow. CALLS. A dry *pit-ti-tic* or *prit-tic.* In late afternoon and evening may render a *pri-tic, pri-ter, pri-tic, pri-ter* pattern. SONG. Like that of the Robin, but hoarser and much faster in tempo as *cheero-chee-wee, cheero-chee-wee, cheero-chee-wee.* HABITAT. Prefers open coniferous and mixed coniferous-deciduous woodlands at all elevations. Foraging, singing, and nesting carried on in the middle and upper parts of the canopy, though may use lower branches for perches in flycatching. RANGE. Spring and fall migrant and summer resident and breeder from northern B.C. south in coniferous forests through the Northwest. Rare north of B.C. Visits deciduous growth only during migration. Rare winter visitor in southern Idaho and western Oregon.

WOOD WARBLERS

153. Yellowthroat (Pole)

Warblers are slender, brightly-colored, very active birds that are smaller than sparrows (except the Chat) and usually have considerable yellow in their plumage. Feeding mainly on insects, most warblers are to be found in coniferous or deciduous woods or in dense brush of good size. Most individuals are summer residents or migrants only in the Pacific Northwest, with a few species wintering in the lower more protected areas, particularly in the milder marine climate west of the Cascades. Warblers are active foragers and are often hidden in the dense foliage, so that identification of species of this group must be based on recognition of the songs, consideration of the habitat, and comparison of behavior, as well as careful visual study of the individual bird.

The wood warblers, family Parulidae, are widely distributed in North, Central, and South America, numbering about 110 species. They appear to be most closely related to the buntings and tanagers. In such a large group, it would be expected that a considerable amount of adaptive radiation would have taken place, bringing some species into habit similarity with other groups of birds. Thus, we find sandpiper-like habits among the waterthrushes, nuthatch similarities in the Black-and-white Warbler, titmouse tendencies in the Parula, mimic thrush resemblances in the chats, flycatching methods in the redstarts, and so on.

The different species of the 36 kinds that have been recorded in the Northwest occur in a variety of habitats and one must search various places for them. The songs as a group are usually identifiable, but certain species are very similar to each other in vocal utterances and some experience is needed. This is not an easy group, but proficiency in their determination comes as a reward to assiduous and dedicated field work.

PACIFIC NORTHWEST SPECIES

BLACK-AND-WHITE WARBLER *Mniotilta varia* 5 (128)
This is a heavily-striped black and white appearing bird, the black stripes running lengthwise along the body above and below. The habit of creeping over the trunks of trees, nuthatch-wise, is distinctive. CALLS. A weak *tsip,* a loud *tchink,* and a loud *chee-chee-chee.* SONG. A thin *wee-see, wee-see, wee-see, wee-see, wee-see, wee-see, wee-see.* HABITAT. Occurs widely in deciduous as well as coniferous woods, both successional and climax. RANGE. Summer resident and breeder in northwestern B.C. Rare migrational straggler to other parts of the Northwest, mostly east of the Cascades (a few west of that range). Very rare in winter in the western sections.

BLUE-WINGED WARBLER *Vermivora pinus* 4¾ (121)
A small warbler with greenish upper parts, grayish wings (two white wing-bars) and tail, and yellow head (except nape) and under parts. Female, slightly duller. A narrow black line from bill through eye to ear. SONG. A buzzy *zeeee-bzzzz.* The second note may be doubled or tripled and is lower in pitch. HABITAT. Brushy clearings and woodland edges as well as abandoned fields and pastures that have grown up to brush patches and second growth trees. RANGE. Very rare migrational straggler to eastern Oregon and eastern Washington.

TENNESSEE WARBLER *Vermivora peregrina* 5 (128)
This is a plain-colored warbler looking somewhat like a vireo. It has a grayish head with a conspicuous white line over the eye, a greenish rump and back, and whitish under parts. The best marks are the plain under parts and the streak over the eye. CALLS. A warbler-like *tsip* and a sharp *tsee-zeep* in flight. SONG. A fast staccato *ti-zip, ti-zip, ti-zip, ti-zip, ti-zip, ti-zip, twit, twit, twit, tsee-tsee-tsee-tsee-tsee.* Open brush and bogs in coniferous or deciduous mixed woods, preferring

particularly the edges of woods and more open places. RANGE. Summer resident and breeder from southeastern Alaska and the southern Yukon south to southcentral B.C. and northwestern Montana. Rare to uncommon spring and fall visitor elsewhere in the Northwest; possible summer resident and rare breeder. Several records for the Washington-Idaho border flyway and in northeastern Washington. Seemingly increasing in the Northwest, especially in migration.

ORANGE-CROWNED WARBLER *Vermivora celata* 4-5 (102-128) Figs. 154 and 155

A common brush-inhabiting warbler with light green upper parts and yellowish under parts, and a light yellow eye-ring or stripe from eye to bill. The orange crown is seldom visible. Characterized by absence of wing-bars and other distinctive marks. CALLS. A sharp *chip.* SONG. A weak trill, rising slightly and then dropping in pitch and volume at the end. Occasionally rises in pitch at end of series. HABITAT. Mainly in brushy woods, especially by streams and on dry hillsides, often in clearings, but usually with intermixed trees. Tall shrubs a necessity as is sloping terrain. Seldom found outside of brushy cover, and more likely to be heard than seen. RANGE. Summer resident and breeder from northcentral Alaska and the central Yukon south through the remainder of the Northwest. Often common and widespread in preferred habitat. Winters in western Oregon and less commonly, but regularly, in western Washington and southwestern B.C.; rare in winter in northern Idaho.

NASHVILLE WARBLER *Vermivora ruficapilla* 4-5 (102-128)

A small warbler with a gray head, white eye-ring, olive-green upper parts, and yellow throat and under parts. A brownish-orange crown spot. The MacGillivray's Warbler has a dark throat. CALLS. A sharp *tsip.* SONG. A warbler-like *see-bit, see-bit, see-bit, titititititi.* This resembles the song of the Yellow Warbler, but ends in a trill. HABITAT. Most commonly in open yellow pine woods with considerable brushy understory where foraging and singing are done from 20 to 40 feet above the ground. Often found on hillsides. Nests on the ground. RANGE. Local summer resident and breeder from southern B.C. south through the Northwest, mostly in the interior east of the Cascades in suitable habitat. Wanders extensively in late summer and fall through the region on both sides of the Cascades. Very rare in winter in the lowlands west of the Cascades and as winter visitor on the east side of that range.

VIRGINIA'S WARBLER *Vermivora virginiae* 4-4½ (102-115)

This is a small grayish warbler with a pale breast, yellowish rump, and

154. Orange-crowned Warbler on nest (Boggs)

yellow undertail coverts. The head is gray with narrow white eye-ring and a rufous spot on the crown; breast tinted with yellow. Female and immature, dull and lacking yellow of breast and rufous on head. CALL. A hoarse *tchack.* SONG. A loose *chlip-chlip-chlip-wick-wick.* HABITAT. Prefers sagebrush, juniper, pinyon pine, and mountain mahogany thickets on the higher mountain slopes. RANGE. Sparse summer resident and breeder in extreme southern Idaho. Rare summer resident in eastern Oregon. Very rare late fall straggler to western Oregon (one record).

NORTHERN PARULA *Parula americana* 4½ (115)

A multi-colored warbler in which the male has a bluish head (broken white eye-ring) and back (greenish patch in middle of back), sooty gray wings and tail, and two white bars in each wing. Throat and breast yellow separated by a bicolored bib of black and reddish brown. Belly white. Female similar, but without bicolored bib. CALLS. An emphatic *zip.* SONG. A buzzy series, as *bzzzzzzz.* HABITAT. Deciduous or coniferous woodlands, especially in the more moist parts of the woods. Forages chickadee-like high in the canopy and nests where there is *Usnea* lichen. RANGE. Rare migrational and winter straggler to the Northwest, including Washington and Oregon, both east and west of the Cascades.

YELLOW WARBLER *Dendroica petechia* 4-5 (102-128) Fig. 155

This is the only all yellow warbler in the Northwest. Slight greenish suffusion on the back (dark in the female). Red streaks on breast and yellow in tail in male. CALLS. A sharp *chip* or *chik.* SONG. A rapidly uttered, clear, but variable *chwee, chwee, chwee, zee-zee-zee; chwee, chwee, witsa-wee; weetsee, weetsee, weetsee, weetsee, witsa;* or *see-see-see, wee-wee-wit.* HABITAT. Prefers deciduous woods (willows, alders, cottonwoods, etc.) in moderately moist areas, as the edges of streams and lakes, but also gardens in residential sections. Forages and sings up to 50 feet above the ground, nesting at moderate heights. More numerous in suburban areas than any other of our Northwest warblers. RANGE. Summer resident and breeder from central Alaska and the northern Yukon south, mainly in the lowlands, through the Northwest. Widespread and often abundant, though becoming less numerous in certain areas. Rare winter visitor.

CHESTNUT-SIDED WARBLER *Dendroica pensylvanica* 5 (128)

Male has a yellow crown, greenish upper parts streaked with dark brownish, two white wing-bars, a black line through the eye from bill to ear, white under parts, and a prominent chestnut-red stripe down each side. Female, similar with irregular broken chestnut side stripe.

CALLS. A sharp *tchip*. SONG. Has been rendered as *very-very-pleased to-MEET-CHA;* or, *ta-wee, ta-wee, ta-wee, ta-wee, ta-wee, ta-WEE-cha*. HABITAT. Prefers brushy deciduous second growth woods and thickets in early and intermediate successional stages. RANGE. Rare spring, summer, and fall migrational straggler to the Northwest, including eastern Washington, northern and southeastern Idaho, western and eastern Oregon, northwestern Montana, and southwestern and eastern B.C. Most records for east of the Cascades. Recorded in early summer in southern Idaho.

BLACK-THROATED BLUE WARBLER *Dendroica caerulescens* 5¼ (134)

A large strikingly-marked warbler with deep blue upper parts; black throat, face, and sides; and two white wing-bars (the second broad like a patch), as well as white patches in the outer tail feathers. Female has dull green upper parts, pale greenish yellow under parts, line over eye, and white patch in wing. CALLS. A sharp *tchip*, like that of a junco. SONG. Lazy slurred *zwee, zwee, zwee-a-zwee* that rises in pitch on the last note. HABITAT. Prefers brushy deciduous or mixed woodlands. RANGE. Rare pre- and post-migrational straggler to eastern and western Oregon and northern Idaho as it filters southward through and spreads out from the tri-state migrational corridor. A few may linger in winter.

BLACK-THROATED GRAY WARBLER *Dendroica nigrescens* 4-5 (102-128)

Male, crown, throat, and broad line through eye black; rest of face white; remainder of upper parts grayish, streaked with black; under parts grayish white, streaked on sides with black. Female, similar but throat white. Yellow spot between eye and bill in male. CALLS. A sharp *tchip*. SONG. Very similar to that of the Townsend's Warbler, but slower and more buzzing, as *zay-zay-zay-zee-zee* or ascending as *zee-a, zee-a, zee-a, zee-a, zee*. HABITAT. Prefers open lowland coniferous woods where it forages toward the tips of the branches of trees. Requires dense dry coniferous foliage and feeds in the upper half of trees. Found in juniper woods in southern interior of our range and also in oak woods and open timber bordering west-side prairies. RANGE. Summer resident and breeder from southwestern B.C., western Washington, and southern Idaho south. Rare winter visitor west of the Cascades. Rare local summer resident and migrant east of the Cascades in Washington and Oregon. A lowland species.

TOWNSEND'S WARBLER *Dendroica townsendi* 4-5 (102-128) Fig. 156

Male, crown, throat, and broad line through eye black; rest of face yellow; back greenish; wings and tail blackish; under parts yellow; sides streaked with black. Female, similar to male but with yellow throat. CALLS. A sharp *tsip.* SONG. A clear, bright, but unhurried *dzwee, dzwee, dzwee, tzwee-tsee,* or *zeea, zeea, zeea, zu-zip.* Similar to the song of the Black-throated Gray Warbler, but is slightly more musical and less buzzing; also shorter. HABITAT. Prefers the tops of tall coniferous trees in fairly dense forests in the medium and higher parts of the mountains. Less common in the coniferous timber in the lowlands. Forages and sings in the highest parts of the forest canopy where often difficult to observe. RANGE. Summer resident and breeder from southern Alaska and the central Yukon (rare) south to Washington, Oregon, and central Idaho. Winters from southwestern B.C. and central Washington southward.

HERMIT WARBLER *Dendroica occidentalis* 4-5 (102-128)

A warbler of the tall conifers with a bright yellow head, black throat, gray back (streaked with black), and white wing-bars, outer tail feathers, and under parts. Female, similar, but with duller head (crown marked with blackish) and white throat mottled with dark. Almost no streaks on under parts. CALLS. A loud bright *ying, ying, ying, er, chip-chip; wee-zee, wee-zee, wee-zee, lee-o-leet;* or *zeea, zeea, zeea, zeea, ti-dee-dee-dee* (ascending; last phrase very rapid). Very similar to the song of the Townsend's Warbler, but is louder and more musical. HABITAT. Prefers the highest parts of the coniferous canopy where it forages and sings as well as nests. Favors Douglas fir, yellow pine, and larch. Occasionally seen singing on tips of dead trees and snags. Difficult to separate by voice from the Townsend's Warbler and should be identified by sight. Scattered and irregular in occurrence. RANGE. Uncommon, irregular, local summer resident and breeder in mostly the lower mountainous terrain in Washington, Oregon, and northern Idaho. Very rare winter visitor west of the Cascades. Apparently most numerous in western Oregon and the southern Cascades of Washington. Numbers may be increasing in western Washington.

BLACK-THROATED GREEN WARBLER *Dendroica virens* 5 (128)

A strikingly-marked warbler in which the male has a green back, yellow face, black chin and throat (and upper breast), small yellow patch in center of breast, and white under parts streaked on sides with black. Wings black with two white bars. Female, similar, but black of throat and breast replaced by sooty spots. CALLS. A warbler-like *chip.*

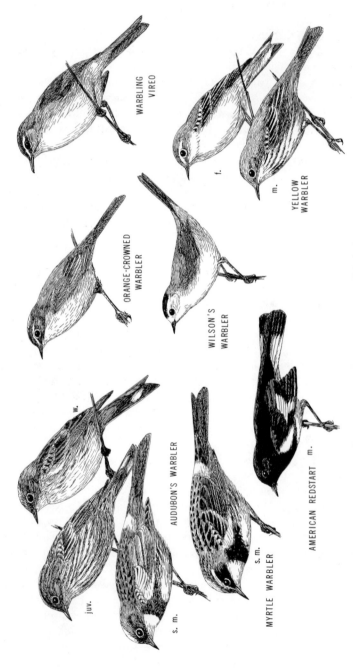

WARBLING VIREO

YELLOW WARBLER

f.

m.

ORANGE-CROWNED WARBLER

WILSON'S WARBLER

AUDUBON'S WARBLER

w.

juv.

s. m.

s. m.

MYRTLE WARBLER

s. m.

AMERICAN REDSTART m.

155. Some Pacific Northwest Warblers (Schultz)

288

SONG. A lazy high-pitched *zee, zee, zee, zee, zee, zee, zee.* Several variants to this pattern. HABITAT. Prefers coniferous forests, especially if mixed with birch, alder, or aspen. RANGE. Rare summer visitor to eastern and western Oregon. Very rare in B.C. and eastern Washington.

CAPE MAY WARBLER *Dendroica tigrina* 5 (128)
Male, blackish crown, greenish back (streaked with dark brown), yellow rump, sooty tail, yellow face (with chestnut red ear patch and yellow area behind the ear-patch), yellow line over eye; yellow throat, breast, and sides streaked with black spots, and white lower belly. Dark wings with white patches. Female, similar, but without black crown, reddish ear-patch, and with two white bars in the wing. Yellow neck patch in male is distinctive. CALLS. A light *chip.* SONG. A weak high-pitched *seep, seep, seep, seep, seep, seep.* HABITAT. Coniferous and mixed woods, particularly along the edges of forest openings. RANGE. Summer resident and breeder in northeastern B.C. Rare spring and fall migrational straggler elsewhere in the Northwest.

BLACKBURNIAN WARBLER *Dendroica fusca* 5¼ (134)
A contrastively-marked warbler with a bright orange throat, crown, stripe over eye, ear-patch, and partial ring under the eye. Remainder of the head and back (white stripes and wing patches) black. Sides are white, streaked with black, and the belly is white. The female is similar, but duller. The black and orange markings of the male are unmistakable. CALLS. Sharp *chips.* SONG. A thin, high-pitched, but variable, *wee-see-see-see-zi-zi-zi,* rising sharply in pitch toward the end. HABITAT. Typically prefers the coniferous woods, but as a straggler in our region, likely to occur anywhere in the lowlands. RANGE. Very rare summer straggler in southwest Idaho; one record, late summer, for Ocean Shores, Washington. Recorded spring 1980 in lower Yakima Valley.

MAGNOLIA WARBLER *Dendroica magnolia* 5 (128)
A strikingly-marked, black, white, and yellow warbler. Male, upper parts black (top of head gray) with yellow rump patch and white patches in wings and tail and line over eye. Throat and under parts yellow, striped on breast and sides with black spots. The broad white stripe across the under surface of the tail is distinctive as is the black ear-patch. Female, similar, but with bluish-gray head, greenish back, and weakly streaked sides. CALLS. A heavy clipped *tlep.* SONG. A rising *wisha, wisha, wisha, wit-see.* HABITAT. Coniferous or mixed woods near swamps and muskegs, particularly second growth spruce. Forages low in trees. RANGE. Summer resident and breeder in

156. Townsend's Warbler on nest (Boggs)

northeastern and eastern B.C. Rare spring and fall migrational straggler east and west of the Cascades in the Northwest, including Oregon, Washington, and Idaho.

MYRTLE WARBLER *Dendroica coronata* 5-6 (128-153) Fig. 155 Similar to the more common Audubon's Warbler, but with white, instead of yellow, throat, ear-patches, black instead of gray, white eye-stripes, and two narrow white bars instead of large white patches in each wing. Female, duller than male. CALLS. A soft *tsip* or *tsup.* SONG. A simple song pattern, as *chee-chee-chee-chee-chi-chi-chi.* HABITAT. For breeding, prefers open to semi-open coniferous or mixed coniferous-deciduous woods. Variable in migration, but perhaps favoring deciduous growth along water. RANGE. Summer resident and breeder from northcentral Alaska and the northern Yukon south to southern Alaska and northern B.C. Passes in migration through the remainder of the Northwest in spring and fall (mostly west of the Cascades) and winters from southwestern B.C., southern Washington, and southern Idaho southward.

AUDUBON'S WARBLER *Dendroica auduboni* 4-5 (102-128) Fig. 155 Male in spring and summer, upper parts bluish gray, streaked with black; upper breast and sides black; throat, crown, rump, and patches on sides yellow; large white patches on wings; belly white. In winter, upper parts brownish; under parts whitish, somewhat streaked with dark; throat and rump pale yellow. Female, pattern similar to that of male but gray replaced with brown, and large white patches absent. In winter, female similar to male. CALLS. A moderate *tchip.* SONG. Like that of the Yellow Warbler, but richer and rising in pitch, as *djeer, djeer, djeer, djeer, zwee, zwee* or *wheelia, wheelia, wheelia, witsee, witsee.* HABITAT. Prefers open coniferous or mixed coniferous-deciduous woodlands. Forages and sings well up in trees. Does considerable flycatching. More variable, habitat-wise, in winter. RANGE. Summer resident and breeder from central B.C. and southeastern Alaska south in suitable habitat through the remainder of the Northwest. Uncommon, though regular, winter visitor and resident from southwestern B.C. and northern Idaho southward, probably being most numerous west of the Cascades, although common in a few places east of that range, as at the Tri-Cities, Washington and the Lewiston-Moscow, Idaho areas. *Note.* Some ornithologists solve the matter of researching the ecology and behavior of this species and the Myrtle Warbler by combining the two. For those who are well familiar with the two species in life, there is little doubt that they are separate.

PALM WARBLER *Dendroica palmarum* 5¼ (134)

A lightly-marked warbler with a constantly wagging tail. Crown chestnut red, upper parts greenish, yellow line over eye, dark ear-patch, throat and breast yellow, streaked on sides with brownish; belly white. Under surface of tip of tail with white patches. Wing-bars obscure. CALLS. A moderate *tchip.* SONG. A flat weak trill, often increasing in volume at end. HABITAT. Spruce bogs of the north with their scattered stunted trees and low brush with occasional bare ground. Like many of the northern warblers, it feeds to a considerable extent on berries and seeds and commonly forages on the ground. RANGE. Summer resident and breeder in northeastern B.C. Of uncommon, but regular — and rapidly increasing — occurrence elsewhere in the Northwest, mainly in the coastal region as a spring and late fall and early winter visitor. Very rare in summer. Recorded rarely east of the Cascades. Increasing as a winter visitor in certain areas, such as the ocean coast, southwestern Washington, and northwestern Oregon.

BLACKPOLL WARBLER *Dendroica striata* 5-5¾ (128-148)

Similar to the Black-throated Gray Warbler, but the male has a black cap and white cheeks. This little striped fellow is olive-gray, streaked with black on the back; white on under parts, heavily streaked with black along the sides of the throat and breast; two white wing-bars. Female and immature (also fall male), similar but more olive above and crown yellowish-green streaked with black; under parts dingy yellowish white. CALLS. A moderate *chip.* SONG. A high-pitched, rising, then falling *zi-zi-zi-zi-zi.* HABITAT. Spruce woods and brush along creeks, as well as logged and burnt areas. RANGE. Summer resident and breeder from the limit of trees in northern Alaska and the northern Yukon south to southern Alaska and central and eastern B.C. Often the commonest warbler in the far northern habitats, especially in brush along streams. Rare spring and early summer visitor and fall migrational straggler in the Northwest states.

BAY-BREASTED WARBLER *Dendroica castanea* 5½ (140)

Male, a dark-headed warbler with a striking pale buffy spot behind the black patch surrounding the eye and over forehead. Crown, throat, breast, and sides chestnut. Remainder of upper parts dark-striped and grayish (two white wing-bars). Belly white. Female, similar, but much paler, except for chestnut crown patch. CALLS. A warbler-like *chip.* SONG. A high-pitched *zee-a, zee-a, zee-a, zee-a, zee,* though somewhat variable. HABITAT. Frequents the edges of openings in the northern spruce woods, as well as the margins of bogs, ponds, and clearings. RANGE. Rare spring and fall migrational straggler in

Oregon and southern Idaho, mostly east of the Cascades. Also, a record for B.C.

AMERICAN REDSTART *Setophaga ruticilla* 5 (128) Fig. 155
A medium-sized warbler of the deep deciduous or mixed woodlands with black head, throat, and upper parts and salmon-red patches on sides, wings, and tail. Female, similar, but black of male replaced by sooty brown and red by yellow. CALLS. A sharp *chip*. A loud bright *tsee, tsee, tsee, tsoo-weet* or *weet-see, weet-see, WEET-SEE,* given rapidly with emphasis on the ending. Also may be rendered as *tsee-a, tsee-a, tsee-a, TSEE-A.* HABITAT. Occurs mostly commonly in our region in deciduous or mixed deciduous-coniferous groves of trees near water where it forages and nests from 15 to 40 feet above the ground, mostly in the lowlands. Willows and/or alders a deciduous necessity. RANGE. Local summer resident and breeder from the southern Yukon (where rare) and southeastern Alaska south in the interior of the Northwest to eastern Oregon. Rare summer and fall straggler west of the Cascades. Summer resident in northern Idaho, but mostly a migrational transient in the southern part of that state.

OVENBIRD *Seiurus aurocapillus* 5½-6½ (140-168)
A large thrush-like ground warbler often seen walking along the surface in groves of deciduous trees. Sexes alike: upper parts olive-green, except orange stripe down middle of crown bordered on each side with black; under parts white, streaked with black on sides of throat and across breast and down sides of belly. Immature, browner above and buffy below. SONG. A long series of two-noted phrases starting softly, becoming louder and louder, as *teacher-teacher-teacher-teacher-TEACHER-TEACHER;* accented on first syllable of each phrase. HABITAT. Deciduous woodland with more or less open floor of leaf litter. RANGE. Summer resident and breeder in northeastern B.C. Rare spring, summer, and fall straggler from Alaska southward through the remainder of the Northwest region, particularly east of the Cascades and along the Idaho-Washington-Oregon migrational corridor. A recent late June record for western Washington.

NORTHERN WATERTHRUSH *Seiurus noveboracensis* 5-6 (128-153)
A large warbler characterized by its streaked thrush-like appearance, white line over the eye, and preferences for wooded ponds and swamps. Upper parts solid dusky brown; white line over eye; throat, breast, and sides heavily streaked with dark brown; belly pale yellowish white; bill and feet dark. CALLS. A sharp metallic *tchip* or *klink.* SONG. A loud, rapid, descending series, as *chwit, chwit, chwit,*

chwit, chew-chew-chew-chew-it or *chee-chee-chee, chip-chip-chip-chew-chew-chew.* HABITAT. Occurs in deciduous brush, such as willows and alders, along streams and pond shores. Also in swamps and bogs. Margins of fresh water a necessity for foraging sites. More numerous in the spruce forest lake and pond area of the northern parts of the Northwest. RANGE. Summer resident and breeder from northern Alaska and the central Yukon south to southern B.C., northeastern Washington, northern Idaho, and western Montana. Uncommon migrant and migrational wanderer elsewhere in the Northwest. Rare in winter in the southern part of the region, but has been noted as far north as the Skagit Flats, Washington. Very local breeder in the Oregon Cascades.

WORM-EATING WARBLER *Helmitheros vermivorus* 5½ (140)
A dull-colored warbler, head greenish buff with contrastive black lines on each side of crown and through the eyes, with a light line over the eye (between black crown and eye lines), rest of upper parts dark greenish, and under parts light green or buffy-green. Sexes similar. A slow-acting ground forager with tail cocked wren-like. SONG. Like trill of Chipping Sparrow, but louder and faster. Flight song resembles that of the goldfinches. HABITAT. Second growth deciduous woods with considerable underbrush, often near water. RANGE. Very rare visitor (fall) to the Oregon coast (Cape Meares). One record.

PROTHONOTARY WARBLER *Protonotaria citrea* 5½ (140)
Male, head, neck, and under parts bright orange yellow; back greenish; wings, tail, and rump bluish gray. Bill black. Female, similar but duller. Wing-bars absent. Some white on sides of tail. CALLS. A soft *chip* or loud *pink.* SONG. A loud *tweet, tweet, tweet, tweet, tweet.* HABITAT. Swampy or flooded woods and bottoms as well as wet riparian growth. RANGE. Rare migrational straggler in the Northwest states, mostly east of the Cascades.

COMMON YELLOWTHROAT *Geothlypis trichas* 4-5 (102-128) Fig. 153
A swamp-inhabiting warbler with a black mask through the eyes, greenish upper parts, yellow throat and breast, and buffy belly. Female lacks black mask. CALLS. A husky *tchek.* SONG. A hurried *rees-wittee, rees-wittee, rees-wittee.* HABITAT. Occurs in dense growths of cattails or young deciduous brush, such as willows, in or near fresh water, mostly in marshes and swamps. Forages in lower few feet of cover above the water surface where it also places the nest. RANGE. Local summer resident and breeder from southeastern Alaska and the southern Yukon (fairly common) south through the

Northwest in preferred marshy or riparian habitats. Rare to uncommon winter visitor in Oregon, though erratic in numbers and at times locally common.

KENTUCKY WARBLER *Geothlypis formosa* 5½ (140)
Male, forehead black, remainder of crown gray and black spotted; yellow eye-ring and line to bill; black patch below eye from ear to bill; remainder of upper parts greenish; under parts yellow. Female, duller, with black markings more restricted. CALLS. A sharp *chip.* SONG. A clear loud *tur-dle, tur-dle, tur-dle, tur-dle, tur-dle.* HABITAT. Prefers dense, brushy, deciduous woodlands near water. A ground forager. RANGE. Rare post-breeding straggler to southern B.C.

CONNECTICUT WARBLER *Geothlypis agilis* 5¾ (147)
Male, head, neck, and breast light gray (complete white eye-ring); upper parts greenish; under parts yellow. Female, similar, but hood is brown, not gray. SONG. A loud ringing *beecher, beecher, beecher, beecher.* HABITAT. Prefers spruce and tamarack bogs, but in northwestern part of range (Alberta and northeastern B.C.) seeks brushy openings in aspen and poplar woodlands. RANGE. Summer resident and breeder in northeastern B.C.

MOURNING WARBLER *Geothlypis philadelphia* 5½ (140)
Male, very similar to the MacGillivray's Warbler, but lacks the white eye-ring of that species. Female, head, neck, and upper breast grayish. Some ornithologists consider the Mourning and the MacGillivray's Warblers to be the same species. SONG. A loud *teedle, teedle, teedle, teedle.* HABITAT. Prefers dense brush, especially in young second growth in burns and clearings; also the margins of bogs and muskegs. RANGE. Uncommon summer resident in northeastern B.C.

MacGILLIVRAY'S WARBLER *Geothlypis tolmiei* 5 (128) Fig. 157
A loud-voiced warbler of the dense brush. Male, green-backed yellow-bellied warbler with a gray hood and white eye-ring. Female, similar but paler; throat light gray or buff. CALLS. A moderate *chuck.* SONG. A loud *sweeter-sweeter-sweeter-sweet-sweet* or *sneaker-sneaker-sneaker-snick-snick.* HABITAT. Prefers dense, damp, dark patches of brush without tree growth, preferably on hillsides, from lowlands to subalpine areas. Forages in lower strata above the ground and comes to the top of the bush only for singing. Much more often heard than seen. RANGE. Summer resident and breeder from southeastern Alaska and southwestern Yukon south in proper habitat through the Northwest. Rare in winter in the lowlands west of the Cascades.

157. MacGillivray's Warbler on nest (Boggs)

HOODED WARBLER *Wilsonia citrina* 5½ (140)
Male, easily recognized by its black hood and large yellow mask; rest
of upper parts greenish; under parts yellow. Female, greenish above,
yellow below, with yellow face separated from greenish crown by a
broken streak of black. CALLS. A sharp *chip*. SONG. A clear ringing
weetoo, weetoo, weetoo. HABITAT. Deciduous forests, particularly
near water. RANGE. Very rare winter and summer visitor to western
and eastern Oregon and western Washington.

WILSON'S WARBLER *Wilsonia pusilla* 4-5 (102-128) Fig. 155
A warbler of the dense forest and brush. Male, greenish above; yellow
below; jet black cap on head. Female, similar, but with smaller cap.
CALLS. A sharp *tchep*. SONG. A series of *tcheps* increasing in intensity. HABITAT. Prefers low dense brush and thickets in the fir-
hemlock forests where foraging is done on branches below six feet
above the ground and nests are either placed within a few feet of the
ground or between the roots of a small conifer. Shows increasing use
of shrubbery in gardens and parks in residential areas of cities, at least
for migratory cover. Moist shade a necessity. RANGE. Summer resident and breeder from northern Alaska and the northern Yukon south
through the Northwest. Rare winter visitor in certain protected places,
mostly west of the Cascades, especially in southern Oregon.

CANADA WARBLER *Wilsonia canadensis* 5½ (140)
Male, upper parts grayish with black-spotted crown, black face (yellow eye-ring and line to base of bill), and yellow under parts marked across the breast with streaks of black spots. Female, similar, but duller, the black necklace reduced. CALLS. A loud *chip*. SONG. A loud, rich, irregular series of notes, beginning with one or two detached *chips*. HABITAT. Dense brushy undergrowth in mature woodlands, dense riparian growth, and brushy swamps. RANGE. Very rare fall migrational straggler in the Rocky Mountain Trench migrational corridor to Washington and Oregon.

PAINTED REDSTART *Myioborus pictus* 5¼ (134)
Upper parts, breast, and sides black with large white patches in the wings and white outer tail feathers; belly red. Lower belly white. CALLS. A finch-like *cheereo* or simple *pee*. SONG. A clear mellow *cheery, cheery, cheery, chew* or *weecher, weecher, weecher, chew, chew*. HABITAT. Timber and riparian woods in the deep canyons of desert mountains; occasionally on pinyon pine slopes. RANGE. Very rare fall straggler in southwestern B.C.

158. Chat (Schultz)

YELLOW-BREASTED CHAT *Icteria virens* 6-7 (153-178) Fig. 158
A large sparrow-sized warbler with greenish-brown upper parts, yellow throat and breast, white belly, and white eye-ring or "spectacles". Like the Mockingbird in personality. CALLS. A mellow *kook* or *kee-yuck*. SONG. Various calls and notes alternating with a loud, clear,

rolling whistle. HABITAT. Prefers dense riparian growth, especially of willows, along streams and ponds. Must have heavy thick cover for foraging and the proper supply of insects, spiders, and berries. Foraging and nesting below 10 feet and singing done in the upper, but well-covered, areas of the brush. Much more often heard than seen. Will occur in dry-slope brush, but only when seeking mates. RANGE. Local summer resident and breeder in suitable habitat from southcentral and southwestern B.C. southward, mostly in the interior east of the Cascades; recorded uncommonly to the west of that range. Very rare in winter in western Oregon. *Note:* This species may not be a true wood warbler.

VIREOS

159.   Red-eyed Vireo (Pole)

Vireos are small-sparrow-sized, greenish- or grayish-backed, warbler-like birds similar in habits to warblers but slower and less active. The bill is heavier and slightly hooked. Their songs are short and lack the high-pitched quality of the other group. These are common birds in wooded areas during the summer and their songs make up an

298

important part of the wild chorus. The vireos specialize in feeding on crawling insects which they secure from the foliage of trees by slow careful searching. The word "vireo" means "I am green" in Latin and an earlier name for the group was indeed "greenlets".

The family is confined to the New World and amounts to some 44 species, divided into three groups, the typical vireos, the fruit-eating shrike-vireos, and the large-billed pepper-shrikes. The Vireonidae show little relationship to other birds. Six species have been recorded, some rarely, in the Pacific Northwest.

Our only resident vireo, the Hutton's, is small, drab, and easily overlooked. To find it, one must search through the deciduous thickets in the lowlands west of the Cascades. It is more often heard than seen, but its call note is unique and easily recognized. Fifty years ago and more, the Seattle Audubon Society used to make an annual field trip to Mercer Island, then a cutover wilderness accessible only by ferry from the west shore of Lake Washington. One of the principal goals of the excursion was to locate the Hutton's Vireo which was numerous on the island in those days. Those were times also when the Newport Flat was excellent for shorebirds. How times have changed!

PACIFIC NORTHWEST SPECIES

HUTTON'S VIREO *Vireo huttoni* 4½ (115) Fig. 160
This is a small greenish-gray vireo with two prominent white wing-bars, an incomplete eye-ring, white spot between eye and bill, and yellowish under parts. CALLS. A light *kip* or low *tschuk*. SONG. A ventriloquial *chu-weem, chu-weem, chu-weem,* or *zu-zeep, zu-zeep,* etc., delivered on the same pitch every few seconds with clock-like regularity. HABITAT. Prefers dense deciduous and mixed deciduous-coniferous woods in the lowlands. RANGE. Resident and breeder from southwestern B.C. south in the Northwest west of the Cascades. Some northern individuals move southward in winter. Very rare east of the Cascades. Extra-limital records should be made with care, as the species has often been confused with the Ruby-crowned Kinglet.

BELL'S VIREO *Vireo belli* 4¾ (121)
A small dull-colored vireo with a gray head (obscure white eye-ring), greenish upper parts (two narrow white wing-bars), bright greenish rump, white throat, and buffy under parts. The eye is dark. CALLS. Three rapid notes in scolding. SONG. A rapid series of coarse *chips,* alternately slurred upward and downward in typical vireo "question and answer" pattern. HABITAT. Deciduous riparian thickets along streams. Often found feeding on or near the ground. RANGE. Rare

299

160. Three frequently confused species: Hutton's Vireo (top), Ruby-crowned Kinglet (center), Golden-crowned Kinglet (bottom) (Schultz)

spring visitor to extreme southwest and eastern Oregon. Prefers low cottonwood and willow thickets in that area.

SOLITARY VIREO *Vireo solitarius* 5-6 (128-153)
A greenish-backed vireo with a dark gray head, white eye-ring, two white wing-bars, and dirty white under parts. The flanks usually have a yellowish tint. CALLS. Low purring notes. SONG. A series of detached questions and answers, two-noted, slow, and low-pitched. Similar to the song of the Red-eyed Vireo, but slower in tempo and lower-pitched. HABITAT. Prefers semi-open coniferous timber with brushy understory, mostly in low to intermediate elevations. Seldom found in deciduous woods. RANGE. Summer resident, breeder, and migrant from central B.C. south in suitable habitat through the remainder of the Northwest.

PHILADELPHIA VIREO *Vireo philadelphicus* 4½-5 (115-128)
Very similar to the Red-eyed Vireo, but smaller, with dark eye, more grayish head and upper parts, more obscure markings on the head, and with pale yellow breast. SONG. Similar to that of the Red-eyed Vireo, but higher pitched and slower. About the tempo of the Solitary Vireo's song. HABITAT. Prefers edges in deciduous and mixed woodlands, aspen parklands, and thickets of willows and alders along the water. RANGE. Summer resident and breeder in northeastern B.C., straggling rarely southward through the Northwest, both east and west, to Oregon in spring and (mostly) fall migration. Possibly summer resident.

RED-EYED VIREO *Vireo olivaceus* 5-6 (128-153) Fig. 159
A greenish-backed vireo with a black-bordered white line over the eye, dark-gray crown, white under parts, and red eyes. Wing-bars are lacking. CALLS. A querulous *quee*. SONG. A monotonous series of questions and answers like those of the Solitary Vireo but higher in pitch, more regular, and three- to four-noted, instead of one- to three-noted as in the Solitary, and in faster tempo. This species usually sings from deciduous tree tops. HABITAT. Prefers tall deciduous growth along water in the lowlands. RANGE. Common summer resident and breeder from western Washington and southern and northeastern B.C. south in the lowlands to northern Oregon, northern Idaho, and western Montana. More numerous in the interior of the Northwest. Scattered, but increasing, summer resident elsewhere in the southern part of the region (especially in Oregon).

WARBLING VIREO *Vireo gilvus* 5-6 (128-153)
A nondescriptly-colored vireo, similar to the Red-eyed Vireo, but with only an indistinct white line unbordered by black over the eye; little or

no gray on crown. CALLS. A buzzy *twee;* drawling nasal *shree, shree.* SONG. A squeaky wavery *zeekery, zeekery, zeekery, zeek.* T. Gilbert Pearson of early Audubon Society fame rendered it as "If I could see it, I would seize it, and squeeze it, till it squirts." HABITAT. Frequents deciduous and mixed deciduous-coniferous woods, mostly in the lowlands. Forages and sings in the upper parts of trees. Proximity of water not a necessity, as in the Red-eyed Vireo. RANGE. Summer resident and breeder from southeastern Alaska (rare), northern B.C., and the southern Yukon south in low to moderate elevations through the Northwest. Often common and widespread in occurrence.

TROUPIALS

The troupials (Icteridae) are a very diverse family in which adaptive radiation has proceeded to a very marked extent. We have in the family such diverse species groups as orioles, blackbirds, bobolinks, grackles, caciques, meadowlarks, oropendolas, etc. The vocal notes for the most part are raucous and not particularly attractive, although one, our Western Meadowlark, has a very fine and famous song. Birds of the family have stout legs and feet, vigorous direct flight, strong pointed bills, and much black or yellow in the plumage. These are primarily tropical birds with a relatively few penetrating the upper part of the Temperate Zone. They feed mostly on insects and a number of them forage extensively on the ground. All seldom visit more than bushes and low trees. Another interesting feature of the group is the extreme sexual dimorphism in plumage patterns that is common. That is, the two sexes of a species are often quite different with the female much duller and more protectively colored. Many habitats have been invaded by members of the family but most of our Northwest species are migratory.

Approximately 100 species make up this strictly New World group of which some fifteen have been recorded, commonly or rarely, in the Pacific Northwest. They are an interesting, extroverted, and noisy group and very attractive to the birder. There seems to be a pattern of southern Orioles wandering north along the coast to the western or southwestern part of the Pacific Northwest. Oriole students should keep a close watch on all orioles they find, especially in the fall and winter months. Winter plumages may be tricky and careful work in identification and note taking is advised.

161. Red-winged Blackbird (male, l.; female, r.) (Fisher)

PACIFIC NORTHWEST SPECIES

SCARLET-HEADED ORIOLE *Icterus pustulatus* 5½ (217)
Male, head bright scarlet with black bib and patch before eye; wings black with broad white wing-bars; back orange, streaked with black; under parts orange yellow; tail black. The striped back is unique in Northwest Orioles. CALLS. A *reep.* SONG. Similar to that of the Bullock's Oriole, but less emphatic. HABITAT. Broken brush, open woodlands, and thickets in the desert country, especially mesquite. RANGE. Very rare visitor to the southwestern part of the Northwest.

HOODED ORIOLE *Icterus cucullatus* 8 (204)
An orange-yellow oriole with black face, throat, breast, back, and wings (two white wing-bars); remainder of head (back and above eye) and under parts orange yellow to yellow. Tail black. CALLS. High-pitched notes and various oriole chatters. SONG. Various whistles, chatters, and warbles. HABITAT. Deciduous woods and groves along water, as well as in city parks and wooded residential areas. RANGE. Rare spring and fall migrational visitor in Oregon, both east and west of the Cascades (very rare in winter in western Oregon). Possibly very sparse summer resident in the southeastern corner of that state.

303

BULLOCK'S ORIOLE *Icterus bullockii* 7-9 (178-230) Fig. 163
Between a large sparrow and a robin in size. Male, bright orange and black with large white wing-patches and a black stripe down the center of the throat. Female, upper parts grayish, suffused with yellow on head; wings dark with white wing-bars; sides of throat and breast yellow; rest of under parts whitish. CALLS. A sharp *kip* or *tyew;* also a sharp twittering *che-che-che-che,* etc. SONG. An accented *kit, kit-tick, kit-tick, whee-oo, wheet.* HABITAT. Prefers tall deciduous trees, especially cottonwoods, in riparian growth along streams or in other moist places. Nests placed at medium to high locations. Nearby fields or meadows for foraging desirable. Also occasionally found in wooded parks and residential areas. RANGE. Summer resident and breeder from southern B.C. southward through the Northwest, mostly east of the Cascades. Local and regular west of that range. Rare winter straggler west and east of the Cascades. Strongly restricted to large deciduous trees.

BALTIMORE ORIOLE *Icterus galbula* 8 (204)
An entirely-black-headed oriole with a black back, wings (white wing-bars), bib, and tail (margined with orange). Rump, patch on shoulders, and under parts bright orange. Female, similar, but black of head and back replaced by brown streaks on greenish. CALLS. A whistled *tewly;* harsh chattering notes. SONG. A series of loud mellow whistles, often varied in pattern. HABITAT. Open woods and scattered deciduous trees as well as shaded residential areas in towns and cities. The author has found them in aspen parklands in northeastern B.C. RANGE. Summer resident and breeder in northeastern B.C.; rare summer and early fall visitor to the Northwest states.

ORCHARD ORIOLE *Icterus spurius* 6-7 (153-178)
A dark-colored oriole with black head, wings (white wing-bars), back, and tail. Rump, shoulders, and under parts deep chestnut red. Female, very similar to some other female orioles and not easy to call. CALLS. A blackbird-like *chuck* and various other notes. SONG. Robin-like, but the ending is a slurred-downward note or notes. HABITAT. Open deciduous woods and scattered trees. Found commonly in orchards and shaded residential areas. RANGE. Very rare spring straggler in southeastern Washington and adjacent northern Idaho; occasional summer resident and breeder in southwest Idaho.

SCOTT'S ORIOLE *Icterus parisorum* 8 (204)
A black oriole with yellow rump, shoulders, sides, and belly. Yellow margins to upper sides of tail. Two white bars on wings. Female, more greenish than most female orioles. CALLS. A harsh *chuck.* SONG. A

series of rising and falling whistled notes, similar to the song of the Western Meadowlark. HABITAT. Junipers, pinyon pines, and other desert vegetation, as well as riparian growth in canyons. Particularly seeks yuccas and agaves. RANGE. Rare summer resident and breeder in extreme southern Idaho in the juniper-sage flats. Very rare winter and early spring straggler to western Washington (one record, Chehalis, February to April, 1980).

YELLOW-HEADED BLACKBIRD *Xanthocephalus xanthocephalus* 8-10 (204-255) Fig. 163
A brilliantly-colored blackbird of cattail and tule marshes. Male, head, throat, and breast yellow; rest of body black; except for white patch on wing. Female, mostly dark brown with light line over eye and light yellow throat and upper breast. CALLS. A liquid *klook* or *klack*. SONG. A leering gurgled *ca-caow-ow, ca-caow*, etc., or *kluck, glook-glook, gaah, gaah,* the last two notes drawled and very harsh. HABITAT. Nests in cattail and tule patches standing in permanent fresh water in the deeper parts of sloughs and ponds. Forages widely over adjacent meadows, fields, and marshes. RANGE. Local irregular summer resident and breeder from central B.C. south through the Northwest, mostly east of the Cascades. Uncommon as late summer visitor west of that range and north to central Alaska. Winters from southern Washington, southeastern Oregon, and southern Idaho southward. Rare in winter elsewhere in protected places in the Northwest. Preferred breeding habitat a necessity.

RED-WINGED BLACKBIRD *Agelaius phoeniceus* 7-9 (178-230) Fig. 161
Male, a jet-black bird with red shoulder patches. Female, brownish heavily-striped bird with characteristic blackbird bill and habits. CALLS. A harsh *keck* or *tee-er*. SONG. A liquid gurgling *o-ker-leer-lup* or *o-ka-lee*. HABITAT. Prefers freshwater swamps, cattail-filled drainage ditches and canals, marshy backwaters on rivers, with nearby fields, pastures, and meadows to forage in. Occasionally nests or sings in trees in swamps, but these not a necessity. RANGE. Summer resident and breeder from the southern Yukon and southeastern Alaska south in suitable habitat through the Northwest. Winters irregularly through much of the breeding range.

TRICOLORED BLACKBIRD *Agelaius tricolor* 7½-9 (191-230)
Male, very similar to the male of the Red-winged Blackbird, but there is a band of white along the back edges of the red epaulettes which is quite noticeable in flight. The red in these patches is darker than in the Red-winged. Female, similar to the female Red-winged but darker.

CALLS. A nasal *kemp* or *kape*. SONG. A nasal *on-kee-kaaaagh-a,* with a definite braying quality. HABITAT. Nests in cattail or tule marshes and perches in nearby trees during the day. Forages in adjacent fields and meadows. RANGE. Summer resident and breeder in eastcentral and southern Oregon. Rare spring visitor to eastern Washington and to western Oregon; rarer in fall and winter, though occasionally locally common. Rare in summer and possible breeder in southwest Idaho. Possibly increasing northward extension of range.

WESTERN MEADOWLARK *Sturnella neglecta* 8-10 (204-255) Fig. 163
A chunky short-tailed bird, slightly smaller than a Robin, with brown upper parts streaked with black and yellow under parts crossed on breast with a black V-shaped collar. CALLS. A soft *turk* and a loud rolling trill. SONG. A short, flute-like, gurgling phrase, something like *eu-hew, whee-licky, whee-licky,* rapidly uttered and ventriloquial in effect. HABITAT. Frequents grassy and sage-covered plains, northern shrub deserts, alfalfa fields, and other large open places where rocks, fence posts, and scattered stubs provide singing posts and herbaceous vegetation in which to place the nest. Foraging done on the ground. RANGE. Summer resident and breeder from central B.C. south through the Northwest, being most numerous and widespread in the interior east of the Cascades. Has occurred in Alaska. Winters irregularly, but often in good numbers, in scattered protected places in the Northwest, both east and west.

GREAT-TAILED GRACKLE *Quiscalus mexicanus* 16-18 (408-459)
Similar to the Purple Grackle, but much larger (the male almost as large as the Northwestern Crow). The male is an iridescent steel blue, while the female is a lighter brown than the female Purple Grackle. NOTES. Squeaky calls and harsh gurgles. HABITAT. Marshes, swamps, and mudflats. RANGE. Very rare straggler to the Northwest. One record, Malheur, Oregon, May 1980.

PURPLE GRACKLE; COMMON GRACKLE *Quiscalus quiscala* 11-13½ (280-344) Fig. 162
A black bird larger than the Brewer's Blackbird and smaller than a crow. Male, black; head, neck, upper breast and flight feathers with purplish iridescence; rest of body with bronze-green reflections. Tail long and keeled; beak black, heavy, slightly decurved at tip. Eyes yellowish-white. Female, duller and smaller. CALLS. Harsh *chuck* or *chack*. SONG. A harsh squeaky series of notes, ascending in pitch. HABITAT. Fields, moist meadows, golf courses, marshes, aquatic margins, or open woodlands, where ground surface foraging is possi-

162. Purple Grackle (Fisher)

ble. RANGE. Rare migrational, winter, and early summer straggler to the Northwest from central Alaska southward on both sides of the Cascades. Recorded breeding in western Montana (Deer Lodge). Several fall and winter records for northern Idaho, as well as several spring records for southern portion of the state.

RUSTY BLACKBIRD *Euphagus carolinus* 8½-9¾ (217-249)
Male, a glossy-black blackbird with a bluish-green sheen on head; similar to the Brewer's Blackbird, except for the iridescence of the plumage (Brewer's has purplish sheen on the head and greenish cast on the body). Some feathers of the present species have rusty tips. Eyes yellow. Female, like male, but slate-colored without iridescence. In fall, the adults and immatures are brownish with most feathers rusty-tipped. Could be confused in spring with the grackles which have white eyes and longer tails, and the cowbirds which are smaller and have dark eyes. CALLS. A short *chack*. SONG. A creaky *kuck-a-lee* and *kush-lay* mixed together. HABITAT. Wet woods, swamps, shrubbery, aquatic margins, etc., where foraging may be done. RANGE. Summer resident and breeder from northern Alaska and northern Yukon south to central B.C. Rare late summer and fall straggler

307

163. Some typical troupials: Western Meadowlark (upper left), Brown-headed Cowbird (upper right; immature, male, and female), Bullock's Oriole (center, female and male), Yellow-headed Blackbird (lower left, female and male), and Brewer's Blackbird (lower right: female and male) (Schultz)

elsewhere in the Northwest. Rare to occasional winter visitor from Alaska southward, especially in wintering flocks of Brewer's and Red-winged Blackbirds.

BREWER'S BLACKBIRD *Euphagus cyanocephalus* 8-9 (204-230) Fig. 163

Male, a wholly black blackbird with a white eye and a purplish reflection on the head. Female, entirely brownish gray and with a dark eye. CALLS. A harsh *check* or *chup.* SONG. A wheezy *check, check, korree* or *kee-yay.* HABITAT. Prefers open lowland country with brush patches and thickets where there are plenty of insects. Commonly to be seen along roads and highways where moisture in the bordering ditches and brush and fences for perching are available. Resorts to open areas at the higher elevations after the breeding season where it may be seen in large flocks. RANGE. Summer resident and breeder from central B.C. southward through the Northwest. Winters irregularly through the breeding range. Rare in Alaska, mostly in the southeastern part.

BRONZED COWBIRD *Molothrus aeneus* 8½ (217)

Similar to the Brown-headed Cowbird, but larger and longer billed. Somewhat similar to the Brewer's Blackbird, but has a red eye. Appears blackish in color, but a good light will reveal a bronzy iridescent sheen. The female is black, lacks the bronze sheen, but has a red eye. Bill is heavy and more sparrow-like. Size and red eye are distinctive. CALLS. Various rattling sounds. SONG. Very similar to that of the Brown-headed Cowbird, but higher pitched and of a longer duration. HABITAT. Similar to that of the Brown-headed Cowbird. RANGE. Occasional migrant and rare summer resident in southwest Idaho.

BROWN-HEADED COWBIRD *Molothrus ater* 7-8 (178-204) Fig. 163

A small brown-headed blackbird with a short, conical, sparrow-like bill. Female, grayish and weakly speckled. Immature, pale brownish with buffy scale-like markings on the back. CALLS. A liquid gurgling *gloo-gloo, whee-eet,* or *gloo-gloo-eeee,* and a shrill whistled *whee-eeet;* notes often resembling the sounds of a squeaky barn door. HABITAT. Frequents woodlands, tall brush, orchards, meadows, and pastures, usually in the immediate vicinity of cattle in the case of the latter two habitats. Forages on insects on the ground. Penetrates woodlands and open forests for nest parasitization of tree-nesting birds. RANGE. Summer resident and breeder from western and northeastern B.C., the southern Yukon, and southeastern Alaska south through the

Northwest. Less common and tending to be more local in southern Idaho. Common to uncommon winter visitor in the Northwest states.

BOBOLINK *Dolichonyx oryzivorus* 7 (178)
The male is a black-and-white sparrow-sized bird of open fields and meadows. The upper back is mostly black; shoulders, lower back, rump, and upper tail coverts are white. The nape is yellow and the under parts wholly black. Female, buffy colored, streaked with blackish, except on under parts; black stripes on crown above eyes. CALLS. A soft *tchink*. SONG. A reedy bubbling series, gradually ascending in pitch; difficult to describe. HABITAT. Occurs in moist open meadows of considerable size, such as wild hay fields and large flats with tall grass. RANGE. Local irregular summer resident and breeder from southern and eastcentral B.C. south through the interior of the Northwest. Rare west of the Cascades as a migrational straggler. To be found in summer mostly in large lowland prairie-like areas, as the Bonner's Ferry, Idaho and Cusick Prairie, Washington localities, as well as in Okanogan, Yakima, and Stevens Counties. A large colony now at the Malheur National Wildlife Refuge in summer. Recorded from the Olympic Peninsula in spring.

FINCHES

164. Pine Grosbeak (female, above; male, below) (Fisher)

The finches are sparrow-like birds with short, stout, conical bills (except the crossbills). The tail is short to long, but notched at the tip. The feet are small and weak. This is a varied group in appearance. Some forms are more or less solidly reddish in color with heavy streaking. Others show considerable amounts of yellow. With the exception of the goldfinches and a few others, these are for the most part birds of the coniferous trees where they forage among the branches, a fact separating them from the sparrows which are primarily birds of the ground and low trees and bushes. Careful attention must be paid to details in identifying these birds and the carpodacine finches are probably best told apart by their vocal notes. We are not at all impressed with the so-called ability of most people to tell these very similar birds with variable sex and age plumages apart visually.

Some 125 species are included in the family Fringillidae as now recognized by authorities. These are birds strongly adapted for handling hard seeds. Superficially, they resemble other seed-eaters, such as the American bunting sparrows, but the resemblance is purely a matter of convergent evolution. Seed eating is a fairly common alimentary habit among a number of birds and the necessary adaptations for this habit are much the same. Many of the species in this family are highly colored and to us, with our living in a northern clime, these are common and familiar birds. Some show strong ecologic restrictions and one must go to where they occur. This is particularly true of such species as the Gray-crowned Rosy Finch.

PACIFIC NORTHWEST SPECIES

BRAMBLING *Fringilla montifringilla* 5¾ (147)
Male, a black (summer)- or brown (winter)-headed finch with a prominent white rump and lower back. Throat, breast, and shoulders orange, wings (two white bars) and tail black; belly white. Female, light brownish with dark buffy nape (bordered by dark brown lines), two white wing-bars, and prominent white rump. CALLS. A harsh *tzack* or *chunk* in flight, also a *djee-ek* call. SONG. A twittering series of monotonous notes. HABITAT. Open or mixed woods, frequently the parks and gardens in towns in winter. RANGE. Very rare winter straggler west of the Cascades, mostly along the coast.

PINE SISKIN *Carduelis pinus* 4-5 (102-128) Fig. 165
A small sparrow-sized brownish bird, heavily streaked with dusky; yellow often showing conspicuously in wings and tail in flight. Similar to the Redpoll, but without red cap and black chin. CALLS. A high-pitched *pi-ti-tic* in flight; also a loud *clee-ip* and a buzzy *shur-ree-ee-ee;* a *klee-klee* note for the flight call. SONG. A rapid succession of rattled notes which resembles the *klee-klee* call but also has some short warbled notes interspersed. Often sings on the wing while flying in a wide circle. HABITAT. Frequents coniferous or mixed coniferous-deciduous woods at all elevations; also common in parks and residential areas in towns and cities where coniferous trees are preferred for perching. Nests in conifers and forages in trees as well as on the ground, as on snowbank flats in the forest. Perches high in tree-tops when not foraging. A common and widely-spread species in the Northwest. RANGE. Summer resident and breeder from southern Alaska and the southern Yukon south in coniferous forests through the Northwest, wintering very irregularly at lower levels throughout much of the breeding range.

AMERICAN GOLDFINCH *Carduelis tristis* 5 (128) Fig. 165
A striking yellow and black bird of the late summer thistle patches. Male, in spring and summer, bright yellow with black forehead, wings (white wing-bars), and tail. In winter, like the female, but with black and white wings. Female, upper parts brownish green; wings and tail

dark with grayish wing-bars; under parts dull yellow. CALLS. A rollicking *ka-chee-chee, ka-chee-chee,* given in flight; a clear *sweet* call and an odd *kool-dear.* SONG. A sustained, twittering, canary-like warble, often given on the wing or at a tree-top perch. HABITAT. Breeds in willow and alder riparian growth and orchards, foraging out in the open in fields and bushes where favoring the seed heads of composites, especially thistles, in late summer. Roams widely in fall, winter, and spring, seeking particularly trees along water. RANGE. Common summer resident and breeder from southern B.C. south, wintering irregularly through much of the breeding range.

LESSER GOLDFINCH *Carduelis psaltria* 3½-4¼ (89-108)
Male, similar to the American Goldfinch, but with a black cap, greenish back, dark rump, and noticeably smaller size. Female, similar to American Goldfinch female but greenish with a dark rump. CALLS. A plaintive *tee-yee* (rising) and *tee-yer* (dropping). SONG. Musical, with notes often in pairs. HABITAT. Weedy fields and pastures, as well as open brush and scattered trees. RANGE. Resident and breeder in western Oregon. Rare visitor and possible breeder in extreme southwestern Washington. Has been found nesting near Lyle, Washington on the north bank of the Columbia River where it may be resident. Listed as accidental in B.C. Rare in summer in southwest Idaho as a visitor.

LAWRENCE'S GOLDFINCH *Carduelis lawrencei* 4¼ (108)
A gray goldfinch with black cap and bib, yellow rump and wing-bars (on dark wings), and yellow breast. Female, similar, but without black on head. CALLS. A light *tinkle* or *tink* in flight; a harsh *kee-yerr.* SONG. A typical goldfinch series of tinkling notes. HABITAT. Open woodlands, riparian thickets, and trees and shrubs in gardens and parks. RANGE. Rare summer straggler in western Oregon.

COMMON REDPOLL *Acanthis flammea* 5 (128) Fig. 166
A small, streaked, grayish-brown, sparrow-sized bird with dark red patch on forehead and black chin. Whitish under parts are conspicuous in flight. The breast of the male is washed with rosy. The rump is grayish white and streaked. CALLS. A twittering *chet-chet.* SONG. A series of *chets* followed by a trill. HABITAT. As a winter visitor in our region, prefers open country, particularly open woodland, orchards, weed patches, fence rows, and trees and shrubs in urban areas in the interior. Occurs in pure flocks or mixed in with Pine Siskins. RANGE. Summer resident and breeder from northern Alaska and the northern Yukon south to northern B.C., wintering from central Alaska and the Aleutians irregularly and sparsely southward through the remainder of the Northwest, mostly east of the Cascades.

165. Common Redpoll (Pole)

HOARY REDPOLL *Acanthis hornemanni* 5¼-5½ (134-140)
Similar to the Common Redpoll, but with an immaculately white
rump (streaked in the Common Redpoll). Male, paler pink breast than
the male Common and usually unstreaked sides. The ground color is
more or less whitish (rather than grayish) under the streaks and spots.
Female, lacks pink but has crimson forehead, as does male. CALLS
AND SONG. Similar to those of the Common Redpoll, but more
emphatic. HABITAT. In migration and winter, open places such as
meadows, weedy and stubble fields, and open flats. RANGE. Summer
resident and breeder along the Arctic slope from the Yukon west
through northern and western Alaska to the mouth of the Yukon
River, wintering south through the Northwest to southern B.C.,
northern Montana, northeastern Washington, and (rarely) southern
Idaho.

GRAY-CROWNED ROSY FINCH *Leucosticte tephrocotis* 5-6 (128-
153)
A dark-colored finch of the mountain peaks in summer and open
places in winter. Male, a dark brownish sparrow-like bird. Forehead
and chin black, rest of head gray; wings and tail black. Belly and

314

shoulders with rosy tint. Female, similar to male but duller, with gray of head reduced. Belly and wings with buffy tint. Amount of gray on sides of head varying according to subspecies. CALLS. A loud *weep, weep;* a harsh *churk* or *tzzt;* a twittering given in flight. SONG. A high finch-like series of notes. HABITAT. Breeds on the high rocky ridges and plateaus above timberline, gathering in flocks in the fall to descend to open areas in the interior where they commonly forage on the faces of road cuts and roost in crevices or old swallow nests on cliffs, as at the famous "Swallow's Nest" rock south of Clarkston, Washington. Feeds on seeds and snow-benumbed insects in the summer. RANGE. Local summer resident and breeder from the Aleutians, Bering Sea islands, and northern Alaska and the northern Yukon south in preferred habitat in the high mountains through the Northwest to the southern Cascades and Olympics of Washington, the Wallowas and Crater Lake area of Oregon, northern Idaho, and northwestern Montana. Winters erratically to the lowlands and moderate elevations in the southern part of the breeding range, mostly east of the Cascades; and occasionally southward into Oregon where it is a summer resident. Breeds throughout the Oregon Cascades to and including Mount Shasta in California.

BLACK ROSY FINCH *Leucosticte atrata* 6 (153)
Similar to the Gray-crowned Rosy Finch, but sooty brown rather than rosy brown. The gray crown is more prominent by contrast. CALLS. A high plaintive *cheew* or *cheep,* repeated. SONG. Similar to that of the Gray-crowned Rosy Finch. HABITAT. Alpine meadows, rocky fields, and tundra in the highest parts of certain mountain ranges. RANGE. Summer resident and breeder in the high mountains of central and eastern Idaho (Sawtooths, Seven Devils, Tetons, etc.), wintering to lower elevations in the interior of the northwest states. Has been recorded in the Steens Mountains of Oregon in summer. Breeds from southern Montana and central Idaho to Wyoming, Utah, and eastern Nevada.

PURPLE FINCH *Carpodacus purpureus* 5-6 (128-153)
Male, more or less solidly reddish-brown; lighter on belly; streaked on neck and back with darker. Female, brownish; heavily striped; light line over eye. CALLS. A dull metallic *pit.* SONG. Melodious warbled *reegura-reegura-reegura; dreetoreet-dreetoree-toree-dreetoree;* or *reeo, reeo, reeo, richity-ree.* HABITAT. Prefers moist shaded parts of the dense coniferous forest, but occasionally seen in parks and residential areas and in orchards. Mostly in the lowlands. Forages at all levels in trees. RANGE. Resident and breeder from southwestern B.C. south through the Northwest west of the eastern foot of the Cascades. Sum-

166. Some Pacific Northwest finches: Evening Grosbeak (upper left), Red Crossbill (upper right), American Goldfinch (center), Pine Siskin (lower left), House Finch (lower right) (Schultz)

mer resident and breeder in northern B.C. and the southern Yukon (fairly common). Casual in southeastern Alaska. A few straggle east of the Cascades as far as western Montana and southwest Idaho. Recorded uncommonly in eastern Oregon. Appears decreasing as the House Finch increases.

CASSIN'S FINCH *Carpodacus cassinii* 6 (153)
Male, upper parts pinkish brown, streaked with dark brown; square patch of bright red on crown sharply defined from brown neck; rump gray-red. Under parts pale pink, fading to grayish white on belly and flanks. Similar to male House Finch, but paler without heavy streaking on under parts. Female, brownish gray above with heavy dusky-brown streaking; dull grayish white below with gray-brown streaking except on belly. Similar to female House Finch, but head and back heavily marked with dark streaks rather than finely marked with light streaks. At a distance, the female House Finch appears unmarked on upper parts. CALLS. A finch-like *tee-dee-yip.* SONG. A lively warble, more varied and richer than that of the House Finch and not ending with a coarse note. HABITAT. Prefers open coniferous woods and groves at the upper part of the montane forest and in the subalpine areas, as well as in the open to semi-open yellow pine belt. Occasionally found in towns in the arid interior. Almost always seen in conifers where it feeds to a considerable extent on the needle buds. Commonly breeds in scattered groves of subalpine firs and mountain hemlocks in the Hudsonian Zone. RANGE. Summer resident and breeder from southern B.C. southward in the foothills and mountains of the Northwest, wintering to lower elevations. Occurs mostly east of the Cascade crest, being rare and irregular west of that range. Selects coniferous timber at all elevations, but seems to prefer that of hills and mountains.

HOUSE FINCH *Carpodacus mexicanus* 5-6 (128-153) Fig. 165
A common finch of the urban areas and very similar to the Cassin's and Purple Finches. Male may be identified by the red, which is confined to the forehead and above the eyes, the breast, and rump; by the sharp streakings on the belly; and by the prominent wing-bars. Female, very pale rusty brown without head pattern; finely marked below with light streaks; and with conspicuous wing-bars. Usually restricted to settled areas, towns, and cities. CALLS. A coarse *wheet.* SONG. A lengthy, disjointed, finch-like song, usually ending with a harsh *chee-wher.* HABITAT. Prefers scattered groves of trees, interspersed with fields and lawns or fruit- or berry-bearing shrubs, and adequate nesting sites such as provided by human habitats. In our region, mostly to be found in the lowlands in the vicinity of towns,

317

cities, and rural settlements. RANGE. Resident and breeder from southern B.C. south through the lowlands of the Northwest. Possibly somewhat more numerous east of the Cascades. Prefers the lower elevations where there is coniferous timber, pure or mixed, but of a somewhat more open nature, and particularly the vicinity of human settlements, large and small. Very common in fruit orchards, especially in the Yakima Valley, Washington.

PINE GROSBEAK *Pinicola enucleator* 8-9 (204-230) Fig. 164
A Robin-sized finch of the high mountains with a stout conical bill and a deeply-forked tail. Male, head, breast, and rump rosy red; wings (with two white wing-bars) and tail blackish; rest of body gray. Female, grayish tinged on head and rump with yellowish or light red; wings (two white wing-bars) and tail dusky. CALLS. A clear whistled *tee-tew* or *tee-tee-tew,* a *twee-del-eet,* a sharp *peer,* and a low whistle. SONG. A rich and melodious warble. HABITAT. Breeds in the semi-open coniferous forests of the higher parts of the mountains but does considerable foraging in deciduous brush and thickets. In migration and winter, descends in lower elevations where it frequents both deciduous and coniferous trees and occasionally may be seen on the ground. A slow deliberate forager and shows remarkable tameness to humans. RANGE. Local resident and breeder from northern Alaska and the northern Yukon south through the Northwest in the subalpine areas of the mountains. Moves to the lowlands on both sides of the Cascades, often cyclically, in winter. The cycle is apparently about eleven years in length, when on the "high" year the birds may invade the lowlands in winter in considerable numbers, always in small flocks.

RED CROSSBILL *Loxia curvirostra* 5-6 (128-153) Fig. 165
A reddish-colored finch of the coniferous forests usually found in large flocks. Male, red with dusky wings and tail. Female, dull greenish gray; lighter on head and rump. Crossed tips of mandibles seldom visible in the field, unless birds are close to the observer. CALLS. A sharp hard *kip-kip, kip-kip-kip,* often alternated with a *chit-chit-zicker-zeen.* SONG. A finch-like warble. HABITAT. Restricted to coniferous forests or groves for all activities. Forages around the tops of trees. May be found cutting off cones and later removing the seeds from them on the ground or feeding on attached cones. Spends considerable time flying about in varying-sized flocks, always alighting near the tops of conifers. RANGE. Resident and breeder from southeastern Alaska and the southern Yukon south in coniferous forests through the Northwest, wandering irregularly, usually in large flocks, through the year.

WHITE-WINGED CROSSBILL *Loxia leucoptera* 6-7 (153-178)
A rare bird of the coniferous forests. Male, rosy red with black wings (with two white wing-bars) and tail. Female, grayish green, streaked with black; two broad white wing-bars. The white markings on the wings separate this species from the Red Crossbill in flight. CALLS. A soft *peet* rapidly repeated a number of times and a dry *chif-chif.* SONG. A beautiful canary-like series of warblings, sometimes interspersed with a loud *sweet*. Very similar to the song of the Brewer's Sparrow, but richer. The characteristic sound in the spruce woods of the north in June. HABITAT. Breeds in open coniferous or mixed forests and spends most of the remainder of its time in similar habitats, perhaps favoring the conifers. Occasionally seen in flocks of Red Crossbills. Easily located on the breeding grounds during the courtship period by its beautiful singing. RANGE. Resident and breeder from the limit of trees in Alaska and the Yukon south to southern B.C., northeastern Washington, and northern Idaho. Wanders irregularly and sparsely through the southern half of the Northwest in fall, winter, and spring. Recorded in July, 1977 in extreme southeastern Idaho and in various places in the Cascades and northern Rockies in summer as far south as Mount Rainier and on Mount Hood, summer of 1979. Has been extending its range southward in summer during the last several years.

EVENING GROSBEAK *Coccothraustes vespertinus* 7-8 (178-204)
Fig. 165
The familiar large-beaked bird of bushes and low trees that is frequently a fall and winter visitor in parks and urban areas. Male, cheeks, neck, back, and breast olive brown; crown, tail, and wings black, with a large white patch in the secondaries; yellow forehead and line over the eye, shoulder, rump, sides, and belly. Female, with gray head and back, whitish spots in secondaries, and yellowish wash on under parts. CALLS. A loud high-pitched *ee-eep, tsee,* or *gr-ree.* SONG. A short irregular warble. HABITAT. Breeds in coniferous or mixed woods, and forages extensively in deciduous growth for buds and berries. At other seasons, frequents deciduous woods and brush, especially in parks and residential areas in towns and cities where the berries of ornamental shrubs and trees are prized. Usually seen in groups of individuals. A common visitor to the bird feeding trays for sunflower seeds. RANGE. Irregular summer resident and breeder from northcentral B.C. through the Northwest, wandering widely in large flocks in winter through much of the breeding range. Casual winter visitor in southeastern Alaska. Our only New World hawfinch.

319

WEAVERS

167. House Sparrow (male, l.; female, r.) (Schultz)

HOUSE SPARROW *Passer domesticus* 5-6 (128-153) Fig. 167
The common sparrow about streets and buildings in almost all settled
areas. Upper parts brownish, heavily streaked with brown or black on
back and wings. Male, dirty-white under parts, black bib, and gray
crown. Female, grayish-white under parts, no bib, and brownish bill.
Also called the "English Sparrow". CALLS. A soft *cheep* and a harsh
chirp or *chees-ick*. HABITAT. Occurs mostly in and around buildings
and houses, sheds, barns, ivy-covered walls, grain elevators, and other
edifices of man, as well as city streets. Seldom penetrates far from
man's activities where it forages mainly as a scavenger. RANGE.
Common resident from central B.C. south in settled areas through the
Northwest. Recorded at Whitehorse, Yukon Territory, February 28,
1980.

STARLINGS

168. Crested Myna (Pole)

PACIFIC NORTHWEST SPECIES

COMMON STARLING *Sturnus vulgaris* 9 (230) Fig. 169
A short-tailed black bird. In spring, all purplish and greenish black
with yellow bill and light-colored dots on back and under surface of
tail. In winter, heavily streaked with light dots, wings brownish, and
the bill is dark. Resembles blackbirds in flight but appears tail-less and
has swift direct course, rather than an undulating pattern. CALLS. A
drawn-out rising whistle, as *whoo-ee* or *tsee-eer*. SONG. A combination of musical whistles and harsh notes; often imitates other birds and
animals. (The author's backyard starling does a good job with tree
frogs!) HABITAT. Occurs commonly in cities, towns, and farming
areas, as well as in wilder country where adequate crevices or holes for
nesting are available. Requires open areas for feeding and scavenging,
such as gardens, sanitary land fills, feed lots, pastures, and fields.
RANGE. Resident and breeder in the lowland areas through the
Northwest from southeastern Alaska and the central and southern
Yukon southward. Scattered records for various parts of Alaska.
Largest numbers are to be found in cities and towns, but in warmer
regions in the interior spreads out to relatively "wild" areas where it
prefers aspen and cottonwood groves. Winters at lower elevations,
often in immense flocks, from the central Yukon (rarely) and northern
B.C. southward.

169.　Common Starling (winter male, l,; juvenile, r.) (Schultz)

CRESTED MYNA *Acridotheres cristatellus* 10 (255) Fig. 168
This is a black Robin-sized bird with large white wing-patches, an up-
turned crest of feathers covering the nostrils at the base of the bill, yellow eyes and bill, and orange legs. CALLS. A loud melodious whistle;
various repeated phrases. HABITAT. Occurs in close proximity to
metropolitan areas (Vancouver, B.C. and environs) where nesting sites
in trees and buildings and foraging areas in fields, gardens, pastures,
and garbage dumps are available. RANGE. Resident and breeder in
and around the city of Vancouver, B.C. Has spread sparsely to Vancouver Island and southwestern B.C.

CORVIDS

170. Pinyon Jay (Fisher)

Toward the end of books on world birds, such as that by C. J. O. Harrison *(Bird Families of the World),* one finds a series of families of jay-like or crow-like birds culminating in the family Corvidae. These are stout-bodied birds with strong bills and legs and feet and a tendency to much black in the plumage. Here are the choughs, magpies, crows, ravens, jays, rooks, jackdaws, and nutcrackers. To quote from the above mentioned book:

"Much of their behavior suggests a highly developed mentality, and it has been suggested that the corvids are the most highly evolved of birds. This is supported by the behavioral adaptability of many species and by the performances of crows in laboratory tests of intelligence. Other characteristics of the family include the absence of any musical song, a tendency to be gregarious and aggressive and powerful flight."

The family contains about 103 species, of which ten have been recorded in the Pacific Northwest.

PINYON JAY *Gymnorhinus cyanocephalus* 9-11 (230-280) Fig. 170
A uniformly dull-blue Robin-sized jay with a short tail and long bill, this bird can be separated from other Northwest jays by its unmarked plumage and its lack of a crest. CALLS. A cawing *kaa-eh* or *karn-eh;* also a jay-like chattering and other miscellaneous notes. HABITAT. Occurs primarily in juniper or pinyon-juniper areas, but also occasionally to be found in sagebrush, scattered pine groves, and oak woodlands. Often seen in flocks, particularly after the breeding season. RANGE. Resident and breeder from central Oregon and southern and southeastern Idaho south; uncommon in central Idaho and rare in southcentral Washington. Wanders often widely in fall and winter.

BLUE JAY *Cyanocitta cristata* 11-12 (280-306) Fig. 171
A blue bird with a conspicuous purplish-blue crest and a narrow black collar about the neck. Nape, back, and rump purplish blue-gray; tail bright blue, barred with black, white-edged on tip. Face and throat white or pale gray; breast (excluding collar) and remaining under parts light gray or white. Wings light azure blue, spotted with white. CALLS. A thin, harsh, rather high-pitched *jee-ah, jee-ah;* a whistled

171. Blue Jay, l.; Scrub Jay, r. (Pole)

172. Steller's Jay (Pole)

too-wheedle, too-wheedle; a good imitation of a buteo; and various other notes. HABITAT. In our area, open woodlands, thickets, orchards, shady residential areas, etc. RANGE. Rare but regular visitor to eastern and western Washington, northern and southern Idaho, eastern Oregon, and southwestern B.C. Records for all seasons but apparently mostly as spring and fall stragglers. Appears to be on the increase, though fewer individuals were recorded in the winter of 1978-79 than in previous winters. The largest influx occurred in the 1976-77 winter; 50 in Idaho, 46 in Washington, 8 in Oregon; and 11 in B.C. (from data furnished by John Weber). A nesting record for the Blue Mountains of eastern Oregon, (1977).

STELLER'S JAY *Cyanocitta stelleri* 12-13 (306-331) Fig. 172
A dark-colored jay, slightly larger than the Robin, with a long tail and a pointed crest. Head, neck, and shoulders blackish; rest of body dark blue. Exhibits typical jay-like curiosity and aggressiveness. Flat gliding flight is distinctive. CALLS. A harsh *shack, shack, shack* or *flitch-flitch-flitch;* also a surprisingly good imitation of the cry of the Red-tailed Hawk. HABITAT. Occurs in dense coniferous forests from sea level to timberline, but possibly most numerous in the yellow pine

325

zone. Often found in and around large city parks where there is coniferous woods. RANGE. Common resident and breeder from southern Alaska and western and southern B.C. south in the coniferous forests of the lowlands and mountains through the remainder of the Northwest.

SCRUB JAY *Aphelocoma coerulescens* 11-12 (280-306) Fig. 171
A crestless jay with blue upper parts, except for brownish-gray back, white line over eye, and blackish sides of head. Under parts grayish white, with streaked dusky collar and blue patches on sides of breast. Bill and feet black. CALLS. A high-pitched jay-like *tschek, tschek,* etc. and a harsh *ker-week.* HABITAT. Prefers semi-open or broken mixed coniferous-deciduous forests and woodlands, particularly oak woods. Found in some suburban areas, as in Portland, Oregon. RANGE. Resident and breeder in southwestern Washington (restricted to the vicinity of the Columbia River, but as far north as Chehalis), western and southern Oregon, and southern Idaho, south of the Snake River. Wanders northward in fall and winter to the Puget Sound region as far north as Seattle, southeastern and central Washington, and northern Idaho. Records for Buckley and Seattle in summer. Range increasing in the Northwest.

GRAY JAY *Perisoreus canadensis* 9-11 (230-280)
A grayish Robin-sized bird with black nape and brownish-gray back and tail; forehead white and lower hind neck grayish; bill short and black. Amounts of light and dark on the head vary according to subspecies. Like a little gray ghost in the dark woods as it glides through the trees. CALLS. A soft querulous *whee-oo,* a raucous *horee,* and other sounds. HABITAT. Occurs in the denser coniferous forests of the mountains in the Northwest states and in similar habitat in the lowlands farther to the north; working to lower elevations in winter. Frequently seen in the vicinity of campgrounds and forest cabins where it mooches food and has gained the name of "camprobber". RANGE. Resident and breeder from the northern limit of trees in Alaska and the Yukon south in coniferous forests through the Northwest. Tends more toward a montane distribution in the southern part of the range.

BLACK-BILLED MAGPIE *Pica pica* 18-21 (459-536) Fig. 173
A large black and white land bird with a long sweeping tail; white belly, flanks, shoulders, and patches on wings. Remainder of bird black. CALLS. An *eck* uttered singly or in series; a moderate *bay-bee;* a low *charr;* and a *maag, maag, maag.* HABITAT. Prefers scattered brushy thickets in open areas, often near water or ranch buildings. A dry

173. Magpie (Fisher)

country bird, though occasionally visits the mountains and western lowlands during the non-breeding seasons. RANGE. Resident and breeder from southwestern and central Alaska and the southern Yukon southward, east of the Cascade crest through the arid parts of the remainder of the region, wandering widely in winter, especially rarely to areas west of the Cascades.

CLARK'S NUTCRACKER *Nucifraga columbiana* 12-13 (306-331) Fig. 174
A jay-like bird slightly larger than the Steller's Jay. Body grayish-white with black wings (white wing-patches) and black tail bordered with white. Separated from the Gray Jay by the plain head and white patches on wings and tail. CALLS. A rough grating *kra-a-a;* various other sounds. HABITAT. Occurs during the breeding season in the subalpine areas of the mountains, often along the high ridges near timberline. Wanders to the lowlands in winter and often passes through them in considerable numbers in migration. RANGE. Resident and breeder from central B.C. south through the higher mountains of the Northwest from the Cascades eastward, wandering in winter to the adjacent lowlands and to the southern Yukon and central Alaska. Occasionally breeds in scattered lowland and foothill areas.

174. Clark's Nutcracker (Fisher)

175. American Crow (Schultz)

Migrates back to the high mountains in loose flocks. Occurs in scattered groups in groves of trees in lava bed areas in Oregon and southern Idaho.

AMERICAN CROW; COMMON CROW *Corvus brachyrhynchos* 17-20 (434-510) Fig. 175
The well-known black bird, larger than the blackbirds and smaller than the Raven. Wings are held above the horizontal when gliding. Tail is square-ended. CALLS. A loud insistent *caw* or *awk*. HABITAT. Occurs mostly in the lowlands where it frequents open woodlands, cultivated fields, swampy places, towns (becoming common in such places as residential areas in Seattle), and farmsteads. Prefers moist places and often seen along riparian growth. RANGE. Summer resident and breeder from central B.C. southward through the Northwest, wintering mostly south of the U.S.-Canadian border west of the Cascades and in the extreme southern part of the Northwest east of that range, though scattered wintering pockets have been found north in the interior to southeastern B.C.

NORTHWESTERN CROW *Corvus caurinus* 16-17 (408-434)
Like the American Crow in color, but separated from that species by the slightly smaller size, faster wing-beat, voice, and habitat preference. CALLS. A coarse nasal *cah* or *car;* a crackling *wok-wok-wok-wok,* etc.; the *cah* note distinctly lower-pitched than the *caw* of the American Crow. HABITAT. Occurs in the immediate vicinity of saltwater beaches where it scavenges along the tide lines. Common around Indian villages located along the seashore. Seldom strays more than a few hundred feet from salt water, except for roosting. RANGE. Resident and breeder from southern Alaska (Kodiak area) south along salt water to the Columbia River which it ascends to the Portland area. Winter visitor and migrational straggler to the northern Oregon coast.

COMMON RAVEN *Corvus corax* 21-26 (539-663) Fig. 176
A large entirely-black bird, noticeably larger than crows. The Raven flies hawk-like, alternately flapping and soaring on horizontal wings. Tail is wedge-shaped and the throat feathers are long and loose. CALLS. A loud, harsh, metallic *krawk, krawk,* or *kr-r-ruck,* etc. also various other notes. HABITAT. Prefers wild, open, non-cultivated country in the lowlands and mountains where it forages as a scavenger. Occurs also along the seashore. Seldom overlaps the range of the American Crow. Strongly attracted to sanitary landfills to which it may travel many miles for nocturnal roosting. RANGE. Resident and breeder from northern Alaska, the northern Yukon, and the

Aleutian Islands south in suitable habitat through the Northwest. Most often to be found in the wilder non-human-occupied areas, from sea level to the summits of the high mountains, but now showing a tendency to be seen more frequently in towns as it, along with many other species, adapts to man.

176. Common Raven (Fisher)

INDEX

335